HIDDEN FORTUNES

*How to Profit from the
New Opportunities of the 1980s*

Albert J. Lowry, Ph.D.

SIMON AND SCHUSTER *NEW YORK*

Published by Simon and Schuster
A Division of Simon & Schuster, Inc.
Simon & Schuster Building
Rockefeller Center
1230 Avenue of the Americas
New York, New York 10020

SIMON AND SCHUSTER and colophon are registered trademarks of
Simon & Schuster, Inc.
Designed by Irving Perkins Associates
Manufactured in the United States of America

10 9 8 7 6 5 4

Library of Congress Cataloging in Publication Data

Lowry, Albert J.
  Hidden fortunes.

  Includes index.
  1. Real estate investment.   2. Real property—Finance.
3. Real estate business.   4. Mortgages.   I. Title.
HD1382.5.L679   1983   332.63′24   83-12070
ISBN 0-671-42721-0

IN APPRECIATION

The author acknowledges his sincere appreciation to Keith Monroe, Calvin Wheelock, Frederic Hills, Dave Chodack and Hal Morris for their valued contribution and assistance in research, editing, and documentation of this manuscript.

CONTENTS

8

10

12 | How to Fend Off Foreclosure

13 | Negotiating with Tricky Sellers

14

1

Welcome to the New Opportunities of the 1980s

Oh yes indeed, the times they are a-changing, as an old song says.

Even in real estate.

Throughout the 1960s and 1970s the whole world seemed uprooted, yet the real estate business changed only slightly, and usually for the better. Mortgage money was plentiful and moderately priced, as it had been since the 1930s. Cities kept growing. Subdivisions sprang up almost overnight like fields of wildflowers. Most people became homeowners.

Not until 1950 had more Americans owned their homes than rented. And by 1970, home ownership by Americans rose to 63 percent, and at the end of that decade the percentage was still going up. Of families making more than $20,000 a year, 84 percent owned their homes.

So the 1970s were joyous for investors in real estate, and even for speculators. Housing prices kept chugging upward right through the stock market breaks of 1970 and 1974, both of which were associated with credit crunches, when interest rates jumped and credit became hard to get. In some areas—California, to mention one—property values rose at an annual rate of 25 percent. Inflation transmuted even bad investments into good ones, and tax laws sheltered much of the profit. In 1976 more than three million homes changed hands. Realty investment opportunity seemed unlimited.

The Revolution of the 1980s

But now we're in the throes of what some observers call a real estate revolution. After a half-century of virtually no change, mortgage financing of today is as foreign as Mars to the financing of the late 1970s. Despite the ever-growing variety of flexible-rate mortgages, people find it fearsomely hard to qualify for any kind of mortgage at a conventional lending institution, and harder still to pay the heavy interest each month. The traditional thirty-year mortgage at a fixed one-digit interest charge is as obsolete as 60-cents-a-pound steak.

In fact, only about 12 percent of all families can now afford even a median-priced new home—as compared to 43 percent in 1970—according to the National Association of Home Builders. Unwise home-buying is one of the big reasons why foreclosures and personal bankruptcies have hit their highest peaks since the 1930s. Real estate agents have disappeared by the thousands. Their easy deals of yesteryear are gone.

You probably know why the lending institutions virtually stopped lending. Their vaults are full of old mortgages worth little because of inflation. Some savings and loan associations still have as much as $500 million rented out at 7 percent and less. No matter what happens, that group of borrowers keeps paying the same driblets each month, though of course the loans are slowly being liquidated. To get more money to lend on new mortgages, the banks and S&Ls must borrow elsewhere—at rates more than double what they paid ten years ago.

I've heard statements such as "This is the most illiquid real estate market in the last fifty years." Disaster lies ahead, in the view of some seers; they say property values will tumble tragically.

I've been hearing those statements for several years now—while I've watched numerous people move ahead in real estate. The speeded-up change in this field offers opportunities that these investors are using to their benefit—as smart investors always do. There are ways to prosper whether it's a buyer's or a seller's market—whether money is tight or easy.

What Makes Millionaires?

The Internal Revenue Service says there are now at least 575,000 millionaires in this country. That's more than twice as many as in 1970, by IRS and Census Bureau calculations. According to *Forbes* magazine, there are roughly four hundred centimillionaires. Probably the only kind of millionaire worth an awed glance nowadays is the kind whose annual income, after taxes, is $1 million or more. Of these, 642 are known.

Most of the centimillionaires either inherited great wealth or acquired oil land when it was cheap. But the plain, ordinary, common variety of 1980 millionaire is self-made from humble beginnings. I'm one of these, and I'm acquainted with many others like me.

The multitudes of people who have attained wealth in the last few tough years are living proof that an almost sacred myth, "It takes money to make money," is false. Recently the Research Institute of America surveyed thousands of people who had accumulated $100,000 to $500,000 in hard wealth. It found that a large majority started with little or no "seed money" and only average or below-average pay.

It was ever thus. Why does one person amass enough capital so he'll never have to worry while another, with comparable income and obligations, is always hurting financially? I think it has little to do with brains, luck, or boldness. Successful accumulators, at least in real estate, typically follow a rather plodding and predictable course.

Virtually without exception, the most prosperous real estate investors have learned—by trial and error or instruction from others—about a relatively small number of specific money-multiplying methods. These techniques are fairly simple, and can be mastered about as easily as any other basic skill.

Why This Book?

Of course the techniques must be adjusted to changing conditions. That's why I've felt it worthwhile to write this book less than two years after revising and updating my previous best-seller, *How You Can Become Financially Independent by Investing in Real Estate*.

The basic methods I worked out for myself by years of experimentation—methods for choosing a good investment, negotiating a good buy, guarding against fraud and legal pitfalls, and selling at a profit—still work as well as ever. I won't repeat or rehash them in this book. What I will do is to build on them, adding refinements and innovations to help you surmount the current difficulties and cash in on the emerging opportunities of the 1980s.

Difficulties? Sure, new difficulties have arisen lately.

Of course, there is a comparative lack of liquidity in real estate. There's a lack of mortgage money from conventional lenders. At current interest rates we can't get the leverage we used to. And now with disinflation, unemployment, and business failures making people wonder if another Great Depression could be coming, it's hard to visualize real estate prices rising much in the near future.

Will Housing Prices Crash?

After the breathtaking decades-long frenzy of house-buying and mortgaging, the conventional wisdom is that there must be a bust. "What goes up must come down" says the adage.

You look at houses that have quintupled in price and you wonder if this is a bubble, a craze, like the seventeenth-century tulip frenzy in Holland when the growers bid up the price of one tulip bulb to half the price of a stout ship.

"Bubble," said the *Wall Street Journal, Business Week, Forbes, Barron's, Financial World* and *Money* in 1980. "No boom lasts forever," warned *Forbes*. "All such obsessions have ended in crashes," warned *Business Week*. A study quoted in *Barron's* forecast that the break in housing prices could be as bad as the 1929 crash in the stock market.

Could there be a crash in property values? At least, there could be a shakeout of foolish speculators, and there has been. Obviously if someone buys ten condos and pyramids them, using unrealized paper profits from one to borrow for a down payment on the next, that speculator can get foreclosed. If rents don't cover debt service, if taxes go up faster than cash flow, if the turnover game slows down, speculators are vulnerable and so are property prices. Bidders pull back when they suddenly see plenty of property for sale.

A crash in one town doesn't necessarily cause a ripple ten miles away. All the Iranians in Beverly Hills can sell out and move to Mecca, and it won't change the price of property in Oceanside. There is no central market for real estate, as there is for stocks and commodities, where the whole country reads the same prices and reaches for a phone. Moreover, in most places, speculators do not own ten condominiums.

In central markets, falling prices trigger selling if people believe prices will go still lower. But the current generation of homeowners isn't likely to sell, even when prices dip; they are more likely to hold on and wait, because they need a place to live. There are 56 million houses owned by the people who live in them—and if too many had to sell at sacrifice prices, any government that let it happen wouldn't stay in office much longer.

Another reason why I can't see a crash: prices are set by supply and demand. Demand seems slow now, because people are saving instead of spending, and because borrowing is so costly. But the pent-up demand for housing is enormous and makes itself felt wherever possible, because this demand far outruns the supply. Look around and you see few empty houses, few vacancies in apartment buildings.

And the demand must grow. More than forty million people will reach their thirties in this decade, the largest such group in U.S. history to enter the household-forming age in one period. Married or single, those thirty-year-olds don't want to live with their parents. They want houses or apartments—in most cases, houses, if possible. Even high interest rates and a major recession won't completely stifle their demand. How can prices crash when housing is scarce?

What History Tells Us

Look at the history of housing prices. The Census Bureau tells us that house prices were not depressed by the panics of 1893 and 1907, nor by the lesser depressions of 1913–14 and 1920–21.

Prices did indeed fall during the Great Depression of the 1930s, as thrift institutions slammed down their loan windows and eventually closed their doors. But the National Housing Act of 1934 —one of the New Deal's most valuable and lasting innovations —stabilized house prices and kept them stable through the rest of the decade. Prices began to move up in the 1940s and have never stopped since.

In 1974 the stock market dropped almost 50 percent, interest rates hit new highs, and housing starts shrank 65 percent. Yet the national average of home prices kept climbing. It was still climbing—though slowly—in 1981–82. The whole history of real estate shows that houses and apartments resist the economic storms around them.

Although it's highly unlikely that we'll have a crash, we could have the end of the house as a wonderful inflation hedge, at least for a while. The price tags should go up intermittently (as most experts now predict) but whether they stay above the inflation rate may depend on the area of the country and the size and location and attractiveness of the particular dwelling. This simply means that successful investors must be more selective in the properties they buy.

Attractive Financing Is the Key

House prices have outdistanced the ability of the traditional buyers to carry the mortgage. That's another way of saying that property lacks liquidity. This condition may be eased soon by a law enacted late in 1982 that lets banks and S&Ls compete on even terms with money-market funds; it may bring in enough new deposits to stimulate mortgage lending.

Personally I doubt that it will. I think the solution to the liquidity problem is to be found in sophisticated alternative ways to finance real estate. There are several such ways, old and new, as you'll see in reading this book.

Call it creative financing. Call it give and take. Call it barter. Call it buyers and sellers cooperating to keep a real estate deal alive. It's a matter of finding who has the money to lend during this financing crisis, learning what these lenders look for, and figuring out a proposition that will be profitable to both sides.

There's plenty of money available from little-known sources. This book will show you where it is, and how to borrow more for less. It will show you how to tap your own hidden capital reserves; how to turn fixed assets into cash without selling or losing control of them; how to find the best private or institutional lenders for your special needs.

Uncle Sam Will Help You

The big reason lenders still like real estate is that tax laws are still stacked in favor of real estate investment—more strongly even than in the 1970s.

Sellers are allowed to avoid capital gains taxes by rolling over the sales proceeds of a house into another house, even if cash is taken out from the sale by getting a bigger mortgage on the newly acquired house.

Even for investors, capital gains taxes weigh less heavily than in recent years. And if they buy income real estate, they take depreciation deductions based on the full purchase price—even if they bought mostly with borrowed cash. And they can write off the full cost in just fifteen years, compared to the former varying period of thirty or thirty-five years—thus doubling the amount of depreciation or tax shelter allowed. Better yet, many can take accelerated depreciation for bigger and faster deductions.

As before, owners and investors can continue to deduct all their mortgage interest and their property taxes. Unlike non-real estate investors, they can take unlimited interest deductions on any borrowing on real property.

Only investors in real estate can use capital without risk. Their loan is secured just by the property in which they invest, not by any personal obligation. They can use as much borrowed capital as they wish, yet treat such capital as if it were their own money.

Sometimes the deductions and credits on real estate investment are so generous that they wipe out all tax on the profit, with some left over to reduce taxes on other investments. Thus Uncle Sam may turn a money-losing investment (before taxes) into a profitable one (after taxes). More and more people have discovered this in the last few years. So now we see group investing, public and private limited partnerships in real estate, and shared-equity arrangements. These developments are analyzed in detail in this book.

New Tactics For a New Era

Despite pressures of high interest rates, discouragement from institutional lenders, and a lagging market, hundreds of real estate investors are flourishing because of their adaptability to new conditions. "Five years ago the biggest game in town was to buy single-family houses, hold them six months, then unload at a fat profit," an investor said recently. "Today we play by a new set of rules."

Some rules, briefly summarized, that you should be following:

You'll generally hold on to properties longer than in the 1970s.

You'll be more selective in rehabilitating or refurbishing. "It used to be that what you did to the property could dictate what you sold it for," I tell my seminars. "Now, what you can sell it for dictates what you do to it."

Either as buyer or seller, you'll usually help the other party find an attractive, safe financing plan.

You'll tend to concentrate on a narrow slice of the market such as foreclosed or distressed properties, redesigned properties that attract special types of buyers or renters, or other kinds of real estate that the typical untutored investor never thinks about. (Another reason I'm writing this book is to explain such unusual segments of the market.)

Real estate fortunes are made by buying in bad times, like now, before they turn again into good times. When times are tough, bargains abound. Read on and you'll see!

2

Getting Ready for Your First Investment

So you've decided to invest in real estate. It can be the most profitable decision of your life. How do you get started?

To start right you'll need: (a) knowledge, (b) time, (c) money.

You'll get the know-how you need by reading this book. I suggest you skim through it, at least, before looking for your first investment. Later, as you become active in the field, you can reread a particular chapter to guide you through whatever you're doing at the time. (However, you'll also need the know-how of professionals in law, taxation, and other specialized subjects—as I'll explain in detail in this chapter.)

Time? That should be no problem. Presumably you have it available, or you wouldn't be delving into this subject.

Money? Maybe you haven't much to spare. That's okay. You don't need much to get started. And there still are simple ways to raise sizable sums. However, the money question is so important that I'll devote most of this chapter to it—and all of the next four chapters.

How Much Money Will You Need?

Conceivably you can start with only a thousand dollars. Or, if you're really determined, you can start by buying property with no down payment—as I did when I started, and as I explain in my Real Estate Investors Seminar. But let's be conservative.

Let's assume that you haven't yet studied any creative financing methods, so you flinch at the thought of owing six-figure sums of money. (Later, when you get the feel of using other people's money, you'll be as glad to use it as they are to lend it.)

Very well, we'll start with the assumption that you haven't the experience and mental agility for anything ambitious right now. So we'll be conservative. We'll say you should have at least two thousand dollars, either as a nest egg or within easy borrowing reach. Two thousand is enough to give you a smooth start.

Maybe you think you don't have that much to spare. I'll bet you have much more than you realize. Your financial position is probably stronger than it looks at first glance.

Take an Inventory of Your Financial Assets

Get a pencil and fill in the following form. If you don't know the exact amounts, use approximations. A few dollars more or less won't matter.

TANGIBLE ASSETS

estimated market value of your home, less balance due on mortgage: _____

estimated value of other real estate minus mortgages or outstanding loans: _____

market value of car, less loan: _____

cash value of life insurance and annuities: _____

amount you could withdraw now from pension plan: _____

market value of jewelry, furniture, and other personal effects you could easily sell: _____

LIQUID ASSETS

savings accounts: _____

average minimum balance in checking account: _____

value of all securities (stocks, bonds, mutual funds, etc.): _____

MISCELLANEOUS ASSETS

interest in business or profession if you are self-employed; money credited to your account in a profit-sharing plan; estimated value of a patent; etc.: _____

CASH FLOW

total annual take-home pay, less total expenses per year: _____

annual income from social security, pensions, trusts, etc. _____

net income from dividends, income properties, etc.: _____

expected income tax refund: _____

TOTAL ASSETS _____

LIABILITIES

personal debts not secured by any assets listed: _____

contingent liabilities such as co-signed notes: _____

taxes payable during next 12 months: _____

dues payable during next 12 months: _____

TOTAL LIABILITIES _____

When you subtract your liabilities from your total assets, the result is your "net worth," as financial people call it.

If your net worth is $7,500 or more, you are in the upper half of the population. If your net worth is more than $10,000 you're in the upper eighth.

$2,000 Is Enough

However, even if your net worth is as low as $2,000, don't stop reading. In all likelihood you can borrow the additional money you'll need for a modest start. In a moment we'll look at ways you can do this.

But first, save the tabulation you've just made. Why? Because your net worth is a key number in the eyes of lenders with whom you'll be negotiating.

They'll want a financial statement from you—sometimes in considerable detail, itemizing each stock you own, each piece of property, each debt, and so on. Put it all down now, before it's needed, on whatever form your bank gives you for doing so. Once your bank has this on file, the bank's lending officers will be ready to consider advancing money to you.

Keep several copies of this financial statement. You'll need one whenever you request a loan from any bank, insurance company, savings and loan association, or other lender. Some will accept a photostat of your statement to your own bank. Others use their own special forms, but they'll want the same basic information.

This brings us to an important point. Your borrowing power is as much a financial asset as the money you have on hand. Which means that your assets are really just a fraction of the amount that you can put into a down payment on an investment property.

In other words, it's perfectly possible—and prudent—to invest several times your net worth. What counts is your borrowing power, not your money available to invest. If real estate investors had to operate on cash alone, then not much property would ever change hands.

I'm not suggesting that you invest your total assets in one project. As a prudent person, you'll certainly keep an ample reserve to protect against emergencies.

But maybe you don't need a lot of cash for emergencies. If you
work for a corporation, it's fringe benefits may include payment
of virtually all expenses connected with a family illness. Likewise, if you're well along in years, you may have a pension plus
Social Security benefits or Medicare protection.

On the other hand, if you're a self-employed professional such
as an architect or attorney, you may have little to fall back on
except your savings and investments. You'll take such factors
into account in deciding how much of your own assets to put into
a real estate investment that may not be easily liquidated.

Build Your Fortune with Borrowed Money

You'll find that credit is available from so many sources that it
seems endless. Business runs on credit. Everyone gives and gets
credit.

When you deposit your savings in a bank, you're lending your
money to the bank, which uses it to earn more money by lending
to someone else at a higher rate of interest. When you buy a bond
you're lending to the issuer of the bond.

A manufacturer borrows to buy the materials he uses. You
borrow from him when you use a credit card or an installment
plan to buy what he manufactures.

The only way a car dealer can keep cars in his showroom is by
getting a bank or finance company to lend him money on them.
Almost all American homeowners have used mortgage credit.
Insurance companies owe four dollars to policy-holders for every
dollar in assets—which is considered perfectly sound by financial
experts and government regulators.

The old-time Puritan ethic that it was sinful to go into debt
made good sense in the days of cash-and-carry, COD, and low
incomes for most of the population. It was the age of the automobile that changed all that. The auto was the first mass-pro-
duced consumer item that cost more than 10 percent of a family's
annual income; it could never have been widely sold if General
Motors hadn't introduced the "installment plan." Commercial
banks, which were the logical institutions to finance installment
sales, resisted and even opposed this new style of purchasing.
"The bankers believed that the extension of consumer credit to

the average man was too great a risk," recalled Alfred P. Sloan of General Motors. "Furthermore, they had a moral objection to financing a luxury, believing apparently that whatever fostered consumption must discourage thrift." In 1926 the American Bankers Association advised its members not to finance installment purchases. But by the early 1930s the banks themselves were in the installment credit business. And before World War II they were vigorously seeking customers for installment loans. That was when the expression "down payment" entered the American language. By 1963 General Motors' Time Payment Plan had financed nearly fifty million car buyers, and installment buying was common for radios, refrigerators, washing machines, and countless other kinds of consumer goods. We were transformed from a cash-paying society into a credit-using society.

Credit enables borrowers to buy or do something they couldn't afford if they had to pay in advance. Borrowing to invest is usually more justifiable than borrowing to spend. Reckless borrowing for any purchase can still make life miserable for people who don't have a plan for repaying. Ordinary people who know what they're doing, and budget part of their income to pay off their debts, can be just as prudent and successful as corporations that rely on banks to supply working capital.

Whenever you consider using credit, the important questions to ask yourself are: "Can I afford the interest rate?" and "Where will I get the money to pay the principal?"

Most people get answers to these questions by applying—consciously or unconsciously—the concept called cash-flow accounting.

Cash Flow: Your Key to Successful Borrowing

They plan to keep the amount of money coming in from every source a little larger than the total going out for every purpose. By using credit they can postpone payments, if necessary, to keep outflow smaller than inflow.

For example, suppose you borrow $90,000, and add it to $10,000 of your own cash to buy a $100,000 property. If rentals of the property, or other income from it, produce only a $1,500 a year cash flow (the amount left after all fixed expenses and the

payments on the $90,000 mortgage) then you're in good shape.
You're earning 15 percent on your $10,000 cash—not counting
the bigger gains you may eventually get through tax savings,
through the higher market value that inflation adds to your property, and through the growing value of your equity in the property
as you pay off the mortgage month by month.

So even if you borrow at high interest, cash-flow accounting
can show that this is worthwhile if the borrowed money will bring
you back more than enough to pay the interest and any other
fixed expenses. Using credit wisely is like using cash wisely—
it's a matter of making sure that what you get is worth the price
you pay for it.

Find the Less Expensive Lenders

Cash for rent! Renting cash to borrowers is a widespread, profitable business. Plenty of people in the business are all too eager
to say "Okay, here's your cash," to almost anyone who will sign
certain papers. The more eager the lender, the tougher the terms
he is likely to demand.

Shop for credit just as you'd shop for a car. Money is for rent
cheaply or expensively. All lenders lose money on idle funds, so
they try to keep their money out working for them. Their interest
rates vary from lender to lender, and from state to state, and
sometimes from day to day, depending on the supply and demand
for credit.

In general, the "rental price" of the cash you borrow—the
interest charges—will be set according to the lender's opinion of
how good a risk you are. If the facts indicate that you're a long-
established, reputable person with a good record of paying what
you owe, you can get a lower rate than someone with no record
or a bad record.

Let's look at some of the less expensive arrangements you can
consider if you need additional cash to put together your recommended $2,000 grubstake.

Low-Rate Loans on Insurance Policies

If your life insurance policy has a cash surrender value, you can
borrow on it. Life insurance companies are willing to lend to

their policy-holders, up to 95 percent of the policy's cash value. You can borrow on older policies at only 5 or 6 percent interest —the lowest rate you're likely to find anywhere. The interest rate on policies issued more recently is likely to be 8 to 10 percent, which still is a bargain.

Since your insurance policy itself serves as security for the loan, you won't be asked to pay anything but the interest. Of course the loan reduces the benefits your family would receive if you died before paying it back. But wasn't your purpose in buying the insurance to guarantee a good future for the family? And aren't you likely to provide an even better future by using some of the insurance for a more profitable investment?

Low-Rate Loans from Credit Unions

A credit union, if you belong to one, is another source of low-interest loans. A credit union is a voluntary association of people with some common tie, such as employment by the same company or membership in the same church. A member can borrow a substantial amount on his signature alone. He can borrow even more if he puts up some form of security. Interest is likely to be about 12 percent a year. It's worthwhile to join a credit union if you can.

Passbook Loans Are Bargains

Did you know that your savings passbook is good security for a loan? Such loans also carry a low interest rate. Just by handing your passbook over to the bank where you keep your savings, you can get a loan from the bank—and your savings will continue to earn interest for you.

Of course you're borrowing your own money and paying for the privilege, but it's a good deal for you as well as the bank. Since the bank is making a no-risk loan, it is willing to accept less interest than usual. Your net cost (the interest the bank charges you, minus the interest the bank pays on your savings) may be only a few cents for each dollar you borrow.

To illustrate, let's assume that the bank's rate for passbook loans is 6½ percent on the average balance, if your repayment schedule will pay off the entire balance in a year. And we'll say the bank pays 5 percent on your savings. This means you'll be charged $35.60 to borrow $1,000 for a year. (Remember, during a year's time the balance due will average only a little more than half the total lent to you at the start, because you'll keep whittling it down.) Meanwhile your $1,000 savings earn $50 interest—but the fraction of the $1,000 that's actually at risk if you default keeps dwindling as you pay off the debt, so the net earnings on your passbook account would amount to $14.40 after the interest on your loan is paid. And there's also a tax savings if you itemize deductions for interest paid. So, if you're in a 30 percent tax bracket, the net interest on your bank account would have been over twenty dollars, and you still had the use of the $1,000 you had borrowed from the bank.

At many banks you can now borrow $1,000 or more just by writing a check, even if your checking account is almost empty. Instead of bouncing the check, as they used to, certain banks will honor your overdraft and call it a loan. Most of them don't even require you to apply for this overdraft privilege. You get it automatically if you maintain a checking account. This can be so useful that I'll cover it in detail in Chapters 3 and 4.

Another Way to Borrow: Pledge Stocks

You've got additional borrowing power if you own stocks or bonds listed on the New York Stock Exchange, or if you own shares in any listed mutual fund. Just by handing the certificates to your bank as collateral—that is, "hypothecating" them, to use a banker's word—you can borrow at least half of their current quoted price.

Bank loans secured by stocks are cheap compared to the interest on a personal loan or an auto loan. And the dividends on the stock continue to come directly to you. Even though the certificates are kept in the bank vault, your name still appears on them as owner, and you retain control of them—more or less. Any time you want to sell them you can tell the bank to do it for you, clear up your loan, and pay you whatever is left over. Or you can bring in other stocks and exchange them for those in the vault.

If You're a Property Owner, You've Got Credit

If you own a house, a vacant lot, or other real estate, it can provide the money you need to get started. If the property is free and clear, and even if it isn't, you can borrow against your equity in it. You pay no taxes on the cash you receive.

Even if the property is mortgaged, you can do what most big investors do when they need cash—increase the mortgage on it or acquire a second mortgage. Either will cost more than other types of loan, because they are cumbersome procedures. You may pay several hundred dollars in fees, service charges, and the like.

However, your credit standing won't be investigated so closely. A mortgage loan is granted on the value of the property rather than on the character and assets of the borrower. The security is the land and its improvements.

Friends and Relatives: Possible Partners

A well-off friend or relative who wants to invest is the last resort. If you simply can't get enough cash to get started on your own, maybe you should ask someone close to you to join with you in a real estate investment. Human nature being what it is, there's danger in any partnership within a family or between friends. Personal conflicts can embitter the business dealings, and a conflict with someone close to you is hard to walk away from. On the other hand, two heads can sometimes be better than one, and a partner may be able to do various things that you can't, including spending time on details when you're busy with other things.

A Seller May Offer You Credit

If you want to buy property from someone but can't find the money, the property owner may help you by taking a "purchase-money" or second mortgage in lieu of the cash down payment. In effect he is lending the difference to you. His security is the mortgage; he can foreclose and take back the property if you don't meet the payments. This is a fairly common arrangement.

Sometimes the real estate agent who handles the sale may

suggest this, or may help you borrow elsewhere. Like the seller, he wants to help you solve your financing problem in order to make his profit on the transaction. But both will want to be sure you are a good risk. That means you need a good credit rating.

First Step: Establish Your Credit Rating

Before you start shopping for loans, get yourself a credit rating if you don't already have one. Lenders probably haven't met you and don't want to. They prefer verifiable facts to personal impressions.

They'll get some of these facts by asking you to fill out a loan application. They'll also ask for the financial statement I provided on page 27, and perhaps for a photostat of your last income tax return.

Credit applications don't ask whether you pay bills on time or have a lot of money. Instead they ask where you work and live, how long you've been there, where you bank, and where you have credit accounts. These are signposts that guide an investigator toward other facts he wants.

Whoever is thinking of lending money to you may occasionally do some investigating on his own, like telephone your employer to verify that you work there. But usually he calls a credit bureau, which is likely to have a computerized file dating back to the first time you ever formally applied for credit anywhere. If a creditor ever reported that you were slow to pay bills, this may pop up from the file. Have you ever been in police trouble? Ever been sued? Have you hopped from job to job? Your file probably shows this.

Credit bureaus used to clip newspapers, comb police blotters, and take note of every recorded property transfer. Maybe some still do. But it's more likely that, if you check your report, you'll be surprised at how little they know about you. They don't have time or money to send investigators out checking on you.

How to Get Your Credit Record

You can see your credit record whenever you want. Ask a store or bank which bureau it uses, or look in the yellow pages of the phone book under "credit-reporting agencies." Then call to arrange a personal interview. Legally you have the right to be told what is in your file. This may cost you a small fee (two to five dollars) unless the report has led to your being turned down for credit, in which case the bureau must show you the record free.

Credit bureaus make mistakes—often by getting two people with similar names mixed up, or by recording nonpayment of a bill without showing any reason for nonpayment, which could be that you returned the goods or that you never received the bill.

Misleading information in a credit-bureau file may damage your life wherever you go, because a bureau's computerized memory core is probably available nationwide. Under the 1971 Fair Credit Reporting Law, you have a right to correct or add to a bureau's report on you. You can probably set the record straight within a week.

If you have trouble getting credit although you know your record is clear, find out whether a credit bureau has made a mistake. For that matter, you can check your credit file even before you apply for a loan.

Maybe there's no file on you, especially if you're new in the community. In that case, it may make sense to put up some collateral and take out a bank loan even if you don't need it. Paying it back quickly will do a lot to give you a good local rating. Many small investors borrow increasing amounts they don't need, simply to build a record of repaying larger and larger loans. Another good idea is to get several credit cards and use them enough to establish a record for prompt payment.

When someone refuses you a loan he probably won't volunteer any reason, but you ought to ask. Under the law, he must then tell you if he's received a bad credit report on you and must identify the source of the report. But there may be other reasons for his refusal. He probably asked why you wanted the money, and he may have judged that the property you plan to buy isn't worth as much as you propose to pay. This could be worth knowing.

If your credit file does contain unfavorable (and correct) data about you, you can still get credit by assigning your lender the right to seize and sell assets of yours that are worth considerably more than the amount you want to borrow.

Next Step: Find Good Advisers

So now, we'll assume, you've got at least two thousand available to invest in real estate, or know where you can get it. You're almost ready to look for a piece of property.

But first you'd better find a few competent advisers, so you can get their advice quickly when you need it. Real estate transactions can be tricky for a novice. The possible troubles range from honest mistakes to sharp practice to downright fraud.

Of course, some lucky people choose a property, bargain for it, sign the papers, take possession, and live happily ever after without the help of a lawyer, an accountant, or a realty broker. But if you're unwilling to trust to luck, you'll want to spend a little money for expert help.

You'll Need a Good Real Estate Lawyer

You don't want a general-practice attorney. You want one with plenty of experience in real estate practice, so he can advise you in negotiating for property as well as in closing the deal. Maybe you'll find him in a big law firm, which usually contains one or more specialists in real estate law. The same firm may have partners who know income taxes and estate taxes, who'll be useful in planning transactions to get the maximum benefit of tax write-offs later on, when your buying and selling and borrowing become bigger.

Make your contact now. Begin by asking around among your friends, relatives, business and social acquaintances. Have they ever used an attorney to handle real estate matters? Did he give good help, or was he "out" too often when they needed guidance? Did he seem familiar with the laws affecting deeds, mortgages, contracts for the sale of real estate, encumbrances, liens on title, zoning, foreclosures, and so on? How much did he cost?

There are other sources of information too. An officer of your bank can probably recommend someone. You can ask the local realty board. You certainly should ask some successful real estate investors, if you know any. You can ask the bar association; probably it will give you not only a list of specialists in real estate law but also a schedule of minimum fees for the various services likely to be involved.

Don't be shy about asking for a preliminary interview with any attorney on your prospect list. You can explain that you have no legal problem at the moment, but will be making real estate investments in the range of $100,000 or more, and wonder if he might be available on fairly short notice. You are just a prospective client, wanting to get acquainted.

A good lawyer won't charge you for such a visit. If you like him, and he agrees to be on tap, you'll want to jot down his home phone number as well as his office number, and keep them as handy as your physician's numbers. But before you go, ask him to give you an idea of the fees he charges, if he hasn't already made this clear.

REAL ESTATE ATTY. FEES

As a rule of thumb, a real estate contract and title closing will commonly run 1 percent of the purchase price, or about $500 on a $50,000 building. This jumps by $300 or so if an independent title search is involved. And if the attorney represents you in negotiations, he'll make an hourly charge (anywhere from $40 to $250) for his time.

It's important that you find a lawyer with whom you feel comfortable and confident. Then you won't wonder if he is deliberately building up a fee when he says there may be a "defect in title" to a property you want to buy. There may be legal thickets ahead, and you need a guide you can trust.

Just as an example, you may decide not to buy a property only to find yourself in court a year later, listening to something like this: "Your honor, my name is Lucius Grabb. I am a realtor. I worked like a dog to bring about this deal and finally got the buyer and seller together on every detail. Then at the last minute this man changed his mind and wouldn't buy. I found out he made a deal for another building elsewhere. I claim there was a meeting of the minds . . ."

A good attorney can guard you from the Mr. Grabbs of this world. One precaution he'll urge on you—and be sure to do this, from the beginning—is to buy a notebook and keep a careful log of all you do in investigating properties: their locations, prices quoted, conversations, names of all people involved, dates, times, everything.

In addition to this daily diary, put a file folder in your desk and drop into it every newspaper ad, letter, envelope, memo, invoice, receipt, and other slips of paper connected with your realty project. Very soon you'll find you can hardly lift this folder. But later you'll be glad you don't have to hunt everywhere for these records when you need them.

Good Brokers Are Useful

Licensed real estate brokers or salesmen can show you properties worth considering. But don't count on them for impartial advice. They're working for the seller. He pays their commission. The bigger the price they persuade you to pay, the better for them and their clients.

Nevertheless, a good broker can save you time and maybe money. He knows what properties are on the market. He can probably tick off the good and bad points of a property as he walks through it, and estimate rather closely what it should sell for—not will, but should. He probably won't let his clients price themselves out of the market, since he'll lose a sale if he does.

There are more than a million real estate brokers and salesmen in the country. They sell three-fourths of all property that changes hands. Those who call themselves "real estate brokers" are licensed by the state, and must pass an examination to get this license. Of the brokers, about 526,000 identify themselves as "Realtors" and "Realtor Associates." These terms are copyrighted. They can only be used in advertising by someone who is a member of the National Association of Realtors.

A realtor with G.R.I. after his name means that he is a Graduate of the Realtors Institute. This is a fairly new designation, given to comparatively few brokers and salespeople who have had courses such as real estate law, appraisal, transactions, and other instruction in the fine points of their profession. Any G.R.I. has very broad knowledge, but doesn't usually specialize. Fewer than 1 percent of the realty salespeople can use these initials after their name. So you can assume that a G.R.I. knows his business.

R.E.C.I. after a realtor's name means that he is a member of the Real Estate Certificate Institute. To get this label (which is quite similar to the G.R.I. designation) a real estate professional must take an impressive array of college courses in general realty subjects. Only a few hundred people hold the R.E.C.I. designation.

A member of the Appraiser's Institute—designated either as S.A.I. or M.A.I—can be useful to you later, after you've found a piece of property that looks interesting. You'll need a professional appraisal to determine the property's fair market value. An S.A.I. or M.A.I has studied the subject for years and has passed intensive written exams. He probably helps banks and other lending institutions make decisions about their real estate investments.

Sooner or later you'll probably need advice from such an appraiser, but you should know that appraisal isn't an exact mathematical process. An appraisal is only an estimate. Ten appraisers evaluating the same property on the same day, for the same purpose, may come back with ten different figures. These figures should be within a reasonable range of each other, but this isn't always the case.

Bankers can often help you get a sound appraisal—on the conservative side, naturally. They don't thrive by lending more than a property is worth. At least they know values rather well and can point out various advantages and disadvantages of a possible investment. A banker is usually glad to give free advice on the chance it will lead to more business for him.

Other specialists who can help you later are the C.C.I.M., the C.P.M., and the S.E.C.

The first set of initials means that the bearer is a Certified Commercial Investment Member of the Realtors National Marketing Institute (that's the association which regulates this designation). This person is a specialist who used to be called a certified property exchanger. When you own property and start to think of selling it, a C.C.I.M. will probably be able (for a fee) to suggest complicated solutions that will enrich you: exchanges, leasebacks, combinations, or other transactions that benefit all parties concerned. At times you'll come out ahead by trading rather than selling your interest in a property. It can be tossed in as a sweetener in acquiring more profitable property—if you have expert advice on how to do so. To find a C.C.I.M. ask your bank or the realty board.

A C.P.M. is a Certified Property Manager. You may need one

if you buy an apartment building or a string of homes, unless you plan to manage the property yourself, which involves all kinds of detail work.

Good management of sick property is one of the best ways to make your money grow. There are only approximately five thousand Certified Property Managers in the nation. To get this credential they must have years of on-the-job experience in managing properties, after which they must pass stiff examinations. When you come across a C.P.M., make a note of his name and phone number. Someday you may want to consult with him on short notice. His consultation fee will probably be $40 to $75 per hour, but he makes most of his money on management fees, not consultation fees. A management fee will usually be about 5 percent of the rent roll.

An S.E.C. is a member of the National Society of Exchange Counselors. At this writing there are only approximately 150 members. As their name suggests, they work out exchanges that are profitable for all owners involved.

So now you know where to get the various kinds of expert help you may need.

In today's market of inflated prices and steep interest rates you may think big profits for realty investors are scarce—but that's not true. If you know where to look, you can still pick up countless bargains. Starting with Chapter 7, you'll learn where to look for the bargains, and what to do when you find them.

Naturally you'll need operating capital—first in small amounts, maybe in big wads later if you decide to expand. I think it's clearest to cover the whole financing subject first. So in Chapters 3 and 4 I'll show you how to raise a thousand or two at a moment's notice. In Chapters 5 and 6 I'll explain a number of financing strategies for bigger investments, even though you may not need them until later in your realty career. Just knowing they exist will give you more confidence. Then we'll move on into a whole flock of chapters showing you how to use your capital profitably.

KEY POINTS TO REMEMBER

⊙Keep a personal financial statement handy to give to prospective lenders.

- ◑ Before you borrow for an investment, figure how much cash flow it will bring. Inflow should be larger than interest charges and any other fixed expenses.
- · You can borrow at low interest on an insurance policy or savings passbook.
- · You can pledge stocks for a loan at comparatively low interest while continuing to receive the dividends.
- · Real estate you own can be borrowed against.
- ◑ An owner who wants to sell to you may take a purchase-money mortgage.
- · Check your credit-bureau rating and make sure it is correct.
- · Before starting to buy real estate, establish contact with a good lawyer, accountant, and realty broker.

3

Give Yourself Credit

A point I made in the previous chapter is worth repeating here: "Your borrowing power is as much a financial asset as the money you have on hand. If real estate investors had to operate on cash alone, there wouldn't be much property changing hands."

So let's consider how to strengthen your borrowing power.

The institutional lenders (banks, savings and loans, mortgage companies, insurance companies and the like) are no longer such good sources of real estate loans as they used to be. I needn't go into the reasons. If you've been reading the newspapers, you know what the long climb in interest rates did to these institutions.

Today it's simpler to finance realty transactions by dealing with private lenders and investors. They are numerous, approachable, and less entangled in red tape. I'll show you how to get sizable loans from them in Chapters 5 and 6.

However, having said this much, I'm now going to contradict myself slightly. For smaller loans—$1,000, maybe $5,000 or $10,000—banks have become the best place to go. That's what this chapter is all about.

How to Borrow Instantly—For as Long as You Like

Maybe you've noticed that most banks want customers nowadays. Their new broad smiles and big hellos are part of a nation-

43

wide upheaval in the banking business. I want to explain this change in some detail, so you'll feel at home in the midst of it.

The upheaval is visible mostly in the onrush of electronic banking with its automatic tellers, debit cards, computerized records and telephone bill-paying. But the change most advantageous to you and me doesn't depend on electronics.

It's a rulebook change, put in because bankers awoke to a need. They decided to open up the plain old checking account.

Back in the 1960s, business seers predicted that by 1980 money would dwindle into mere electronic blips in a checkless, cashless society. Obviously this hasn't happened. Banks find that people still need cash. So they're developing ways to make it available almost any time, almost anywhere.

The best way to do this, they're finding, is to put automatic credit at the fingertips of depositors.

Many banks no longer require a depositor to hock something or sign a promissory note when he wants to borrow. He just whips out his checkbook. Quite likely he can keep the money as long as he wants.

Better yet, he can probably postpone paying interest as well as principal for months and even years. All this is legal—and simple, once you understand how to use the newer kinds of checking accounts offered by a majority of banks across the United States.

What caused this startling change? Let's take a quick look at banking history. In the aftermath of the 1933 bank panic, when scores of banks became insolvent and closed their doors permanently, laws were passed prohibiting banks from paying interest on demand deposits—i.e., checking accounts. The purpose was to prevent banks from bidding deposits away from other banks in the cutthroat deflationary struggles of the Depression.

The need for this law soon faded. But the law stayed on the books, which pleased all bankers, since it saved them a heap of money. Their customers remained willing to pay a bank a monthly service charge just for holding their money, bundling up their checks, and keeping track of their balance.

This strange situation persisted for more than forty years. But in the late 1970s it began to change. By then all the checking-account balances in the country added up to more than $200 billion—a sea of "free money" which the banks cherished. But a few bold bankers saw how to siphon more of this sea into their own banks, away from duller competitors.

They did it by cutting down on charges to customers: on service fees for checking accounts, on requirements for minimum balances, on the old-style 10-cents-per-check charges. Some even advertised "free" checking.

Meanwhile their rivals, the S&Ls and other "thrift" institutions, found they could legally permit depositors to write checks against interest-bearing savings accounts. They attracted so many new customers that bankers screamed "Unfair competition!"

Such a windstorm was stirred up in Congress and the legislatures that laws were passed allowing banks as well as S&Ls to pay interest on checking accounts through Negotiable Order of Withdrawal (NOW) accounts.

How Overdraft Checking Works

This was helpful, in a minor way, to banks and to small depositors. But the banks needed something bigger and better. Now they've found it.

They have waved a wand over their computer programs, instructing the computers to let you overdraw your checking account without suffering the old-time consequences such as a check returned unpaid, urgent phone calls, hasty trips to put cash in the bank, rewriting of checks, damage to your credit standing, an average $5 penalty to your account, and the accompanying unpleasant churning in your gizzard.

Instead the bank simply pays the check, using its own ample funds. It notifies you by mail. Your bank balance swells by at least the amount of your overdraft—but probably by more, since a bank normally makes such deposits in $100 multiples. And of course the bank charges you a specified daily interest rate (a few pennies per $100) for each day you're in debt to the bank for that amount.

These expandable checking accounts are known by various names. Different banks call them Automatic Credit, Cash Reserve, Ready Reserve, Guaranteed Reserve, Check-o-Draft, Chextra or something equally cute. Some banks issue you a special set of overdraft checks, just to dramatize how easily you can borrow.

Why the Banks Loosened Up

A good many banks now offer credit reserves of $5,000 or $10,000, or even more, on checking accounts. Why such liberal credit? Because the banks are profiting by their liberality. They're attracting many, many new checking accounts.

The business of banks is to pull in money and use it to the fullest all around the clock. When they can use it by putting it in your checking account, and charging you a healthy rate of interest, fine.

Whenever they can't rent out as much money as they pull in, they fret. They want every buck in the bank to be earning interest for them somehow, somewhere. That's why they were disturbed in the 1970s when they realized they weren't attracting as many "good" borrowers as in the past. Why weren't they? Because of the retirement of old-style bankers whose respectable cronies had kept borrowing from them. The newer bank executives didn't have as many good connections, because people were on the move more than they used to be. Nobody lived a lifetime in one town anymore and did all his business with one bank.

If banks were to put their surpluses to work, they would have to make a lot of small loans to small borrowers. But this realization was slow in dawning on them. They had always believed it unwise to lend to barbers, bartenders, beauticians, musicians, actors, writers, cooks, waiters, waitresses, counter clerks, hotel employees, housewives, dock workers, salesmen on commission, nurses not connected with hospitals, and various other types whose occupations put them in what were called "problem categories." Anyone in a problem category is viewed by banks as a person who might squander a loan instead of putting it to productive use and paying it back.

Could You Pass This Secret Test?

If you ever go around to banks in search of an old-style loan—personal or business—you'll find that the ordeal is practically the same at all banks. You are told to fill out a loan application, which is mainly a questionnaire about your personal way of life. When you complete it, a receptionist asks you to wait: "Our loan representatives are busy at the moment, but someone will be with you shortly."

You are waiting because a loan rep is evaluating whether you are a good risk. He does this with pencil and paper, applying a secret scoring formula to your application. If you admit being in one of the problem categories mentioned above, he starts you off with a minus score. Then he gives low scores for not living at your current address long enough, not working for your present employer long enough, not being married, not being older than thirty, not having a listed telephone, and so on. You get pluses for good traits like owning real estate.

When the loan officer reaches the bottom of the application he adds up your total, which he applies against the bank's yardstick. A score of 40 or less means no loan. Above 80 means almost automatic approval. In fact, if a loan officer rejects an application with 80 points or more, he has to justify this to the installment-loan division. Whenever a score falls in the big swampy area between 41 and 79, the officer must write to headquarters explaining whether the loan was approved or rejected and why.

Let's say your secret test score is reassuringly high. Does a loan officer hand over the cash? Indeed not. "Everything looks okay," he says. "But since it's your first application it has to go to the installment-loan division for approval. Probably you'll get good news soon." This means the bank is now about to check your credit.

Danger—Credit Bureau at Work

Credit bureaus want to give banks a reason to reject a loan. A bureau looks good when it saves a bank from making a possible mistake. Contrariwise, when a loan goes sour, the bank will look back to see whether a credit bureau warned against it—and if not, why not?

So the credit bureau will bad-mouth you if it can. Then your loan application will be rejected, and you'll have to go through the procedure I explained in Chapter 2 for uncovering the reason why you're classed as a bad risk, and for correcting whatever errors may be in the credit bureau's report.

Who needs all that bother? Why apply for a loan if you can get the money automatically through your checking account?

Thousands of Americans found the obvious answer. Don't bother with loan officers. Write overdrafts instead.

Of course this sounds as if the cautious custodians of bank vaults had suddenly turned foolish. Well, not exactly. To understand why overdraft loans haven't bankrupted the banks, you still need a bit more background.

Banks Do Make Big Bad Loans

Banks are fearsomely prudent about personal loans and small business loans, as you can see from the way they screen the loan applications. But their big loans, arranged in the elegant offices of vice-presidents, cause startling losses now and then.

For instance, the six mightiest banks in New York City charged off $39 million in uncollectible loans in 1969. These were loans made by the shrewd experts at Chase Manhattan, Citibank, Morgan Guaranty, Manufacturers Hanover, Bankers Trust and Chemical New York.

If 1969 was a good year for fleecing the banks, 1970 was better; in that year the same big six lost $166 million. Each year, deadbeats and fools cost banks more money. By 1973, net losses on loans at the nation's 473 biggest banks ran about $26 for every $10,000 outstanding, up from $21 the year before. In 1974 United Virginia Bankshares (headed by a former chairman of the Federal Deposit Insurance Corporation) had to write off $3,800,000 in loans secured by fake inventories of cheap wine.

So much for the banks' credit reports and scoring systems. Combine these with their credit losses, and you see a nationwide banking problem. Banks were using a lot of manpower and paperwork to evaluate loan applications, yet were making bad loans.

Meanwhile the "good" loans they needed to make—the short-term, high-interest, low-risk loans—were seldom seen. Hence the banks were plagued by their surplus money as well as their losses.

And so we come back to the advent of overdraft checking loans —a way to put surpluses to work while getting rid of the waste motion and lost time that goes into processing small loan applications.

Overdraft checking was pioneered in this country way back in 1955, when First National Bank in the staid old city of Boston set up a "check credit" plan whereby any depositor who paid off one loan from the bank became automatically entitled to write a check for as much as $3,000 exceeding the amount in his account. Amazingly, this bank found that defaults ran less than ¼ of 1 percent of the overdrafts.

First of Boston was merely copying a system British banks had used for generations. One difference between England and America is that Americans think of a bank as a place to put money, while English view it as a place to get money.

Of course, the only people who get money from British banks are the well-to-do. Their bankers are sternly selective about whom they accept as "depositors." American banks, on the other hand, bestow checkbooks on anyone who shows up with cash and can sign a signature card.

This was why the British overdraft system was thought unworkable in America. But when First of Boston tried it and didn't get burned, other banks one by one began to copy it.

Today most American banks realize that the easiest and fastest and safest—and thus the most profitable—way to make a personal loan is by giving a depositor overdraft privileges. Based on the financial statement you submit, the bank will set an initial overdraft limit of from $2,000 to $5,000. It cuts out the interviews and paper shuffling. More important, it puts a bank's idle capital to work, in the hands of hundreds of customers who had always refused to go through the rigmarole of applying to a bank lending officer, explaining why they wanted a few thousand, filling out a financial statement and loan application, and maybe coming up empty anyhow. Several of my own friends have used overdrafts to raise substantial capital for their businesses after the commercial loan department spurned them.

So go ahead and take what the bank offers you, if you know you can afford the interest charges.

The next step, as you expand your real estate investments, is to arrange for the bank to let you borrow more and more. That's what the next chapter is all about.

KEY POINTS TO REMEMBER

· Most banks now lend automatically for indefinite periods, through overdraft checking accounts.
· Use overdrafts, when possible, in preference to negotiating personal or business loans from a bank.

__4__

How to Borrow More at Lower Interest

Most banks which offer the overdraft privilege don't even require that you apply for it. You get it automatically if you maintain a checking account.

And the repayment terms aren't harsh. The typical overdraft plan calls for you to amortize 5 percent of the deficit each month. In this sense, overdraft accounts are rather like credit-card accounts.

Yet bank programs are even more flexible than the usual credit-card account, which bills you monthly and imposes "late charges" on top of interest if you don't make at least partial payment within a set number of days. And no two banks are quite the same. You'll be smart to shop around and perhaps open checking accounts at several different banks.

You Can Owe the Same Amount Indefinitely

Some banks automatically subtract a partial repayment (commonly $25) from your balance each month if the balance is big enough. Others will wait indefinitely for the principal as long as you pay the interest. Still others don't even require you to pay interest immediately (although they keep charging it against your account) as long as you stay within your credit limit.

Thus if your credit limit is $3,000 and you borrow $2,000 at 16 percent, conceivably you won't have to make any interest payments until almost three years later. Those are better terms than you get on some mortgages.

Furthermore, if you need $10,000 without putting up collateral and without paying interest for an indefinite period, you can probably get it by opening accounts at five different banks which offer this type of overdraft checking, and take $2,000 from each.

Test Your Overdraft Limit

Just how much can you be overdrawn at a bank before it clamps down? This varies from area to area and from bank to bank. It depends partly on how solid a customer you are. You can find out your personal limit by testing, if you wish.

The usual ceiling is somewhere between $500 and $5,000. But if you slightly exceed the ceiling a few times, and pay off immediately, you may gradually stretch your limit without anything being said. But if you need a higher limit than normal, and don't feel safe in pushing it up without asking, you can probably arrange this just by asking for an application over the phone, filling it in and mailing it back.

The Quick Refill System

Even if a bank insists that you repay part of your debt every month, there are ways to owe the same amount indefinitely. One way is by overlapping your repayment with any monthly installments due on a mortgage or car.

Here's how. Suppose the bank requires an overdraft payment by the fifth of each month. And suppose you get a salary check or rent check on the first of the month, from which you would normally make payments on the mortgage. Instead, use that monthly check to pay the overdraft debt. So now you're not delinquent at the bank, and your line of credit is intact again. Four days later you use this newly refilled credit line, again overdrawing to make your usual payments on your installment debts.

This procedure keeps you owing the bank the same amount for years on end, except for the few days between renewing your credit line and reusing it each month. The bank feels safe. And of course the lenders on your home, auto, or whatever get their monthly installments from you as usual. Your interest cost on the bank debt is only a few dollars a month.

When *Not* to Use Overdrafts

Keep in mind that you're charged daily interest from the day the check is posted until you pay off. At this writing, most banks charge an annual rate of around 18 percent, which is less than credit cards and finance companies charge, but more than credit unions, and more than the same banks charge when they promote "bargain rates" for car loans.

Try not to use overdraft borrowing from any bank that charges more than some other bank nearby. Investigate all the banks in your area, if you expect to need credit in the high four figures or more. In general you'll find that small and middle-size banks tend to charge lower interest. The big ones, being slow to change, usually charge higher.

Regardless of which bank you choose, you must realize that those pleasant folks behind the counter are telling you in effect, "Go ahead, be our guest. Buy, buy, buy, the good old American way." Beware of the temptation to splurge.

The best plan is to use a bank's line of instant credit strictly for short-term purposes, repaying fast. Overdraft borrowing is an expensive way of financing a long-term purchase such as real estate—although it can be handy in covering a temporarily negative cash flow from rental property.

When your checking account is low and you feel the urge to buy new clothes or take a vacation trip, ask yourself, "Exactly when and how am I going to repay this overdraft debt?" If you don't have a good answer, you'd better not borrow. Overdraft credit is even more seductive than those handy credit cards. Hundreds of thousands of families are forced to declare personal bankruptcy because easy credit got them in too deep.

Bank Cards Can Be Handy Too

For short-term cash advances, overdraft checking may be cheaper than bank card borrowing because the initial fee is small or nonexistent. But with a bank card you don't have to borrow in multiples of $100. So if the loan is of an odd size, you may do better by using your bank card. (A $102 overdraft usually means you're charged interest on $200.)

When you charge purchases to a credit card such as Visa and then pay the bill within twenty-five days, no interest at all is due under most card arrangements—although some are starting to charge a dime or more per transaction. So when you can pay a bill quickly it's better to use credit cards, because in effect you're borrowing the amount of the bill for as long as twenty-five days, interest-free. In this way you may be able to borrow as much as $2,000 on one card. But check the rules of your particular credit cards, and your bank.

Some big banks now insist that personal loans under a certain size be put on bank cards or overdraft checking. But if you go to a smaller bank or credit union, you're likely to get that same sum on a single-payment loan or a personal installment loan, which may well be cheaper—although it may also take longer to arrange.

If you need the money for only a few weeks, compare the total interest you'll have to pay. A single-payment loan may include sixty or ninety days' worth of interest, or even more. An installment loan ties you to a schedule of repayments which may seem small, yet include more total interest than you'd pay on a short-term overdraft.

When Overdrafts Help

1. Overdraft loans are ideal for certain business needs since you pay interest only during the days you use the money. Sometimes a few thousand dollars, available by writing an overdraft check, can be the difference between making a down payment on real estate—or a cash binder—and losing the chance to buy.

2. If you own and manage furnished rental property, you can save money by dipping into an overdraft account when you spot

a real bargain that's needed in your property—furnishings or appliances on sale at a big discount, for example. Here the interest you'll pay can be comfortably covered by your savings on the buy, assuming you repay the overdraft in a few weeks or even a few months.

③ If you're a sloppy bookkeeper, the interest on overdrafts may be smaller than a pile of "late charges" and interest on overdue bills from creditors. Just get in the habit of paying all your bills in one check-writing session at the beginning of each month, regardless of the balance in your checking account. That's the beauty of overdraft checking: you don't get hit by one of those $5 "service charges" whenever your check exceeds your balance by even 50 cents.

④ Conversely, if you're a sharp-pencil type, overdraft borrowing will help keep the idle dollars in your checking account down to a minimum, so that most of your surplus money can draw daily interest elsewhere as long as possible.

Riding the Float

You do this by taking maximum advantage of the float—the period between buying something with a check or credit card and the actual subtraction of the purchase price from your bank balance. If you time it right, the float on a credit-card purchase can be as long as two months.

Even the float between mailing your check to a distant city and having it processed at your own bank can be ten days. The day the check is deducted from your balance, you'll be notified by mail. As soon as you receive the notice, you should go into the bank and pay off immediately by depositing the amount due, including the interest for a day or two. The bank teller can look up the exact amount for you. Just be sure that your deposit—or, preferably, a check to the bank, drawn against the new deposit —is marked "overdraft repayment" and acknowledged as such by the teller, in writing.

If your overdraft check was for $1,000, say, you've had the use of $1,000 for about ten days at a total cost of perhaps 50 cents. Meanwhile your $1,000 awaiting transfer into your checking account might have been in a money-market fund earning interest compounded daily. Even if the interest rate is only 10 percent annually, it would earn about $2.75 in ten days. Over the course of a year, your accumulated extra interest could buy you several good meals.

5. When you need money in a few hours to meet some emergency, your overdraft account may be the only traditional source you can tap. Where else could you borrow overnight? Only from a finance company, pawnshop, or loan shark. And you know what kind of interest they demand.

6. When there's a chance to lower your tax bill by prepaying various deductible expenses, an overdraft brings you the needed cash. Suppose you're near the end of the tax year, and you'll owe a big tax come April 15. Is there any way to reduce your taxable income before the end of the year? Sure, if you have cash to do so. You owe a bunch of bills that will be tax-deductible— medical and dental costs, job-related expenses, and the like. You've planned to make some tax-deductible charity contributions. Maybe a property tax comes due next February. By making these payments before December 31, you can pull yourself down into a lower bracket. You can do it with overdraft checks. In January—or later, as your budget permits—you can pay off the overdrafts. And don't forget that in the following year the overdraft interest, like most interest expenses, will also become a taxable deduction.

7. If you're self-employed, or if your income suffers short but temporary sinking spasms, overdrafts may be worth their cost just to ease your jangled nerves.

This Insurance Costs Nothing Until You Use It

Maybe you're so prosperous that you think you'll never need overdraft privileges. Maybe there's an abundant cash flow from which you pour money to cover checks as fast as you write them. What a soothing feeling!

But take my advice anyhow: Just in case, find a bank that provides an automatic line of credit with checking. Make sure it requires no minimum balance, charges nothing for checks, levies no "service" fees. (Such a bank can be found in almost any town.) Open a checking account there.

You've nothing to lose. And some day, in a totally unforeseen pinch, you could be glad the extra money is instantly available. It's almost like having insurance coverage for which you pay no premium. Zero cost, until you use it.

KEY POINTS TO REMEMBER

⊘ Ask about overdraft checking plans at all banks in which you could conveniently keep accounts. Some plans are better than others.

⊘ By maintaining accounts at several banks, you may multiply the total you can borrow quickly.

⊘ After opening an account, test the limit of your credit and try to raise it.

⊘ Use a monthly refill system to owe the same amount for months or years.

⊘ A bank charge card may be better than an overdraft when you need an odd amount for a short time, because it doesn't force you to borrow in multiples of $100.

_5_

A Beginner's Guide to Private Financing

This chapter is about the uses of a magical, flexible substance called "private money." Innovative financing ideas that I'll show you in this book are often made possible by private money, rather than by the slower-flowing funds from conventional institutions such as banks and S&Ls.

Private financing becomes especially useful when you advance from small investments into bigger ones. Presumably you're not ready yet for transactions involving a quarter-million dollars or more. But when you do reach that stage, you'll need to understand private financing, and I'd better explain it now, since you may find the background useful even in smaller transactions.

Learn the Language and the Rules

If you're new to the field you'll run into unfamiliar language and unknown rules. I'll cover them here. Old hands at real estate may prefer to skip ahead to Chapter 6.

Maybe you're wondering, "What's so great about private lenders? What's wrong with borrowing from banks or S&Ls?"

Banks and S&Ls are useful and necessary, of course. But they won't be much help to you in a tight-money period, because they dictate borrowing terms and are very choosy about borrowers.

58

Under their current standards, few would-be buyers of real estate can qualify for a mortgage loan from them.

It would be different, perhaps, if you were a millionaire with old money, or if you represented a sizable corporation. Such high-level borrowers can get short-term loans from a bank on their general reputation and credit rating, without pledging specific assets. The rest of us usually have to hock some property in order to wangle a loan from a financial institution, and then have to pay interest at a rate considerably higher than the "prime rate" available to the best customers.

So there isn't much room for creativity or flexibility when you try to arrange a mortgage or a trust deed with your good old statewide bank, or with your dear friends at the savings and loan association. Financial institutions tend to be stodgy. And indeed they should be, most of us feel, since we entrust our rainy-day reserve funds to their care.

To start our definitions from the beginning, "private" money comes from sources called *private lenders*. Sometimes these are called risk capital investors. Who and what are they?

Where to Find Private Lenders

Usually they're individuals who have bags of their own money to invest. This money might otherwise be paid in taxes, so they often accept higher risks than a lending institution would. And they seek higher returns.

You can find potential private lenders almost anywhere except in jail. They can be college professors, playboys, shopkeepers, or thrifty Army sergeants. More commonly they are prosperous doctors, lawyers, executives, or entertainers. Occasionally they may be your in-laws or your bachelor uncle.

Whoever they are, they have one nice trait.

Most of them are looking as hard for you as you are for them —maybe harder, because they hate to let their money lie idle.

Furthermore, the recent easing of capital gains taxes has made them even more receptive to investment ideas. As I'm writing this, a top-bracket investor can hope to pocket or reinvest $80 from every $100 in capital gains, instead of the $50 out of $100 on ordinary income that he is allowed to keep. Consequently investors are starting to take profits they disliked taking in the past, thus freeing cash for new commitments.

If you can't locate the right private lender among your acquaintances, be patient for a few minutes. In the course of this chapter I'll show you how to find as many private lenders as your larynx will allow you to talk with. Finding them is the easy part. The harder part is convincing them that your investment proposal will bring them a satisfactory yield—and this isn't particularly hard when you know enough about real estate.

How Much Will Private Investors Lend?

No individual is likely to lend you more than $99,000. Six-figure sums tend to flow into corporate ventures, high-priced art objects, rare postage stamps and the like.

Within this five-digit limit, any astute lender will generally apply other yardsticks in deciding how much to invest with you.

First of all, he'll want to know the value of whatever you pledge as collateral or security for his loan—as guarantee of payment, that is—just in case you disappear or go broke. He'll probably insist that it be appraised by an outside expert. The appraiser will use one of three standard methods, or a combination of these, to figure out the current market value of the real estate you propose to sign over.

I say "real estate" because that's the most common collateral. If you put up diamonds instead, a lender will want something like the Gemological Institute to examine them. If you offer negotiable securities, he'll look them up in the daily stock quotations, and perhaps in Value Line's quarterly estimates of their future worth. And so on.

After the appraisal, he'll ask, "How much equity do you have in it?"

Rules About Equity

Equity is defined as the owner's share. This can be computed by subtracting mortgages and other liabilities from the market value. Or, if you look at it the other way, your equity is the amount of principal you've paid on property which you are buying on time.

Naturally no lender with an ounce of brains will write you a check for the total amount of your equity. He wants to turn a profit. So he'll compute a certain percentage of your equity, to arrive at an amount he's safe in lending. What percentage? He follows fairly standard rules of thumb. Here they are.

Residential property: 80 percent of the appraised value, minus what you owe on it, or 50 percent of your equity, whichever is lower.

Apartment buildings: 70 percent of the appraised value, minus any existing loans.

Commercial property: 60 percent, minus loans.

Land: 50 percent minus loans—although few lenders accept land as collateral if you owe much on it.

What Scares a Private Lender

Sometimes phrases like "existing loans" in the above rules can loom menacingly. If you've already borrowed heavily against your piece of property, a new lender will be extra careful because he is "taking a secondary position," as money men say. More about that in a moment.

Let's pause here for definitions of a few other terms you'll keep meeting in this book. I'll blend them into a narrative for the sake of easier reading.

Imagine you own a condominium appraised at $150,000 and you need money. You ask the First Reputable Bank for a loan of $50,000. The bank says okay—on condition that you sign a "promissory note" and a "first deed of trust." What do these mean in plain English?

A *promissory note* is like an IOU wrapped in legalese. It's an unconditional promise to pay a certain debt on demand or at a definite date. You'll often hear this document referred to as just a "note." Home and auto loans financed by commercial banks are based on such notes. But notes also have many other uses in creative financing, as we'll see.

A *first deed of trust* (or its near equivalent, a *mortgage*) is legally defined as a formal pledge of property to secure the repayment of a loan. When you sign you say in effect, "If I don't keep my promise to pay $395 per month (or whatever the monthly mortgage payments are), I authorize you to sell my property and pay off the loan with money from the sale." (If the sale brings in more money than you owe, the lender must give you the remainder, unless there are other liabilities against your property, such as unpaid bills from contractors.)

The procedure by which a lender takes possession of property to get back the equivalent of the money he has lent is called *foreclosure,* which will be the subject of a couple of chapters later in this book.

The terms mortgage, deed, trust deed, deed of trust, and first loan are used almost interchangeably in real estate. All five refer to documents that come under the general classification of *commercial paper,* another term you'll often encounter in financial dealings. It covers many different legal papers used in commerce —including such items as checks, notes, bank drafts, certificates of deposit, and similar *negotiable instruments.* There are two types of commercial paper, negotiable and non-negotiable. Negotiable paper can be transferred by endorsement or sometimes just by handing over the paper—if, for example, it's a promise to pay "bearer." This means that the debtor must pay the person who has the paper in his possession.

In a non-negotiable paper, the debtor states that he owes a sum of money to a specific individual or organization and will pay the money only to that legal entity.

Now about your $150,000 condominium. You need more money than the $50,000 you borrowed from the bank. You get more by signing another note and another mortgage—called a *second mortgage, second trust deed, junior loan* or the like.

So you're putting up the same collateral for two different debts. This sounds odd to the novice, but it's routine in real estate. You're not legally limited to one mortgage on your property. While the property itself can't be carved up among different creditors, the proceeds of its sale certainly can.

If you get two mortgages, the date of recording determines the *seniority* of the loan—in other words, which lender gets paid first from the sale of the property if you default.

Some Investors Dislike Second Mortgages

Junior loans are higher-risk investments. As we've seen, the first mortgage takes precedence by law, and the lender on the second mortgage may never get his money back. To rephrase the same hazard in financial jargon, the rights of the *junior* lender are *subordinate* to those of the first lender. Let's see how this works out in practice.

Using the example of your condominium borrowings, if you can't pay, the First Reputable Bank will foreclose and sell your condo for whatever it can get. If it gets only $55,000, then it keeps $50,000 to cancel out your debt to it. The remaining $5,000 goes to Old Fateful Mortgage Company, holder of the second mortgage. If the company lent you more than $5,000, too bad for Old Fateful. You're not obliged to pay any more, now that you've forfeited your property. (Under certain conditions the company might get a court judgment against you, entitling it to seize something else you own, but that's a legal matter beyond the scope of this book.)

Bear in mind that a second mortgage won't scare private lenders if the value of your collateral is far greater than the sum of the first and second mortgages. Therefore *seconds,* as realty people call them for short, are used as tools in various financing maneuvers I'll describe in this book.

Assumable Loans Are Tricky

Institutional lenders and private lenders alike prefer not to make *assumable loans*. In case you need a translation and explanation of that phrase, here it is.

Occasionally somebody buys property without going through the usual channels, by *assuming*—taking over, as a substitute debtor—a mortgage that hasn't been paid off. Bypassing lenders, he deals directly with the owner, paying him whatever amount represents his equity in the property, and agreeing to take full responsibility for the remainder of the payments.

This is delightful for the buyer during years when interest rates are climbing. By taking over the older mortgage he gets a lower interest rate than any currently available. Then too, he saves closing costs, which can add up to several hundred dollars.

Buyer and seller can make this kind of agreement without permission from the mortgage holder, unless the mortgage prohibits it—which it certainly does, in most transactions arranged since 1976. Many mortgages issued before then were assumable because they lacked the "due-on-sale" clause that has been a bone of contention between borrowers and S&Ls. You'll find more about that in Chapter 17.

Technically the responsibility for repaying the original loan stays with the original owner—unless the lender gives him a written release. Lenders are sticky about such a release. Why should they continue a loan made at 8 percent when new loans are being made at, say, 12 percent?

If you yourself assume a mortgage or trust deed, be as careful as in taking on any other big debt. The contract is between you and the seller (the original owner of the property) and doesn't affect the rights of the bank or S&L—the *mortgagee*—which drew up the mortgage. The original owner's legal responsibility for the debt will not help you if he moves away, and you miss a payment. The mortgagee may try to foreclose and grab the property—and may succeed. Talk to a lawyer before assuming an existing mortgage on property you want to buy. It may save you plenty on interest charges, but you should know the legal risks involved, and should be aware that the mortgagee won't feel friendly to you.

Lenders Love Prepayment Penalties

No borrower wants to be burdened with high interest charges any longer than he can help. He'd like to cut down the number of payments, if possible, so there'll be less interest to pay, and perhaps so he can resell his property without a mortgage on it.

But this wouldn't please the mortgagee, the lender. It would be like substituting a shorter, smaller mortgage for the longer, bigger mortgage originally agreed on. In other words, the lender's money wouldn't bring back as big a total return as expected.

Therefore he probably tries to forbid prepayment, or at least discourage it, by means of a clause in the mortgage. The typical clause provides for a stiff penalty charge to a borrower who pays off a note ahead of time. Contrariwise, a shrewd borrower tries to negotiate a different clause: one allowing prepayment without penalty. FHA and VA loans include this no-penalty clause.

Four Kinds of Private Money Loans

Most loans fall into one of four general classifications: (1) fully amortized; (2) partially amortized; (3) interest only; (4) straight loans.

Amortized is another word that trips lightly from the tongues of the money-minded but may confuse newcomers. It sounds sort of grim, like "mortify" and "mortuary." That's natural, since all three words are descendants of the Latin word for "death."

Amortization means paying a debt by installments, thus liquidating it or wiping it out. The common method of amortizing is by equal payments at equal intervals of time. Each payment includes interest on the outstanding debt and a repayment of part of the principal. At the beginning of the loan's term, the proportion of an installment that goes for interest is very big, while only a tiny part of the principal is paid. These proportions gradually reverse until the loan is fully paid off at the end of the specified term. That's the type 1 loan mentioned above. It's generally written for five to fifteen years, although longer terms are also available.

Type 2, the partially amortized loan, provides for an inflated final installment, the so-called "balloon payment," at the end of a three or five-year term. This is because the monthly payments are smaller than they would have to be if the loan were fully amortized during its term.

Those low, low installments sound enticing. And the borrower may think he'll be richer by the time the balloon comes due, or will have resold the property by then. Or the lender may assure him, "You can easily negotiate a new loan if necessary when the balloon comes due." Maybe. Just maybe. Many borrowers have been badly hurt on type 2 loans during years of high interest rates.

Type 3 is even more dangerous to a borrower. Interest-only loans are usually for one to five years, with the entire principal falling due on the day the loan matures—just as it did in *The Merchant of Venice,* remember? The borrower had better be very sure he can produce the money on the due date. Otherwise his pound of flesh is on the chopping block.

Type 4, the straight loan, is the shortest-term kind—generally for no longer than three years, and sometimes for only three or six months, with all the interest as well as the principal coming due on the same day.

So much for the main rules of private financing. Now we'll see where to find such financing.

How to Get Help in Finding Private Money

Make contacts before you need them. Get on chummy terms with some of the people who can steer you to private lenders. Who are these people?

You'll find one of them in the nearest independent bank.

Not in a branch, even the biggest branch, of any of the banking chains that look so impressive. These chains have tight rules. A branch manager can't break a rule without asking the big brothers at the head office. He hates to do this. So he isn't in the habit of thinking inventively. What you want is a locally owned bank, where the main man is accessible. Find a way to get acquainted with him.

One simple strategy will make a good impression on him: establish a record of borrowing from his bank and repaying on time. It can be a personal loan, car loan, home improvement, mortgage, anything. If your note is backed by liquid assets—stocks or bonds, for example, or a savings passbook—the bank probably won't even make a credit check. The next step may be to ask the top man at the bank for counsel and advice on some business problem, even if you already know the answer. This is a way of conditioning him to the idea that he's your problem-solver, a man in whom you have faith.

Bankers Can Be Bluffed

A more elaborate method was explained by a shrewd operator who came into a town with no assets except walking-around money from a business he owned. Here's his story:

"I looked up an aggressive young lawyer who represented several small business firms in town. As soon as we were friends, I got him to take me to lunch with the up-and-coming vice-president of the local bank. At lunch I chatted about various business enterprises I had in mind, sort of giving the impression they were already going strong. I paid for the lunch by peeling off a hundred-dollar bill from the outside of a thick bankroll. (My roll consisted of dollar bills except for two hundreds on the outside.) The banker noticed the hundreds and the thick roll. He was glad to meet me again at his bank.

"At the bank I said I'd decided to put one of my business accounts in his bank. I mentioned that it was the smallest I was working on, and that when I got settled in town I would probably want to transfer larger accounts to the bank as well. I opened a checking account by handing him my other hundred-dollar bill. I explained this was just a token deposit to get things started, and I would transfer other funds as soon as I could arrange to switch the account from the other bank—which I did. So for lunch and a C-note I got a banker to think of me as a successful business man." Later on this banker was happy to introduce him to wealthy people who were looking for ways to increase their wealth by lending.

In whatever ways suit your taste and personality, get close to an independent banker, and to a loan officer at a small S&L. Do what you can to be helpful to their institutions. It doesn't hurt to take these people around and introduce them to other businessmen. Try to bring in a few strangers to open accounts. Then, when you finally come along with a proposition, if the institutions can't finance it because of some rule or policy, your friends near the top of the institutions may take personal pride in helping you find private money.

Look in the Yellow Pages

Your phone book lists many private money brokers. They come in two types. One type arranges second trust deeds on residential property. The other arranges secondary home loans too, but also buys and sells discounted trust deeds. These brokers look for equity and are usually glad to make imaginative financing arrangements where there is good security. An experienced broker is well worth his fees. Use him to your advantage.

In the chapters ahead I'll refer occasionally to private money *brokerage fees,* which can run to ten or fifteen *points* and up, depending on the quality of the loan and terms. Constant changes in the marketplace may make some of the numbers I mention sound unrealistic. Don't let this bother you. Absorb the principles, not the numbers. The principles are valid, whatever the current prices and percentages may be.

Brokerage fees are the charges a mortgage-loan broker levies for arranging a loan. Most states have laws setting a top limit on these fees. The fees cover the broker's costs and expenses, as well as his basic commission. *Points* are one-time charges by any lender for arranging a loan. They are computed as percentages. That is, "one point" would be comparable to 1 percent of the principal. For example, Golconda S&L may "charge eight points" on a loan. So for a $50,000 loan the borrower would fork over $4,000 in points, in addition to the ongoing interest.

Pick up your daily paper and you'll find classified ads offering to lend money, or to buy and sell notes. Make a list of these sources. Drop in and get acquainted. Size up how they do business. They too can help you solve financing problems when the time comes.

You can find investors directly if you are active in your community. At church, in a service club, in a college alumni association, and in many other groups, when you turn the conversation to real estate or the stock market you'll probably discover that some people in the group are actively investing bundles of cash from time to time. Build a list of such people. When you're ready for financing, don't be bashful about approaching them. They'll be receptive.

So much for background. Now let's set up some typical real estate problems and see how the right financing can solve them.

KEY POINTS TO REMEMBER

· For major investments, private lenders are probably your best source of financing.
· Get to know an executive of a small independent bank, because he can introduce you to many private lenders.

__6__

How to Get Quick Cash from Lenders

Now we're ready to explore some financing problems that may come up when you become a fairly big operator. By then you'll be dealing mostly with private lenders. By understanding how they think, you can buy from them, sell to them, or induce them to invest with you—on terms that will be profitable to both parties.

Buy for Less by Offering Higher Interest

Let's say you've met an elderly gentleman named Cal Reinhart who owns fifty acres of good land in Oregon, and wants to sell. You want to buy.

His asking price is $144,000. You offer $139,000. But Cal quickly makes clear that $144,000 is his immovable, non-negotiable price.

Why did he pick this particular price? Figure out what he really wants or needs, and then you'll know how to negotiate.

You keep chatting with him, trying to draw him out. Finally he rummages in his cluttered desk and dredges up an old loan-table book. He shows you a page of amortization schedules, and some penciled arithmetic showing that by selling for $144,000, accepting 10 percent down and lending you the remaining $129,600 (90 percent of $144,000) on a thirty-year mortgage he would get monthly payments of $695.72.

"That's what I'll need every month to get along on after I retire next year, and I can't make it on any less," he says. His calculations are based on carrying charges of only 5 percent—remarkably low in these times.

Suddenly you realize that the only amount Cal really cares about is the amount of that monthly check. So why shouldn't you raise the interest rate to, say, 10 percent? Then your purchase price can come down without cutting Cal's monthly income.

You study the loan amortization tables. You find that at 10 percent interest with the same down payment, and a loan of only $79,279, the monthly payments would be the same:

selling price	$93,678.78	
cash down payment	− 14,400.00	
financing need	79,278.78	($79,278.78 at 10 percent for 30 years amortizes at $695.72 a month for a total of $250,460)

You have taken the all-important monthly payment and worked your way back to the price tag. Despite the big reduction in selling price, Cal will receive the same monthly payments either way. The down payment will be the same. And the total take for Cal or his heirs after thirty years will be the same—$250,462. (This would be the total if $129,600 were amortized at 5 percent for thirty years.)

"But what happens if you prepay the loan?" Cal demands.

To protect him, you write in a sliding prepayment penalty clause that will assure him the equivalent of his asking price in case of early payoff. This penalty has to be so big that the borrower also needs protection, which you provide by inserting another clause permitting transfer of the note to other suitable property.

Your proposition makes Cal explode briefly, but he agrees to sell when you show him he'll get just what he wants—$695.72 a month, and a quarter-million plus over thirty years.

Selling Notes at a Discount

A note, you remember, is a promise to pay. The note has value, so it can be pledged as security, almost like a stock certificate or the certificate of ownership on your car. "If I don't pay you what I owe, you can take the note to court and get a judgment against me—or sell it and keep as much of the proceeds as I owe you."

There's a market for notes, just as there's a market for money and scrap iron and almost anything else. People buy and sell notes as they do bonds.

In selling a note, they get what it is worth in the marketplace —its current value to anyone willing to buy it. This means it is almost always *discounted*. In other words, the buyer pays less than its face value, so he'll make a profit when he collects the face value from the note's signer.

How to Compare Notes

Suppose you're considering several notes. You must figure which one is worth most. Which should you buy? Which should you sell? Which should you pledge for security?

Take a simple problem of two notes you want to sell. Both notes are for $10,000. One is from Drew Blue, the other from Bob White.

Blue's note promises to pay interest of 10 percent. It promises monthly payments (part interest, part principal) of $200 until paid.

White's note carries 9 percent interest included in installments of $400 per month.

Both are equally secured, so you can seize property if the signer defaults. Both are fully amortized—in other words, the principal is paid down month by month during the term of the note until it is fully paid at maturity.

Which should you sell?

Offhand you might say, "Blue's note is more valuable because it pays higher interest." But wait. You'd better analyze the two notes more deeply. To do this you need equipment. For a few dollars any bookstore will sell you a book containing yield tables.

Payback Rate Is More Important than Interest Rate

Yield depends on the repayment period, the *term* of the note. Whoever buys the note is lending money. The sooner he gets his money back plus the discount (profit), the higher the yield for him.

Here's the equation:

$$\frac{\text{monthly payments}}{\text{current balance of the note}} = \text{monthly payback rate}$$

Apply this to the Blue note, and you get:

$$\frac{\$200 \text{ monthly payments}}{\$10,000 \text{ face value}} = .02 \text{ or 2 percent}$$

Applied to the White note:

$$\frac{\$400 \text{ monthly payments}}{\$10,000 \text{ face value}} = .04 \text{ or 4 percent}$$

So the Blue note's payback rate is 2 percent, the White note's rate is 4 percent.

Now open your book of yield tables. Turn to the page on 10 percent interest, since that's the rate carried by the Blue note. You find the figures dealing with "Fully Amortized Note," which is what Blue is. Then you find (on the left-hand column) the payback rate of 2 percent you just calculated.

Now you need to know another number: the current yield demanded by investors in the market. Ask a banker or broker. Let's say it's 17 percent yearly.

Okay, so you run your finger along the 2 percent line until it comes under the 17 percent heading at the top. At that intersection you read 15.44.

This tells you that 15.44 percent is the fraction by which the note must be discounted to produce a 17 percent annual yield on a 2 percent payback note. So you take 15.44 percent of $10,000 and get $1,544 as your answer. This is the discount on the Blue note. By subtracting $1,544 from $10,000 you get $8,456, the market value of the Blue note.

Do the same for White, going to the 9 percent interest table page and using the 4 percent payback rate. Again you search out the 17 percent yield currently demanded by investors, and you come up with 8.64 percent of discount needed to produce 17 percent yearly on a 4 percent payback note.

$864 is the discount on the White note. Subtracting this from $10,000 you find the White note's current market value is $9,136. So White's note is more valuable, even though it looks less valuable to the untutored eye. That's because White will pay off faster than Blue.

Wealthy Lenders Want Income

One reason I've gone into this in such detail is that it shows you a key fact about the psychology of wealthy people, who are the most frequent buyers of notes. The wealthy are primarily interested in placing capital so that it will produce a large and safe stream of income.

In other words, the size of the stream is more important to them than the length of the stream. (In the case of Blue note vs. White note, White's monthly payments were therefore more attractive than Blue's $200.)

There's a corollary to the principle I've just stated: unlike the wealthy, middle-class people who sometimes need financing are primarily interested in directing income so that it accumulates as capital.

They buy real estate, stocks and other things mainly in the hope of capital gains, not so much for dividends or rental income.

Cash from a Pledge Account

Ready for another problem? Here's one, involving a S&L this time.

Because so many good houses are on the market these days, with high mortgage rates barring some home-seekers from buying, you look at these homes in hope of finding a way to buy one as an investment.

You come across one that looks good. The owner has to sell because he's taking a government job in Washington. He accepts your offer of $250,000 with $50,000 down.

We'll assume you have enough cash for the down payment. But there's a hitch. You'll need financing on the remaining $200,000.

You can probably get it by offering a private investor a share of whatever profit you make in reselling the house (see Chapters 16–17). But this time you may do better by borrowing from the Bountiful S&L, a small free-wheeling outfit with which you've built up a good relationship. It knows you have a steady flow of income from investments, so it considers you a good credit risk. You think your loan application will slide through smoothly.

But Bountiful's loan officer gives you a cool stare after the house is appraised. "Based on this appraisal, the maximum loan we can make is $190,000."

So you're still short $10,000.

You don't want to reopen the talks with the homeowner and try to buy for less, because $250,000 is a fair price. Nor do you want to put a second mortgage on the property.

What to do? Well, you have a $10,000 savings certificate at Bountiful. It won't mature for two years yet. You hate the thought of cashing it in, because of the steep penalty you'll be charged.

But you can pledge it. Then it will still keep drawing interest for you. You'll be using the same principle as the passbook loan I explained in Chapter 2.

So here's the proposition you make to the loan officer: "I want this house and I need your loan, but it has to be for $200,000, not $190,000. Here's my savings certificate for $10,000. Will you accept it as a pledge tie to the loan?"

The certificate (or CD, as it's usually called) is virtually as good as cash. If you default on the loan, Bountiful can keep your $10,000 savings. This extra sweetener gives the S&L a risk-free loan. You get the house with a comfortable first mortgage, and you still retain your $10,000 savings in the S&L, although of course you can't make any withdrawals.

But you make one more shrewd move. You get a clause inserted in the pledge account agreement providing for annual reappraisal of the house. When it is appraised high enough to cover the $200,000 loan, the clause provides for release of the CD.

No Savings? Same Strategy

You still may be able to use this strategy without having a CD or even a passbook. I discovered this during my early days in Oakland, California. I was trying to buy a house and the loan commitment was $4,000 below what I needed. I had no savings certificate, no bank passbook. But there was a savings passbook available—the seller's. Now it so happens that sellers are often willing to help finance the buyer of their home. In this case I talked the seller into pledging his own savings account as security for *my* first mortgage loan!

How to Sweeten a Note

Now for another problem. Suppose you need cash once more. The only paper you have that can readily be converted to cash is a note you took back from John and Jill Hill when they bought a house from you two years ago. It's for $10,000 payable at $200 monthly and carrying 10 percent interest with no due date. It's fully amortized.

To keep the example simple, disregard payments the Hills have made. Assume that the current balance is $10,000. What can you get for this note on the market? Loan brokers in your area demand an 18 percent yield.

Using the formula you saw on page 72, you find that the discounted value of the note is only $8,264.

You shudder. Must you pay so heavy a penalty to get the cash you need? Isn't there some way to make your note worth more to a buyer?

Payback rate is the key, remember? How can you improve the payback rate?

Here's how. You go to John and Jill and say, "Hey, I'll cut your interest rate to 9 percent if you can step up your monthly payments from $200 to $400 a month. You'll save in the long run. By paying off faster you'll cut down the number of interest payments, as well as the interest rate itself. So the total amount you pay will be a whole bunch less. Figure it out.''

John and Jill are pleased. They decide they can part with an extra $200 a month in order to reduce the total amount they pay, and get out of debt sooner.

This makes your discounted note worth $9,035, which is $771 more than it was before. By using the principle that money costs less as the payback time shortens, you've solved your problem and saved some money.

How to Put an Equity to Work

All right, you're doing beautifully in your real estate investing. Now let's say you own a nice triplex worth $200,000 on the market. You've found a duplex you can buy at a bargain price. But there's the same old problem: you're $10,000 short of what you need for the down payment.

Should you raise the money by refinancing the triplex? Bountiful S&L holds a $90,000 mortgage on it. "Sure, you can refinance to a $100,000 loan," the friendly officer tells you. "It will cost you four points, and you'll pay 12 percent interest instead of the 9 percent on the old mortgage."

You eye the numbers balefully:

existing loan	$ 90,000
buyer needs	10,000
new loan	$100,000
4 points on loan	4,000
service charge	150
cost of new loan	$ 4,150

You don't want to shell out four grand plus for the sake of getting ten in cash. Nor do you wish to be hooked for 3 percent higher interest payments throughout a thirty-year mortgage. You look for a smarter, cheaper way.

How about a private money loan secured by a second mortgage?

Using the mortgage formula set forth near the beginning of

Chapter 5 ("Apartment buildings: 70 percent of appraised value, minus any existing loans") you jot down these figures:

triplex market value	$200,000
70 percent of value	140,000
less current loan	−90,000
possible second loan	$ 50,000

You don't need a loan of $50,000, of course. All you need is a $10,000 loan, which is easy. It costs you 16 points (16 percent of $10,000, which is $1,600) and will be at 14 percent interest for five years.

The points and interest rate may sound horrific. But not when you compare the total cost of this financing to what it would cost at Bountiful.

second mortgage	$10,000
16 points	1,600
cost of second loan	$1,600

This way you save $2,550 in refinancing charges. And you retain the comparatively low-interest triplex loan of $90,000. You'll pay the higher 14 percent on only the $10,000 you need, for only five years. You're far ahead.

One Way to Put Land to Work

Now let's imagine a tighter spot. You've run out of cash and you're mortgaged to the eyebrows because you're building a racquetball club. To complete its financing, you need $50,000.

Again you scan your resources. The only asset you can pledge for security is a prime piece of commercial land. It's worth $300,000, maybe more. But there's no market for it at the moment. Anyhow, you want to hold it because you're planning a small shopping center on that site.

In Chapter 5 I suggested that you get acquainted with a local independent banker before you need him. We'll assume you've done this.

You've cultivated Bob Bursar, president of Sunken Heights

State Bank. By paying attention when he talks, you've learned that Bob, being a major stockholder of the bank, is concerned about bank yields. Can you use this concern as a lever to pry loose a loan?

Bob knows the area well, and specifically the value of your idle land. And yes, you've kept Bob up-to-date on your various ventures. Only a few weeks ago you managed to be sitting next to Bob at Rotary Club, and in response to Bob's automatic "What's new?" you outlined your idea for the shopping center.

So now, when you're ready to ask for money, you get his immediate attention. You begin, "I'd like to get an $80,000 loan on that $300,000 parcel," knowing full well that Sunken Heights seldom lends on idle land.

(If you're following closely, you may mentally ask at this point, "Why $80,000? Supposedly I need only $50,000." You'll see why in a moment.)

You continue, "I'd also like you to shave the interest rate a bit below what you normally charge on land loans. To do all this, you'll naturally need a financial inducement. Here it is. Your bank is stuck with a stack of low-yield notes. I'll buy $30,000 worth at par."

You and Bob both realize that unloading notes in today's market may be tough. His eyes widen. Perhaps he secretly wonders why you'll buy low-yield notes at face value. But he makes the loan. Why not? He knows you, he knows the land parcel, and he knows about your plans to develop it. So he's sure you'll pay back the loan in good time. Meanwhile his bank is getting off the hook for $30,000 of notes that he might have had to discount heavily.

You're happy too. You still own your vacant land. The bank has now officially recognized its value, which may help later. You walk away with the $80,000 you need—$50,000 for your racquetball club, $30,000 to buy the bank's notes—at a reasonable interest rate, somewhat eased by the interest you'll be collecting on the notes.

It's another illustration of what we've seen before in this chapter: Look for the other party's needs and try to accommodate them.

When to Sell with Strings Attached

Sometimes, instead of borrowing, it's better to get cash by selling property you want to keep—if you can sell with an option to repurchase.

Let's come back to that planned mini-shopping center of yours. You have now subdivided your land into two parts, and you've started building the shopping center on the larger piece. As for the smaller piece, you plan to put a medical building on it later.

Again you're short of cash. (This is a common problem among big-money real estate operators, who understand the benefits of using other people's money.) You need $50,000 to finish the shopping center. Should you hock the land you set aside for your medical building?

That land now has a market value of $120,000. A beady-eyed speculator offers $81,600 for it, all cash, if you'll sell immediately.

Probably some unprintable thoughts flash through your mind. You have no intention of letting your land go for 32 percent less than its market value. And you won't give up your plan for a medical building.

Private lenders hear about your problem and start phoning, ready to lend on the land. Many call but none are chosen. You don't want to take on more debt that you can handle.

You hear that Stan Naylor has just sold his hardware store, and is looking to invest a bundle wherever there's a safe juicy profit in view. So you sculpture a deal that is sure to please Stan.

"I'll sell you my land for half price, $60,000," you tell him. "It's worth $120,000—which you can verify by asking the bank."

Stan chuckles. "I know all about it. I heard you just turned down $81,600 for it. Suddenly you're eager to accept $60,000. What's your angle?"

"Just this. You'll have to give me an option to buy the land back for $85,000 within two years. That's a good deal for both of us."

Stan can't lose. Either he makes $25,000 profit in two years or he owns valuable land at half price.

You stand to gain too. You can put $50,000 to work immediately in finishing the shopping center, and keep the extra $10,000 as a cushion against unexpected needs for cash. You're free of tax payments or other obligations on the land for two years, by which time you plan to start the medical building. You may also have a good-sized tax deduction for a capital loss, if the $60,000 is less than you paid for that part of the land.

Is it sound finance to sell something for $60,000 and repurchase it for $85,000? In this case, yes. In two years the land should be worth more than its present value of $120,000.

Then too, in the long run you're better off losing $25,000 and regaining your land than losing it permanently for $38,400 less than it is worth, in a quick sale to the speculator.

Of course you must get expert legal advice in drawing up the agreement. You can't lawfully prearrange a guaranteed buy-back. You must be "at risk" as you sell the land.

Anyhow, we've seen another way to get cash quickly from a private investor, without ruining your long-term plans. Keep it in mind as an alternative to selling or to taking on heavier loan payments than you can afford.

KEY POINTS TO REMEMBER

☉ Tailor your proposition to the other party's needs as well as your own.

☉ A seller may be mainly interested in how much he'll receive monthly. By offering bigger payments you may be able to buy for a smaller price.

☉ Wealthy lenders are less interested in capital gains than in generating a large and safe stream of income.

☉ Notes can often be bought or sold at discounts. Learn to calculate their payback rate so you can determine how much they must be discounted to produce the "going rate" of yield.

☉ When you have a savings or certificate at a bank or S&L, you can borrow against it.

☉ When assets are tied up in real estate, use them to finance new investments with short-term private money loans. As you analyze the financing, compare not only the points quoted but also the cost of refinancing, terms, and savings on interest.

⊙ Instead of borrowing on property, sometimes it's better to get cash by selling with an option to repurchase.

_7_

Yes, There Still Are Bargains in Real Estate

In an overheated housing market that has often included waiting lines, lotteries, large profits, plummeting sales, and more than a hint of panic and speculation, average prices have jumped far out of reach of small investors. House prices have risen twice as fast as family income during the last decade. At this writing (1983) they are moving up more slowly, but seem sure to keep climbing.

Meanwhile the violent up-and-down cycles in interest rates have become a threat to borrowers instead of lenders, because of the Federal Home Loan Bank Board's decision in April 1981 to let federal S&Ls protect themselves by making long-term loans at interest rates that can change many times during the life of the loan. This ruling means that residential mortgage lenders now give preference to borrowers whose future earnings seem likely to keep pace with inflation. Borrowing comes harder for would-be realty investors who are near retirement age, or past it.

So the era of quick and easy profits in real estate appears to be slowing down, at least temporarily. Nevertheless, investors who are shrewdly selective in what they buy can still find bargains and can still resell profitably.

Where to Look for the Hidden Bargains

Where do the smart investors look? Certainly not in the "good" neighborhoods with easy commuting, handy shopping and excellent schools nearby. Any property that is obviously well located will command a premium even if it's falling apart.

Finding the hidden bargains takes more than a casual drive with a real estate salesman. It requires prowling in supposedly undesirable locations.

Most metropolitan areas are checkered with city and suburban neighborhoods that look shabby or worse. There are grim vistas of decaying dwellings more than a half-century old. Strange as it seems, many of these are today's bargain areas. Younger families are buying and renovating there.

This is happening in city after city. In Boston, the waterfront area is where the action is. In New York it's Park Slope, in Brooklyn. Chicago has its New Town, Wicker Park, North Austin, and Albany Park. Los Angeles has its Venice and Watts.

Homes costing $55,000 to $65,000 around Houston's Medical Center have been bought and restored by ambitious newcomers. Capitol Hill in Washington, D.C., has gone through a major renaissance, and houses sell for $120,000 on what were blighted blocks in 1970.

Get In Early

Do you see what this can mean to you as an investor? More areas like those I've just mentioned are starting into transition all the time. The trick is to spot a rundown neighborhood early in the turnaround stage. Buy old buildings there at sacrifice prices. Dust them off, make them livable, then resell quickly to young people who are eager to move in and undertake most of the improvement work themselves. You're doing these people a service, because they couldn't afford to rent elsewhere while putting a place into move-in condition.

Don't Let Prejudice Worry You

The dark side of the real estate business is prejudice. But it can work to your advantage—and you can help overcome it—as you seek and find low-priced property in so-called "ethnic" areas. In this era of housing shortages, the buyers will come when you show the way.

Families looking for homes depend heavily on real estate salespeople. This helps perpetuate segregated housing. The tradition of the real estate business has been to consider the agent as a kind of gatekeeper to the community. Unless told otherwise, the typical broker takes the safe course of showing white neighborhoods to white families, black neighborhoods to blacks. But now there are high-principled (and thrifty) families who want to break away from that sort of uniformity and are willing to buy in ethnically mixed or segregated areas because of lower prices.

In all parts of the country there are communities almost solidly black, or Mexican, or Puerto Rican, or Cuban, or Jewish, but they are changing. They are being infiltrated by families with dissimilar backgrounds who spend hundreds of hours of their own time fixing up old units, and thereby succeed in raising real estate values. Contrary to common belief, it is almost always the prosperity of a neighborhood's residents, not their race or origin, that makes property values rise or fall. A case in point is Philadelphia's West Mount Airy, an old residential section where values have risen during recent years. It is about half black. If you find similar sections, you can scoop up bargains before the crowd arrives.

Look Farther Out

The fix-up trend is spreading to the suburbs too. Sometimes a young family gets into a good community by converting an ancient barn, firehouse, or corner grocery store. Whenever you find an old, unused building that could be converted to residential use (whether as one-family home, an apartment building, or a condominium) you should investigate. Who owns it, and what is the asking price? One investor, J. Timothy Anderson, made townhouses out of a former jail in Windsor, Vermont; apartments out of a tannery in Peabody, Massachusetts; and a condo from a school in Gloucester, Massachusetts.

Underbuilt areas outside town can be bargain areas too. People will drive a long way for affordable housing nowadays, even with high gasoline prices. Mortgage costs loom a lot larger in family budgets than transportation, and the price saving can make the longer commuting tolerable.

By going thirty miles or more outside Houston, buyers still sometimes find houses under $60,000. You can acquire a home for $70,000 in the blue-collar community of Waltham outside Boston. And in fast-growing Gwinnett and Cobb counties, a half-hour drive north of downtown Atlanta, thousands of lower-priced houses have been sold since 1979. Why not get in your car and look around the outskirts of your own metropolitan area?

Of course you're not the only investor who is awakening to these new possibilities, so you may find yourself bidding against others for an apparently undesirable building. I don't advise you to jump into hot competition on your first realty investment. You need experience to determine just how high you can safely bid on a problem property.

Your Best Bet: Distressed Properties

Instead, I suggest you consider an even less crowded field of real estate which may be one of the best remaining opportunities for sizable investment gains: the field of "distressed properties," as they're called in realty jargon. The term applies to properties that have underlying problems involving "best use," price, financing or construction. I think this field is so promising that I'm going to concentrate on it for the rest of this chapter, and for the next two chapters as well.

To begin with, you should realize that this is an especially tricky type of real estate investment. Buyers need to be watchful for pitfalls at every step.

For example, the owner of a distressed property usually over-prices it. A building that seems to be a bargain at first glance may be structurally unsound, or may have other hidden defects. You can buy a clearer view of its value by spending $200 to $500 for an independent appraisal. But even if the asking price turns out to be reasonable, or even a giveaway, the property may be more costly than you think because of liens for unpaid bills or other legal claims you don't know about.

One thing you do know for sure. The place is a headache for its owner. You must find out why.

What's the Trouble?

Owners stop making payments on mortgages for a wide variety of reasons. The terrain around their property may have changed,

86

so that it is vulnerable to landslides or flooding. Maybe street traffic is getting so bad that people risk an accident whenever they pull out of the driveway. If it's an apartment building, maybe tenants are leaving because of lack of parking. Maybe the neighborhood is becoming a high-crime area.

Stay away from such places. You can find other problem properties with intrinsically sound values.

The owner of a perfectly sound building in an adequate location may be in trouble because he paid a foolishly high price for it, or because he took on loan payments he couldn't handle. Maybe he's sick. Maybe his family has broken up or his job has gone sour.

For any of these reasons, or others, the owner may have decided to bleed the property, collecting rents while letting maintenance slide, paying no taxes, and fending off bill collectors as long as he can. Such an owner simply wants to suck up as much cash as possible before losing his equity.

Sheer mismanagement is the most common cause of trouble in multifamily buildings. It's almost axiomatic that when you buy a distressed apartment complex, one of the first things you usually must do is fire the manager. The place may be so filthy that the good tenants have left and only deadbeats remain. Or there may be a few really obnoxious residents who are driving out all others. Contrariwise, you sometimes find a manager so harsh and strict that nobody wants to stay.

It boils down to this. When you find a property in distress, don't get into serious negotiations until you're sure what the trouble really is. If it is something you can cure, fine. Go further with negotiations.

Acquiring a distressed property looks complicated and mysterious to the average real estate investor. If it looked simple, scores of people would be doing it. But once you understand the process, you'll find it's easier than it looks. So we'll go through it step by step.

A Drama in Three Acts

The process by which a property is taken away from a delinquent borrower is a sad drama in three acts. You can buy during any of the three:

1. A borrower falls behind in payments and is declared to be in default.
2. His property is auctioned off at a foreclosure sale.
3. He is dispossessed, while the new owner faces up to the question of "What should be done with this property?" (Usually the new owner is the bank or S&L that held the mortgage or trust deed.)

Quite often you can wangle the best financing and other terms at the third phase, but good buys may be possible at any moment during the entire drama. Sometimes it depends on general conditions in the real estate market: how many owners are falling behind in payments; how many foreclosed properties the lender has in inventory; and other factors affecting supply and demand.

Your own temperament will also play a part in determining which phase is the best time for you, personally, to go into action. Some investors prefer to negotiate with lending institutions; others do better in dealing directly with distressed owners.

Then too, the approach you take at any of the three stages will differ somewhat depending on whether a single-family or multi-family property is at stake.

We'll consider these possibilities in detail as we go along. But first you need to understand the legal background.

Foreclosure Laws

As most people know, mortgage-loan agreements usually provide that the total amount of the loan will fall due if the property owner fails to meet his regular monthly payments or defaults on his real estate taxes or his insurance payments. In such a crunch the mortgagee, or lender, may foreclose the mortgage and sell the mortgaged property to satisfy the debt.

Most states have detailed statutes setting out the specific procedure and timing that must be followed in a foreclosure action. These laws vary among the states. The laws which apply are those of the state where the property is, even though the people involved may live in other states.

A friend of mine recently lost a $200,000 property he owned in another state because he thought he had ninety days to make good on delinquent payments. (That was the law where he lived.)

But his property was in a state that allowed only thirty-five days. So you see it's important to know the foreclosure laws in any state where you plan to acquire property. I'm going to explain the laws in rough outline, but there could be differences in your state, so be sure to check.

How a Lender Forecloses

When a property owner stops making payments on a loan, or otherwise defaults, forty-five days or so may pass before a lender gets around to filing a notice of default with the County Recorder. Institutional lenders such as banks, S&Ls, and insurance companies are especially slow to file default notices. They prefer to help hard-pressed borrowers by easing the payment schedule in various ways. One reason for this is that lenders who foreclose too often may have trouble with government regulatory agencies. But no borrower can be sure that his particular case will be treated mercifully. At the expiration of the period when late payments can be made without penalty, the lender can file a notice of default immediately.

After this happens, the lender can do nothing further for ninety days (in most states) to force a sale of the property. This is known as the period of redemption, during which the borrower can reinstate his loan just by making up all back payments and paying certain costs and penalties.

When the redemption period ends, the lender doesn't have to let the borrower reinstate the loan. Most lenders are still willing to do so, but they'll make a borrower pay through the nose. Delinquency charges and costs that are $273.14 on the ninetieth day may jump to $1,298.67 on the ninety-first. You see, the law sets certain limits during the redemption period, but generally gives a lender a free hand afterward.

When the redemption period ends, the lender can move ahead toward a foreclosure sale. The first step, required by law, is to advertise the sale. Generally there must be three advertisements over a specified period, usually three weeks. Probably the ads will have to appear in the county legal paper, and possibly elsewhere. As we'll see later, the legal paper is your best source of leads.

The second step is the sale itself. How this is conducted can vary depending on whether a mortgage or a trust deed is involved. Foreclosure will usually be faster if the borrower signed a trust deed. The deed empowers the trustee to sell the property if the borrower defaults and to deliver a trustee's deed to anyone who buys it at foreclosure.

This is why most lenders prefer trust deeds. These commonly give the choice of foreclosing either as a mortgage or a trust deed. If a lender wants a quick and easy foreclosure, he can use the trust-deed laws. But he can also foreclose under mortgage law—which takes longer—if he thinks an immediate sale won't bring in enough to cover the amount lent against the property. (In inflationary periods it almost always brings enough, of course.) The advantage of a mortgage foreclosure is that if the property sells for less than the debt, the mortgagee can go to court and get a deficiency judgment against the property owner for the difference. This isn't possible with a trust deed.

In a foreclosure, under mortgage law, the lender usually must bring suit. The court then orders an auction sale, and appoints the sheriff or someone else as receiver. Then the receiver does whatever advertising is legally required and conducts the sale. He also has certain additional powers, such as collecting rents if an "assignment of rents" clause is included in the loan documents. Naturally a lender likes to get his hands on whatever revenues the property is bringing in.

Solely for this reason, an institution holding a trust deed will often start foreclosure under mortgage law. Later it may drop the court action and revert to trust-deed law—because a sale made under trust-deed law is usually final, while mortgage law gives the original borrower the right to come back and redeem the property, probably any time within a year.

So much for the basic law. Now let's see how you go about acquiring a property during the various stages of its foreclosure.

Hunting for Distressed Properties

If you want to buy during the first stage, when a property is in default but not yet up for auction, your first problem is spotting such a property. A broker seldom knows a house or apartment building is going to be foreclosed on until it happens, even though he himself is listing the property. Owners hate to confess that they're in financial trouble.

A notice of default is a legal paper which the lender must file with the County Recorder. There are services in most counties that pick up this information and publish it for their subscribers. But you can get the same data more cheaply by buying and searching the county's legal paper. This newspaper covers virtually all matters of legal significance in the county—births, marriages, deaths, divorces, lawsuits, probates, and estate sales, as well as foreclosures. Be prepared to scan columns of fine print.

The legal paper usually gives the legal description of the property, the date of the notice of default, and the identities of the parties involved. But your search is only beginning, because the paper seldom gives the street address of the property. Don't ask me why.

You should be able to get the address from the trustee if there is one, or maybe from the lender. Don't expect to get it with one call, however. You'll probably be told that someone in the office will look up the information and call you back. This seldom happens. In reality you'll have to keep calling back, unless the office is more helpful than most of its kind.

If there is no trustee (because the default is a mortgage rather than a trust deed and the lender won't give out the information) you can probably get the address from the receiver, but you may have to look it up yourself at the County Recorder's office.

Screen by Eyeballing

Anyhow, by one means or another you compile a list of properties on which there are default notices. You pick out addresses in areas that interest you, and then drive out to look at them.

Just from your car, you'll eliminate many at a glance because of obvious structural defects, or sites that could cause trouble, or deteriorating neighborhoods. Properties that pass your first rough screening should be photographed, if possible, to help keep them straight in your memory. You also want to jot down notes about them. When you get home, you can rank them for further investigation in order of your personal impressions and preferences.

On your second visit you should explore the neighborhood for several blocks around and chat with nearby real estate brokers to get a feel for the price levels thereabouts. Then, when you think you have a fairly clear idea what the property would be worth after you make whatever improvements are essential, your next job is to locate the owner.

How to Find Owners

The owner may not live on the premises. He or she may even have abandoned the property. But the tenants, if any, will usually know where the owner can be reached. If not, you can try the neighbors, the trustee or court-appointed receiver, the lender, the County Tax Assessor, or the County Recorder.

Suppose you get a "last known address" but find that the owner has left. You can still locate him. The post office serving that address will give you a forwarding address, if it has one, for a nominal fee. You can also ask credit bureaus. As a last resort, try the utility companies, although they probably won't divulge anything unless you convince them there's an emergency.

Start with One-Family Houses

The best way to start investing in distressed properties is with single-family homes. There are far more of these in most areas than there are apartment houses. Their sheer numbers mean that there will be more of their owners in default than owners of bigger properties. Then too, you'll need less capital to buy and fix up a small house. And estimating the costs is easier. Therefore let's consider first how you can buy a house before foreclosure.

When you locate the owner, try hard to see him in person. And when you do, remember that you must be as cheerful and friendly as possible. He's in trouble, and he won't want to talk if he thinks you're just going to bring him more trouble.

Don't Dress Too Well

Try to avoid giving the impression that you're a money man. Wear an old suit or some other slightly shabby clothes. Drive an old car if possible, or at least an unpretentious one in need of a wash. The idea is to make clear that you're not representing a financial institution or a high-powered realty firm. You shouldn't seem too professional or shrewd.

Understanding this, do you see why it's foolish to make your first contact by phone? Visual feedback is lacking; the owner can't see your clothes or car, can't interpret facial expressions and other behavioral clues. You can't project much by your tone of voice; even a hardfisted Scrooge can sometimes contrive to use a friendly telephone voice, and the fearful owner knows this. He'll probably say, "I'm awfully busy right now. Thanks for calling anyway," or something less polite—and hang up.

At the house, if the owner answers the door when you knock, step back one step. This subtly soothes some of his fear. Smile and say something like, "I'm a private party looking for a home in the neighborhood, and thought you might want to sell your home."

But don't give him your business card. Remember, you don't want to seem professional.

If he says, "No, we don't want to sell," repeat essentially what you said before, and add that you understand his home might be going into foreclosure.

Very likely he'll reply, "No, that's all been straightened out."

This is your cue to nod silently, pull out a scrap of paper and write, "I'm a private party interested in buying your home. If you ever need money or change your mind about selling, please give me a call." Sign your name, list your home phone number and hours when you can be reached. If you can possibly avoid it, don't use an answering service or a business number where someone else may answer.

You can slip a similar note under the door if nobody answers when you knock. Then return to your car—but stall in starting it. The owner may be at home but afraid to answer because he's hiding from bill collectors. When he reads your note he may dash into the street after you. Anyhow, if you leave lots of notes, you'll get lots of calls later.

How to Talk with an Owner

When an owner asks how much you'll pay him for the house, reply, "I don't know. I'm not a broker. I'd have to see."

At this point—or maybe later—he'll probably let you inspect the home. As you do so, gently lower his hopes. Don't talk directly to him, but just mutter to yourself, making sure he can hear and understand: "Wonder if I could get by without repainting this room? . . . Looks like the plumbing may have to be replaced before too long. . . . Could I get along without putting in new carpets?" Talk to yourself as you study the drapes, the kitchen, the bathrooms. Jot down notes.

When you finish, offer some friendly remark like "I hope you're successful in getting rid of the place. It's really terrible how the late charges add on every day." You want him to feel that you're sympathetic—but at the same time you want to put across the unspoken thought, "I don't need you. You need me."

The owner will probably ask again, "What will you pay me for this house?" You answer with another question: "Do you want to sell today?"

He'll say yes or maybe. Then you ask still another question: "How much do you want?"

Now the haggling begins. He might say something to the effect that houses thereabouts are selling for $85,000 (or whatever) but since this house apparently needs a little work, he might let it go for $5,000 less than that.

You smile and say, "Oh, c'mon now. What's the very lowest price you'll take?" Then quit smiling.

Maybe he says, "Well, I've been offered $75,000."

You answer, "Gee, we're really a long way apart. What's the lowest price you'll take right now?"

If he again says $75,000, you say, "No, I mean your very lowest price, the absolute bottom dollar you'll accept for an immediate sale. Will you take $66,000?"

If he says yes, your response is, "Well, before I make a firm offer, I'll have to bring my wife over to see it," or some other stall. If he says no, you simply give him the scrap of paper with your name and phone number and hours when you can be reached. Then leave. You've done as much to soften him up as you can. He needs time to think it over.

Your Second Talk

Some time later (depending partly on how near the reinstatement deadline is) the owner will probably phone you: "Remember that $66,000 offer you made?"

Now you play hard to get. "Why, yes, I do remember you, Mr. Jones. But why did you wait so long to call?" There may be a long pause. You can go on to say, "I'm really not very interested now. I thought you wanted to sell immediately."

After another pause there may be some apologies. Then you might say, "I really don't know what I can do to help you now— but you were so nice in showing me the house, I'll come over and talk with you anyway."

At the house, you again act pleasant and cheerful. You ask, "What happened to the fellow who was going to buy for $75,000?" You can go on, "I've pretty well decided on another house now. Still I hate to cut you off. I don't have too much money, but are you ready to make a deal if I give you an offer today?"

What you offer will depend on your judgment of the least he will take. By then he is likely to feel desperate. You might offer him a few hundred more than you think he can get from a real estate broker in a forced sale. If he balks, you might offer him $500 cash to help him move and get settled somewhere else. This will mean more to him, if he's nearly broke, than a much bigger differential in the price of the house.

Another possibility is to offer to pay some of his bills for him if he'll give you a complete list. You would then pay off only those bills that constitute a lien against the house. In paying, offer each creditor just a fraction of the amount owed. Most of them would otherwise probably have to write off the bill entirely, or pay hundreds of dollars in collection costs.

If the owner accepts, make sure he understands that your offer is conditional on your approval of a preliminary title report. He may or may not have given you a complete list of mortgages, liens, and other debts in the correct amounts. You might get a quit-claim deed (this means that the owner relinquishes all interest) to the property for a few hundred dollars only to find that one or more of the loans against the property has a clause requiring immediate payment of the full debt if there is a change of ownership.

Go to the Lender

Your next step, therefore, is to see the lenders and find out what concessions they're willing to make. Sometimes you'll be surprised at their helpfulness—especially if they have a lot of bad loans on their hands. You're offering to relieve them of one headache, and that's worth enough so they won't want to let you get away.

See if they are willing to:

—waive a clause preventing a new buyer from assuming the old mortgage;

—waive service fees;

—grant a moratorium on all payments for six months;

—pay the taxes on the property and add the tax bill to the loan;

—waive prepayment penalties in case you pay off the mortgage ahead of time;

—give you the right to let someone else buy the property from you and take over your mortgage;

—reduce the interest rate;

—lend you additional money to put the property back in good shape.

Turn Second Loans to Your Advantage

Is there a second mortgage? If so, and the holder of the first mortgage lends you any further money on the property, his debt would become junior to the old second—unless the first is an open-end loan. With an open-end provision, the holder of the first mortgage would still have first claim against any additional advances he made that didn't increase the first above its original amount.

If the first isn't open-end, get in touch with the holder of the second. Ask if he is prepared to foreclose, himself, and take over the payments on the first. If not, does he realize he may be wiped out in the pending foreclosure sale? Quite often you'll find that even though his position is quite secure, he just doesn't want to go through all the fuss and bother and is willing to sell his second at a substantial discount. The shakier his position, of course, the more receptive he'll be to any reasonable offer.

Decide Your Price Quickly

In negotiating for distressed property, you need to get an early fix on the maximum you can afford to pay for it. This is because a forced sale is a fast-talking situation, and you mustn't get swayed by your emotions.

To figure your top price, first try to ascertain what the property's fair market value will be after it is put back in shape. Brokers in the area are your best source of information. As I mentioned earlier, the owner can't or won't give you a reliable set of facts.

Take your fair market value and work backward. First subtract 20 percent for profit and contingencies. This may seem high, but you'll be going to a lot of trouble under difficult conditions and your judgment may be off target.

Next you subtract all costs you expect to incur—refurbishing expenses, costs of purchase and resale, anything else you can foresee. This brings you down to the maximum you can afford to pay. Try hard to get the property for less. Make up your mind in advance that you won't pay more, although you'll feel tempted to do so in the flurry of bargaining. If you can't buy at or below your preset limit, move on to other properties.

But don't get discouraged when your first and second offers are refused. This doesn't mean the owner won't sell at those prices. He may say no today and he may say no three weeks later, but as the deadline nears he'll be far more likely to say yes. You see, when the 90-day redemption period begins, he may feel he has plenty of time to solve his problem. But by the seventy-fifth day he'll be stewing. And by the eightieth day he'll usually be ready to accept almost any offer that will enable him to salvage something from his investment.

This is why it's essential for you to know the foreclosure laws. Unless you do, how can you tell how much time a delinquent borrower has left? Sometimes he himself doesn't seem to be aware of the time limit, and if so you should gently bring it to his attention.

The Big Deals: Apartment Houses

Apartment houses in default are much harder to buy at sacrifice prices. Comparatively few are in distress at any given time, and more people are trying to buy them. Still, you'll find golden opportunities now and then. You can set the stage to buy before foreclosure if you know how.

Most apartment owners who fall behind in their loan payments try to sell before foreclosure. If they're unable to do this, the lender tries to make advance arrangements for someone to buy the property as sole bidder at the foreclosure sale. So when you want to buy an apartment property at a forced sale, try to get an inside track with either the owner or the lender.

But don't commit yourself to anything until you've checked the property carefully. Because it is probably being very poorly managed, you dare not rely on the books (if there are any) or anything the owner or manager tells you. You may not even be able to make sure that bills incurred many months earlier have been paid.

Look for These Danger Signals

Here are some factors that unwary buyers often overlook. Be sure to check them carefully:

1. CHARACTER OF THE TENANTS. Do you have families with three or four children living in one-bedroom units? If so, you are going to have to evict them and this can be a horrendous problem. Be sure to take plenty of time to inspect all the units, making sure the tenants are at home.

2. ARE TENANTS PAYING THEIR RENTS? If so, they should be able to produce rent receipts showing what they are paying. If they can't produce their receipts, you have a right to be suspicious unless and until the manager can prove to you the rents are being paid.

3. ARE CARPETS, DRAPES, STOVES, AND REFRIGERATORS ALL PAID FOR? If not, someone may stop by with the sheriff to repossess them. You may also find the refrigerators and stoves you

thought you bought were leased. A search at the County Recorder's office for sales agreements, conditional sales contracts, chattel mortgages, etc., may give you some clues. Invoices and canceled checks substantiating payment for the items in question should be carefully inspected, if available.

4. FURNITURE. There may be several furnished units in the building, and the owner agrees to sell you the furniture. Here, again, you have the problem that some of it may not be paid for plus the fact the tenants may claim ownership of some of it. Get an itemized list of what you are buying, and as soon as possible, get a verification from the tenants that it is not their property.

5. PROPERTY TAXES AND OTHER POSSIBLE ENCUMBRANCES. Be sure to make any offer subject to your approval of a preliminary title report.

The general principle underlying all this is simply to find out in advance about the assets and liabilities of any property you may be acquiring.

Negotiating Step by Step

Let's go through a sample situation. We'll assume you've made as thorough an investigation as possible and have found that a certain apartment building's fair market value, as it stands now, is $100,000—more, with a little fixing up. If you can get it for $80,000 you'll turn a handsome profit.

You check the mortgages on it. You find there is a $50,000 first, a $10,000 second, a $5,000 third, and a $7,000 fourth—a total of $72,000. Payments are several months delinquent on all the mortgages. The holder of the first is foreclosing.

You have several discussions with the owner, but he's stubborn. He insists he won't sell for a dollar less than $87,500. Should you pay his price? No. It would violate our rule of allowing a 20 percent margin for profit and contingencies. Instead, you can try to buy at the foreclosure sale, or afterward. But you may do even better by taking an entirely different approach.

It is the holder of the first mortgage who is foreclosing. Why haven't the holders of the other mortgages done anything? There could be all kinds of reasons. Maybe those people haven't the money to bring the payments on the mortgages ahead of them up-to-date. Maybe they don't even know the holder of the first is foreclosing, which could wipe them out at the foreclosure sale. Whatever the reasons, why not try to buy one of these mortgages and start foreclosure proceedings yourself?

How to Talk to a Junior Lender

You can start by writing to the holder of the second mortgage. Tell him you're in the business of buying seconds and will pay top dollar for them. Ask him to contact you if he has any seconds he would like to sell. Period. You don't want to tip him off that you're hoping to buy one particular second.

If you don't hear from him within a week, follow up with a phone call, explaining that you sent out a lot of letters, and asking if he owns any seconds as of that moment. You inquire about interest rates and payment schedules and so on, then say, "Would you like to sell if I can offer you a good price?" Try to set up an appointment to talk further.

If he nibbles, you might start by offering him $6,000 for the $10,000 second. You can afford to go up to $7,500 or more if necessary. Your goal is to make your profit on the property, not on the second.

When you acquire the second, you immediately put up enough money to bring the payments current on the first, thereby correcting that default. Then you file a notice of default on the second, even though payments on it may be current. This is possible because, in many states, any loan automatically goes into default whenever someone has to advance money to a lender who has a loan in front of it.

A word of caution here. Before you buy the second, you must make sure that it is really a second, not a third or fourth. And you must know about all possible encumbrances that may take priority. If you haven't already had a title search made (which you probably haven't because it costs you money), here's how to protect yourself. Instead of purchasing the second outright, pay the owner $50 or so for an option to buy it at the agreed price. Then, depending on the results of the title search, you can either exercise the option or walk away from it. Or you can make your purchase contingent on a satisfactory proof of title. Whatever you do, there should be some sort of written agreement that will leave you an out.

If the title report shows you're in the clear, buying the second for $7,500 will put you in a comfortable position. The chances are you can buy the $100,000 property at the foreclosure sale for a total cost of around $60,000—the $7,500 you pay for the second, the $50,000 ahead of you on the first, and maybe another $2,500 for delinquent payments, foreclosure costs, and incidental expenses. You may not have to pay off the first—just bring the payments on it current and take title subject to it (but check the applicable laws in that state).

You may also be able to arrange to pay any delinquent taxes over a period of time. If there's an I.R.S. lien, work out some settlement on it. You owe nothing to the holders of the third and fourth mortgages, who usually lose everything in such situations. You will almost always be the only party bidding at the sale, and you certainly won't be bidding with a view to protecting the interests of those other lenders.

Of course there's some risk that one of them may reinstate your second in the same way you reinstated the first. But what would you have lost? Even though you yourself couldn't foreclose, you would have recovered all the money you had advanced except the $7,500 you paid for the $10,000 second. And if the reinstatement came from the holder of the third or fourth, you'd be entitled to receive the full $10,000 face value of the note at the foreclosure sale. So you'd make $2,500 on your $7,500 investment. If it was the owner who managed to reinstate the first, probably you could easily resell your second to someone else for $8,000.

Still, this raises a question: Is there anything you can do to avoid being bought out by the holder of a third or fourth? Usually there is. Most such lenders just want to get back the money owed to them and aren't interested in taking over a money-losing property. So they should be happy if you guarantee in writing that you'll give them a new note secured by a new mortgage against the property for the full total owed to them, as soon as you've acquired it.

Whether there's any need to offer such an agreement will depend on who the holders of the third and fourth are, whether their loans are also delinquent, whether they are aware there has been a default, and how you size up their sophistication as well as their intentions and resources. If you're so inclined, you can decide to protect their interests just to be ethical.

There's also a question of whether you should try to buy the third or fourth, or even all three loans, instead of just the second. Here again it will depend on how you evaluate the circumstances. If the holder of the third or fourth is the Egregious Investment Corporation, you can figure it will go after the property. If it is Mary Doakes, who lives in a faraway small town, she'll just want to make sure she doesn't lose her money.

Be prepared for trouble if the holder of a priority loan wants to snap up the property. He'll probably go to some lengths to avoid accepting payments that will bring his loan current—especially if the deadline for redemption or for the foreclosure sale itself is near. You won't be able to find out how much is due. He will have sent the records to another office or turned them over to an attorney. The attorney will be "away on a business trip." Or if you catch him in the office, he'll say, "I'll have to get all the costs together and call you."

If you offer a check, he may refuse to accept it because it isn't certified. So prepare yourself with a certified check made out to the lender in an ample amount. Hand-carry it to the lender or his attorney or to the title company, trustee, or receiver. Insist on a receipt for it.

Never depend on registered or certified mail in such situations. Whoever you address it to may be out when it is delivered and may not go to the post office to pick it up later.

When you personally thrust a certified check at the lender or his representative, you can demand that it be accepted or else. Or else what? A legal action with heavy penalties. By law, almost everywhere, they must accept it if the tendering is by the owner or any of the junior lien holders.

KEY POINTS TO REMEMBER

· Look for bargains in previously undesirable areas which are beginning to be upgraded, and in underbuilt suburban areas.

- An owner who can't keep up payments may sell for a bargain price. But the property may be intrinsically undesirable because of changing conditions around it.
- To hunt for distressed properties, study lists of default notices, and go to addresses that seem favorably located.
- If a distressed property looks desirable, try to see the owner in person. Be friendly and unpretentious. Always leave your phone number.
- Make sure an owner understands your offer is conditional on a satisfactory title report.
- Never buy a second mortgage until you make sure it is really second, with no encumbrances that could take priority.

8

How to Buy from Today's Hard-Pressed Owners

There's a saying in real estate, "Your profit is made when you buy." It means that when you buy property for less than it will be worth, there's a built-in profit to be taken when you sell. So the name of the game is to "buy right."

Although hundreds of books have been written on salesmanship, it's hard to find advice on buying. This book aims to provide the advice you'll need.

What does it take to buy right? Chester L. Karras, who spent twenty successful years as a negotiation consultant for major corporations and climaxed his career with three years of intensive research on a Howard Hughes Fellowship, found in his research that the business negotiators who did best—including those in real estate—were those with (a) analytical ability and (b) patience.

Slow Deals Are Better

Analytical ability is needed in calculating what price to pay for property. But that ability isn't inborn like artistic ability. It's just a technique that people can learn. The technique is explained from various angles in my first book on real estate investing; fine points are covered at the Lowry Seminars and in my newsletters.

But even without those aids, now that you've read Chapter 7 you're probably analytical and prudent enough to know what maximum bid to make for a house.

During negotiations, however, you may get impatient. You'll be tempted to bid higher than your predetermined limit. That's where patience becomes essential.

We modern Americans crave immediate satisfaction, the easy and the quick; push-pull, click-click, fast foods, windfall profits, overnight wealth. We want things to happen "while we wait." If we don't succeed swiftly, we toss in our cards and look for a new game. But if you want to make money in distressed properties, you must overcome impatience and negotiate slowly. That's why I'll keep stressing patience as we get into more detail about tactics with hard-pressed homeowners. I sketched the basic steps of negotiating on pages 92–95 of Chapter 7. Now it's time to examine each step closely.

Negotiating on the Doorstep

Leo Durocher, the belligerent baseball manager, is remembered for his saying "Nice guys finish last." But in negotiation, as in life, nice guys do win. You can negotiate profitably without bullying a seller. Before you buy, you can set up a relationship where you understand his needs and help him out of his predicament.

The hardest part is the beginning, when you first face the desperate debtor on his doorstep. Be prepared to meet resistance. All humans resist changes in their behavior, in their lifestyle, in their living space. This seems to be true of all life. Each animal has a domain it will fight to protect. Listen to your dog growl if another dog enters the yard!

You are now entering the living space of an extra-hostile person, angry because he's on the verge of losing his home. Mentally his fists are clenched. Nevertheless you're going to make friends with him.

It's important to begin by stepping back when he comes to the door. You seem less threatening, less like a grasping intruder.

Now you'll try to continue soothing him until his fists unclench and he is willing to listen. You'll show that you like him and are genuinely interested in him. Here are tactics to use:

1. Address him by name each time you say something. His
   own name is important to him. Hearing it builds self-esteem,
   which he subconsciously needs.
2. Smile pleasantly. The effect can be magical. A genuine smile
   says you are pleased to see him. His reflex impulse will be
   to smile back. "A smile often counts more than a thousand
   words," said Walter Strong, a noted newspaper publisher.
   (You'll find it easier to smile and feel sympathetic if you
   remind yourself that this stranger isn't necessarily a fool or
   a deadbeat just because he's behind in his mortgage payments. Maybe the company he works for has shut down.
   Maybe a family illness is eating up his savings.)
3. Look in his eyes as you talk to him. Unless you do this
   you'll seem shifty-eyed, and he'll probably get the impression that you don't believe what you're saying. Good eye
   contact is an absolute necessity, but it takes practice. The
   chances are you have a habit in conversation of looking
   straight at the other person while he or she is speaking, then
   looking off into space when you yourself speak. Most of us
   do this. It's a very bad habit in negotiation. Practice good
   eye contact with everyone you meet, so you'll have it automatically when you speak to a suspicious householder.
4. Speak gently—even humbly. Apologize for disturbing him.
   Tell him what your name is. Only then should you say, as
   suggested in Chapter 7, "I'm a private party looking for a
   home in the neighborhood. I think some friends may live
   near here. . . . I wonder if by any chance you might be interested in selling your home, Mr. Blank."

What to Do if He's Surly

He may snarl, "No way in hell I'm gonna sell this place." Then
he may bang the door in your face (whereupon you slip a note
under the door, and go on your way) or he may stand glaring,
daring you to argue with him.

You may have heard talk among salesmen of "overcoming
objections." Trying to overcome Mr. Blank won't get you in the
door. Overcoming implies conflict. Conflict doesn't help when
negotiating a purchase.

There's an old saying, You can't argue with a drunk. It applies
here, because many a distressed property owner is drunk in the
sense that he's irrational, out of touch with reality, and in the
grip of stormy emotion. He's momentarily deaf to reason. No

matter how logical your proposition, Mr. Blank can't understand it just now.

He's rude to you, so you feel like snapping, "You'll have to sell or lose your equity." Or you want to say, "Okay. The hell with you. Phone me when you're ready to talk business." But you don't. You're guided by the Bible's proverb, "A soft answer turneth away wrath."

What kind of soft answer? You might try something like this:

"Oh, don't get me wrong, Mr. Blank. I'm not saying you should sell. I'm glad you're pleased with your home. . . . I'm just looking around. Can you give me any idea what prices are being paid for homes in this neighborhood?" The idea, of course, is to draw him into a calm chat.

Or you could try this:

Nod sympathetically and murmur, "I don't blame you for refusing to sell. I'd probably feel the same if I lived here. I just need your advice, Mr. Blank. I have a little money and I'd like to buy a nice home hereabouts. Do you happen to know of anyone who might be ready to sell?"

Or this:

"I understand how you feel. After all, it's your house. I was only trying to help, because I saw some notice that sounded like you might want to get rid of your mortgage." Then wait for his reply. Don't say another word until he responds, even if a long silence ensues.

On paper, the silent treatment looks as if it might anger the other person. But my experience has been that this tactic usually leads people to start talking more calmly.

The purpose of all the above conversational maneuvers is simply to give Mr. Blank a few minutes to get over the shock of your arrival and your talk of buying his house. He needs time to realize that your money might solve problems for him. So you do whatever you can to hang in there until he mentally unclenches those fists. Don't interrupt. Don't contradict. Listen, listen, listen.

What to Do if He Can't Decide

Occasionally you'll encounter an owner who doesn't snarl or refuse to sell—he just doesn't know what to do. Here again, you're confronting him with a new idea. He's scared and dazed and confused. So he mutters things like "Oh, I dunno. . . . Well, not really. . . . It's hard to say. . . . Guess I'd have to talk to my family about that."

He doesn't seem to understand that he's either going to sell his house or lose it. But be patient and let him reach this conclusion on his own. You can remember being annoyed by pushy salesmen. Don't play the pushy role.

As before, your best strategy is to coax him into low-key conversation and let his brain start to work. Make talk about nothing in particular. Ask casual questions. But don't show enthusiasm; it alarms indecisive people. Just keep the dialogue drifting slowly around neutral matters such as the state of the neighborhood and the price of homes. After a while you can gently steer the talk toward your goal: "You know, I might be able to offer you a bunch of money for this house."

Then if he doesn't answer, play the waiting game. Gaze at him in a friendly way, but keep silent. As the growing silence produces anxiety, raise your eyebrows expectantly. Chances are he'll say something, especially if you've practiced coping with awkward silences yourself.

Getting Off the Doorstep

Whether this owner is surly or just vague, if you can only keep him chatting he'll grow more communicative. As soon as the conversation seems well started, try to get him out of the doorway. Quite likely he's uncomfortable standing there—tired, hot, cold, or simply tense with anxiety. You can make some mild remark like "Gee, I'm tired today. Shall we sit down on the front steps?" He may take the hint and invite you in. He may just sit on the steps. Either way, he'll feel more at ease. It's been found that people are less resistant when they're sitting than when they're standing.

Sooner or later he'll pop the pivotal question: "How much will you pay?"

This is what you've waited for. It signals that negotiations have begun.

You can mention a price above your mental limit, if you hedge it with phrases like "Oh, conceivably as much as . . . but I'm not a broker. I'd have to know more about this property."

Then you can suggest, "We can talk more quietly if you come and sit in my car. Or could we go indoors?" Again he has a chance to invite you inside. Even if he doesn't, he'll answer questions about the property.

How to Probe

Start with inoffensive questions like "How long have you lived here, Mr. Blank? . . . Do you have any idea how old the house is?" Work up gradually to the most important questions: "How many mortgages are there? . . . Does anyone else have claims against the property?"

In between, ask every question you can think of. Take notes on the answers—partly to show Mr. Blank that you're serious, and partly because you need information.

However, there's one key question you'd better not ask.

Gerard I. Nierenberg, founder of the Negotiation Institute, quotes a corporate officer in charge of acquisitions: "I never ask anyone why he wants to sell. I might believe him." Nierenberg adds, "We all want to do as little work as is required. If we believe someone, we might fail to investigate thoroughly."

I realize that in other writings I've advised readers to find out why an owner wants to sell. It's crucial in negotiating with an owner about whom you know little or nothing. But in negotiating with an owner of distressed property, you already know the true, underlying reason why the property is on the brink of being sold. The owner can't keep up the mortgage payments. Foreclosure hangs over him.

He may give you—without being asked—any number of face-saving reasons for deciding to sell. He may say he's had so many offers that he is beginning to realize his property is worth more than he thought. Or he may say he's considering moving to Sicily. Or whatever. If he's smart, he wants you to think he doesn't have to sell, or at least that he has had a number of offers.

Stay Secretly Skeptical

Just nod sympathetically as he talks. Let him save face. Don't hint at disbelief. But secretly discount every "fact" a distressed owner tells you. People in desperate need of money are prone to shade the truth and to say nothing about facts that count against them.

For example, Mr. Blank may say he has brought his mortgage payments up-to-date. Wait a couple of days and check it with the lender.

Or Mr. Blank may neglect to mention that the building has a serious structural fault which isn't visible at first inspection. Don't worry about that today. Just keep in mind that if you eventually offer a purchase contract, it must be "subject to inspection" by whomever you name.

Despite your suspicions, stay friendly. All you need do at the moment is reassure him. Build a bridge of trust—and glean whatever clues you can about the property and his money problems. Conceivably he may throw caution to the winds and tell you all his troubles; if so, you can show sincere interest in helping him.

However, no matter how chummy the atmosphere may become, don't tell him much about yourself. The less he knows about you the better. The only fact you want him to know is that you're looking at several properties. You can say casually, "I'll probably buy something within the next few days." He may realize that he'd better try for a quick sale.

Looking Inside

At some point during your questioning, you need to walk through the house and see for yourself what improvements should be made. If he hasn't yet brought you in, keep planting the idea in his mind with questions like "How's the plumbing, Mr. Blank? . . . Is the kitchen in need of any repairs?"

It's best that he himself invite you to take a look inside. If he doesn't, eventually you can say, "Gee, I've come a long way, Mr. Blank, and I'd sure like to see your house before I go. . . . Aw, don't worry about it seeming untidy. I know how homes look when they're lived in."

If he balks, press further. "Mr. Blank, you and I are interested in the same thing. You're interested in selling so you can get some cash in hand. I'm interested in buying a house and I've got some cash. But I don't know how much to offer for your house until I inspect it. That makes sense, doesn't it?"

Maybe he knows his wife will kill him if he brings you in with the beds unmade and the bathroom and kitchen messed up. If he makes excuses, that's understandable. Just get him to set a time when you can come back and inspect.

Talk to Yourself

At that time, ask him to walk around and show you the property. You may see that it needs an incredible amount of repair work. The doors don't open and close right, the plumbing is balky, the electrical wiring is frazzled, and the kitchen range is a disaster.

Nevertheless, don't say anything to Mr. Blank that implies you are disparaging his house or questioning his reliability, because he would then react defensively and start arguing, and your chances of buying might vanish. Houses in bad condition are the best buys, if they can be repaired and upgraded without too much expense. The idea, buy only good property and hold it for 5 years, then sell on refinance, is the slow way to wealth.

So as you walk with him you should seem to forget about him, and just talk to yourself, appraising the property aloud: "Wonder if I'll have to paint these walls. . . . Could I resell without putting in a new range? . . . Maybe the screens ought to be replaced. . . ."

Take full written notes as you walk. You might even snap photos to assist your memory. Would it be better just to write your notes and shoot your pictures, saying nothing? No indeed. There's a purpose in your soliloquizing.

As painlessly as possible, Mr. Blank must be made to realize all the defects of his property, so he'll expect less money for it. When you set a price you'll bargain from a position of strength, and you must gently establish this before the bargaining begins.

However, he mustn't feel trapped. As Edna St. Vincent Millay observed, "Even the lowly rat in adversity has courage to turn and fight." Mr. Blank might decide to pack up his family in the dead of night and disappear. So you should toss him whatever crumbs you can as you make the appraisal. If the master bedroom is unusually large, with a cozy fireplace setting, say so. Lift up the screen; handle the tongs. Step off the dimensions of the room even though you may already have them jotted down. Show

Mr. Blank that you appreciate good points even while noting the bad.

Afterward you can ask him questions about whatever couldn't be seen during the walk-through. Ask about the foundation. When was the house reroofed? Any troubles with the plumbing or electricity?

Postpone the Price Negotiation

Having finished your inspection, you're probably not yet quite ready to talk price. You'll recall that in Chapter 7 we saw that you must first figure the property's fair market value after it is put back in shape; if you've checked values in the vicinity, you already know approximately the price for which you can resell. From this price you subtract 20 percent for your profit (and for unexpected costs).

But you're not finished. You must also subtract all predictable costs. To do this you'll probably need contractors' estimates of renovation expenses. So you don't know yet what your *maximum* bid for this property can be.

However, there may be no harm in seeing if you can pick it up immediately for a *minimum* bid, say one-fourth or one-third of its ultimate market value. You'll notice that the dialogue ends without your making a firm offer. You merely get the owner to mention an asking price.

There are other possible sounding-out techniques. Immediately after the inspection, instead of asking how much he wants, you yourself can name a tentative figure. Some buyers try what is called highballing, others try lowballing.

Starting at Extremes

Highballing can be used when a buyer thinks other potential buyers may be hovering around. He suggests a price that he knows is unrealistically good. Maybe the seller tries to grab it. The buyer stalls but continues to dangle the lure until his rivals have lost interest. Then he negotiates a lower price without competition. Of course this only works when a property is in dire straits and must be sold soon.

In lowballing, the buyer's first offer is outrageously low, in order to cut down the seller's expectations. Then the buyer can come up a little at a time and seem to be making concessions.

Lowballing can backfire. The owner may simply shut off discussion and tell the bidder to get lost. So if you try it, make clear that it's not a take-it-or-else offer, and be ready to change tactics quickly. You could preface your lowball with remarks like, "Well, I'm just thinking out loud, because I haven't checked to see how much the repairs might cost. But if they turn out to be really expensive, my price might have to be as low as $40,000—especially if you need all cash."

The key information that any buyer would like to have about sellers is their real limits or just how much they will sacrifice to make a deal. In other words, what is the lowest price they will settle for? Once in a great while a lowball offer is accepted almost immediately, with a slight raise or none. It all depends on how little time the seller has left, and how badly he needs money. On the other hand a seller may insist that he's "absolutely got to have" x number of dollars, and thereby fool a buyer into paying this when it wasn't really the bottom.

There is a famous story about negotiations between John Pierpont Morgan, the legendary financier, and Cornelius Vanderbilt, another crafty capitalist with vast holdings. Supposedly they met on a luxury liner and sat chatting about their various properties. Vanderbilt mentioned some iron-ore land that he expected to sell. Morgan, having acquired steel mills, needed ore sources. The story goes that Morgan offered $60 million, which was immediately accepted. One of the nineteenth century's biggest transactions was accomplished with no dickering.

In telling friends about the deal, Morgan chuckled heartily, for he had been willing to pay $80 million. Vanderbilt also loved to tell the story because, he said, he'd hoped to get only $40 million. If true, the tale only goes to show that in this case both the titans were inept negotiators. They didn't know the true worth of the property and they didn't probe to find the other fellow's bidding limits.

Patience pays. Sometimes when you don't know how much to bid, the best tactic is to do nothing. The pressure is on the owner of the distressed property, not on you.

So after a hypothetical price has been mentioned, by you or by the owner, I'd suggest you change the subject momentarily.

Don't Let a Broker Tie Him Up

This is a good time to warn the owner not to sign an exclusive listing with a broker, because this would prevent him from dealing freely with you or anyone else. Some foolish owners give an Exclusive Right to Sell listing to their neighborhood realtor even though they may be only forty-five days away from foreclosure. So you must be sure to impress on Mr. Blank that he has nothing to gain, and maybe plenty to lose, by locking himself up with a broker. If there's a broker's commission the seller usually pays it.

Time Is on Your Side

Having said this much, you probably should postpone any further talk of price. You can glance at your watch and say, "I have an appointment to look at another property, so I'd better be on my way. Why don't we put off talking about price until I've had time to study the figures? In the meantime, maybe you should talk to your banker or tax adviser or anyone else who can help you estimate what you can get for this property."

Remember, a buyer who can afford to walk away from a deal will usually get concessions from the other party. Mr. Blank must be shown that you don't need him; you hope he'll soon find he does need you. At the same time, you must try not to be the bad guy who proves him wrong about the value of his property. The bearer of bad news often gets an angry reception.

Henry A. Kissinger, the foxy Secretary of State who negotiated settlements with such tough bargainers as the Russians, the Chinese, the Arabs and the Israelis, once wrote this about negotiation:

"The side which is willing to outwait its opponent—which is less eager for a settlement—can tip the psychological balance."

You can use this principle continuously. Never be nasty. Whenever you find you're not making progress during a conversation, do what I recommended in the previous chapter—tear off a piece of paper, write your name and phone number on it, and depart in as friendly a manner as possible.

Keep in mind why people resist. Many times they are subconsciously thinking, "Slow down. Let me think about it. You're suggesting something I hadn't thought of, and I need time to consider it."

Throughout your first exploratory conversation and later ones, keep on diplomatically clarifying the position. Keep mentioning that you're working with limited cash—only enough to make one deal now—and are looking at several properties. If you don't emphasize these points, the owner may think you've given him an open offer with no time limit, so he may hope to jack up the price by stalling. He must be shown that this is unrealistic. Tell him that any offer you make today may not be good tomorrow. Remind him how the lender's late charges pile up.

Telephone Tactics

In Chapter 7 we ran through a telephone conversation that might ensue when an owner called you back. As implied then, it's never a good idea to conduct negotiations over the phone. But sometimes this is hard to avoid. Here's how to limit the disadvantages:

Say little. Let the other person explain his position, but don't state yours if there's any chance of continuing negotiations face to face.

Have a ready excuse for breaking off conversation and mention it at the beginning—something like "I'm expecting an important long-distance call," or "I have to leave in a few minutes to pick up my wife."

Don't be rushed, even if the caller says, "I'm ready to sell but I can't wait. If you're going to buy I need to know right now." If you make a hasty oral agreement, he may try hard to hold you to it. For all you know, he has someone listening on an extension and writing down every word you say. Even if he's accepting a tentative offer that you've previously made, the situation could have changed drastically in the past hour. What if the cellar has been flooded, or the water heater has burst?

So you must fend off his demand for quick agreement by offering to come and see him immediately. But remind him that any purchase agreement must be subject to the usual protective clauses.

Another problem that may come up on the phone: A hard-boiled owner may press for a better price. He'll say, "I've thought over what you said, and I've decided you just aren't offering enough money."

Learning to handle the "not enough" argument is important to you. Use tact in challenging it. "I know how you feel" is a good way to begin. "And I want you to get the best price, too. Suppose you check around and see if you can get better offers. Maybe we can talk again if you find my offer is as good as anyone's. Remember, I'm not saying you should sell unless it's to your advantage. That's up to you."

Later, in detailed face-to-face argument, you can use softening phrases like "Based on your assumptions, I'd agree, but aren't we overlooking the cost of the repairs I'll have to make? We seem to be on the same track except for the margin I'm allowing for a new kitchen range and other refurbishing. Let's go over the contractors' estimates together."

If the Owner Doesn't Sell

Sometimes a distressed owner manages to cure a default. If this happens, tell him you're glad he was able to recoup—and ask him to let you know if he hears of anyone who may need to sell quickly. Now that you're on friendly terms with him, he'll probably keep your name and phone number, and your early efforts may pay off handsomely later—because, of all the people who get into default and bail themselves out, fully half are back in default within one year, and 60 percent are in that position within two years.

The owner may have borrowed money to catch up. If so, he'll have to pay back what he borrowed while keeping up with current payments and expenses. The type of person who gets into financial trouble is likely to get there repeatedly. So stay in touch with this owner and let him know that you're interested in his welfare.

Putting On the Pressure

Now let's assume you're negotiating with an owner who hasn't caught up. He must sell. But he's trying to play poker, hoping to extract the maximum from you. How should you handle him? Never say, "It's this or nothing!" That would make it humiliating for him to accept.

Instead, harp on the advantages of your deal. Give him reasons why he should accept. Admit that it's less than he might hope for if he could wait six months or a year, but he can't. Isn't "a bird in the hand" better than the foreclosure he faces?

Point out that each day he waits, his position worsens. He gets further behind on payments. He accumulates more late charges. His taxes pile up. (You should know the law in his state, as I advised earlier, so that you can show him the details of his predicament.)

Remind him that foreclosure will ruin his credit and that he'll have big trouble borrowing in the future or even buying on time payments.

Many owners think that if a lender forecloses and takes their property, that's the end of it, and they're relieved of any further obligation. So you may need to explain that if the property is foreclosed as a mortgage, the mortgage-holder may get a deficiency judgment and keep after the exowner for more money (in some states).

Maybe the price you're offering is considerably less than you're secretly willing to pay. If he flatly and firmly refuses that offer, of course you'll come up a little. But you certainly shouldn't offer to "split the difference." Instead you can play what negotiators call the "monetary-increment game."

Here's what that means. If your first offer is $50,000 and your next offer is $54,000, how much money will the seller assume you can spend? He may well anticipate that you actually have $56,000, $58,000, or even $60,000. Why? Because the jump from $50,000 to $54,000 is so big that he's bound to believe you can make another good-sized jump. Even if you swear that you have only $55,000 and it happens to be true, he's unlikely to think so.

Instead, signal that you're already near your ceiling by upping your first bid to only $51,200, let's say. Then you extend yourself to $51,750. After some delay you go to $52,000. Your next advance is a reluctant $52,143.57. Because you've steadily narrowed the increments instead of bidding like a playboy millionaire, you're much more likely to convince the seller that you've reached your limit.

When a negotiation seems to be deadlocked, you can deliver an ultimatum, but phrase it in soft and palatable words. Example: "I wish I could pay what you're asking, but this is all I've got. Help me solve this for you," or "It's the best I can do under the circumstances."

Remember that most concessions and settlements occur very near the deadline, or even past it. So be patient, and let time work for you. If your ultimatum doesn't work immediately, just say goodbye and wait for the owner to call you back.

Clinching the Deal

Seal the transaction by making a small deposit when you and the owner sign a contract—or else use the money to get an option. In either case your purpose is to buy time to check all financial matters, including any unknown liens on the property.

But your deposit should be very small. Remember you're dealing with a private individual, not a business firm, and he's almost a total stranger to you. Furthermore, he's short of money. If he cashes the check quickly and the deal falls through later, you may never get your money back.

Your contract could prove worthless if it isn't signed by all owners of the mortgage property. So make sure you know who all the owners are, and talk to them.

Delinquency on a mortgage is often the aftermath of a divorce or separation. And sometimes it's hard to get the signature of an estranged wife or husband. But push hard, and enlist the help of whatever owner or owners have signed with you, because one missing signature can invalidate the deal.

It's a mistake for you to go to the lender before you get a signed purchase contract. The lender might decide to undercut you. The bigger the owner's equity, the more important it is that you show the lender you have the legal rights of a purchaser.

KEY POINTS TO REMEMBER

- Guard against getting impatient during negotiations. Try to understand a seller's needs and help him solve his problem. Let him come to his own realization that he must either sell the house or lose it.
- Try to get him to invite you inside. Once in, show him that you appreciate the house's good points, and gently make him aware of bad points.
- Avoid telephone discussions. When this is impossible, say little on the phone. Try to arrange for a face-to-face meeting.
- Go slow. Remember that most settlements occur very near the deadline.

9

Your Best Deal May Be with Lenders

You meet an owner who's on the brink of foreclosure, but absolutely and positively won't sell.

You know there are no other buyers talking to him. It makes no difference. He's just so frightened, confused, or hostile that he won't listen to offers. You try all the tactics suggested in Chapter 8—with zero progress.

This doesn't mean you must give up. There are other ways of buying the property, as we'll see in this and later chapters.

Bypass an Owner Who Won't Sell

Whenever an owner of distressed property won't talk business, your next move should be to feel out the lenders. Maybe they'll make an advance agreement to sell you the property if they get it at the foreclosure sale. In fact, you can often arrange a better buy from them than from the owner.

The holder of the mortgage or trust deed is usually a bank or a savings and loan. Such institutions aren't in the real estate business. Generally they hate to be stuck with houses—especially houses in bad condition, as foreclosed properties usually are. Then too, the law sets limits on how much real estate a financial institution can own. For all these reasons, the average bank or S&L wants to unload its bad-debt properties as fast as it can.

This is especially true of its lending officer. He looks bad when his company forecloses. It's a black mark on his record, because it means he made a loan he couldn't collect. But if he can just get back the money (or even a major part of it) by reselling immediately, the record won't look so bad. Naturally he'll be eager to talk with a prospective buyer.

How to Approach a Loan Officer

He'll hide his eagerness. His job is to drive the toughest bargain he can—which may mean acting as if he's doing people a favor by even negotiating with them.

Make up your mind in advance that you won't be dismayed by his fishy stare or unenthusiastic manner. You're the one who's doing the favor, so act like it from the start.

Never begin by shuffling up to some receptionist in a loan officer's impressive headquarters and asking, "Who should I talk to about the property at 1031 Putrid Place?" Don't even call up and ask such a question.

Instead, try to approach the loan officer indirectly. Look for some friend who'll pave the way for you. Your entry to the bank or S&L should be as high above the loan officer's head as possible.

In earlier times, when life was simpler, an investor and his local banker were usually friends. They knew the same people. Often they belonged to the same church or service club. They knew each other's children. A transaction might be arranged just by strolling in unannounced for a chat.

That old-time relationship seldom exists nowadays. Bank officers come and go with promotions, reassignments to a different branch or a different department, and moves to entirely different banks. Instead of relying on their personal knowledge of someone, today's money men rely mostly on facts and figures in evaluating their clients.

Even so, the human touch is still a factor. Long-standing customers get better treatment than newer ones. A client whose personality impresses a bank may get a yes, while a person with an equally sound proposition may be turned down if he makes a bad personal impression. And looking ahead, your dealings with an institution in future years will be easier if you develop a cordial personal relationship at the outset.

When you want to approach a bank or S&L, try to arrange an introduction to one or more of the higher-ups through someone who knows them—preferably a good customer. Or maybe you yourself already happen to know an officer. If so, by all means talk to him and take advantage of your relationship or your reputation. Any high officer will know who's handling the Putrid Place loan, or can find out if he doesn't.

Ideally, the way to start this negotiation is by going to lunch with one of the higher-ups, or by getting into casual talk with him at a chance meeting (even if the "chance meeting" takes some maneuvering by you). You can mention that you've heard about a property his institution is foreclosing on, and that you might be interested in buying it after foreclosure.

If all goes well, the money man may say, "Let me have our loan officer get in touch with you." If he isn't alert enough to say this, it's almost as good when you say, "Why don't you ask the loan officer to call me?" because he's likely to reply, "Okay, I'll make a note to do that."

This reverses the usual situation. The bank is approaching you about the property, instead of your approaching the bank. The officer has found a prospective buyer. He looks good, the loan officer feels good, and you're bound to get their full attention.

Of course situations aren't always ideal. Sometimes you'll have to settle for a casual word to the loan officer from someone who says, "My friend may call you about buying the Putrid Place property." That's good enough. You can take it from there.

When you do phone the loan officer, try to set up a meeting outside his office—preferably at lunch, or in your home or office, if this provides an impressive setting, otherwise in the office of your attorney or accountant.

You may not succeed in luring the loan officer away from his desk, because he's busy and he tries to protect his time. But at least, with a little maneuvering and some well-placed boldness, you'll be coming through his door in a dignified way. It's worth the effort.

He should be impressed when he meets you. Wear your cost-liest—and most conservative—clothes. Your appearance makes a difference to financial people.

So does your manner. Don't come on dumb, as you did with the delinquent property owner. Mention some background about your experiences in financing or your investments in real estate. If you know any important financial people, casually work their names into the conversation.

Of course you mustn't sound conceited or blustery. Don't let your voice get too loud, or your sentences too long. Just act the part of a calm, pleasant, substantial investor. The idea is to get the loan officer to size you up correctly so he won't try to bluff you.

Don't Talk Money, Talk Trouble

If you've made the right impression, he'll be friendly. He's wondering how to get his money out of Putrid Place after he fore-closes, and he hopes you'll solve this problem. Unless he seems inclined to chat, you should come to the point after a few preliminary remarks I've just suggested. The chances are he'll want to get down to business quickly.

When you talk about the property, don't start by talking price. Talk trouble. Has he seen the property lately? Has he really examined it carefully? Does he realize what condition it's in? Has he estimated how much must be spent to put it back in shape? Has he noticed how the neighborhood has gone to seed? Does he realize that in every rainstorm the water from blocks around drains into that area? Your purpose, of course, is to soften him up so you can negotiate the best possible terms and price.

According to Anthony (Tony) Hoffman, a real estate consultant who gives daylong seminars on how to negotiate with difficult people, one common type of difficult person is the "analyst" because he's afraid of making a mistake. Bankers are often analytical, which makes them tend to say no whenever they're in doubt. The way to deal with these people, Hoffman advises, is to give them plenty of documentation.

I've seen this principle work well in buying rundown property

from a banker. Remember all those notes you took as you inspected the property with the owner? They are good ammunition
for the conference with the loan officer. Hand him an itemized
list of everything wrong, and your estimate of the costs of fixing
it (with written bids from contractors if possible). If the memo
has complicated figures, that's fine. Bankers welcome numbers.
Attach the adding-machine slip or a note saying "I've checked
these figures."

Stick to the Facts

Of course you'll be careful not to mislead him. This is a key
principle in all real estate dealings—or any other transactions,
for that matter. As George Bernard Shaw pointed out, "The chief
punishment of a liar is that he cannot believe others."

Mutual trust is important in dealing with a bank. Honesty is
always your best policy there. The Center for Entrepreneurial
Management says in its published guide, "There are three people
you don't lie to: your doctor, your lawyer, and your banker."

The straight facts are enough. Probably the loan officer hasn't
seen the property himself. Even if he has, he probably doesn't
remember it clearly. Your objective is to make him realize that
the property may be worth less than he thought.

If the property is vacant, or soon will be, tell him, "I'm willing
to do whatever is necessary to preserve this property for you
until after the foreclosure sale." You can offer to board it up, fix
the roof, or clear the weeds and trim the lawn so it will look
occupied.

Negotiating the Price

Most lenders, like other people, want to avoid trouble. They like
things to go smoothly. So they'll make concessions to someone
who can take a troublesome property off their hands.

For example, Francis Greenburger tells in his book on negotiating how he persuaded lenders to sell him a $50,000 mortgage
for $2,000.

A family trust held the second mortgage on a property Greenburger was buying as a result of a foreclosure by the bank which

held the first mortgage. He offered the trust a nominal fee of $2,000 just so he could avoid the legal costs and delays of foreclosing their position. The trustee he was dealing with balked. Why? Because accepting Greenburger's offer would mean admitting to the other trustees that this asset had declined in value by $48,000.

Greenburger saved the trustee's face by offering a written promise to "pay the entire $50,000 contingent on some future eventuality, even if that eventuality were remote and unlikely (such as my sale of the property at five times what I paid for it within three years). That way, he would not have to acknowledge the worthlessness of the mortgage."

Many lending officers are similarly anxious to save face. A contingent clause such as Greenburger offered will persuade them to lower their asking price sharply. On the other hand, they'll begin by naming a high figure and stiff terms.

A lender may ask you to pay assumption charges, late charges, points, escrow charges, title charges, and other discretionary fees. Your reply should be something like "If you'll let me pay less than I've offered you for the property, I guess we can work something out on these charges. But if you insist on the charges without cutting the price, I just can't go ahead."

You should be friendly—but let your unspoken thought show through: "I don't care if I get this property. I can get another one instead." Let the banker know by casual conversation (maybe in the first minute or two after you sit down) that you're considering other buys. You might even strengthen your position by hinting that you'll lose interest entirely if you do acquire other property.

You've already decided the maximum you'll pay. You determined this without paying any attention to the price asked by the owner or the lender. It's no bargain to trim $40,000 off an asking price which was $50,000 too high in the beginning. Once you know the top price you're willing to pay, start with an offer about 20 percent below it.

The name of the game from here on is to find out the bank's true bottom price. Try to be well informed about general conditions in the local real estate market, how many foreclosures the lender has in inventory, how many owners are falling behind on payments, and other factors that influence supply and demand for distressed properties. You can make better buys, of course, when business is poor. If a bank is getting nervous about its portfolio of bad loans, it will come down significantly in price.

Despite its worries, the bank may demand the right to rewrite the terms of the foreclosed loan, including the interest rate. That's common in times when current rates are much higher than the terms at which the old mortgage was written. But this too is negotiable. Remember that you're in a good position. Unlike a borrower, you're offering to free the bank from a burden.

Even though they are indecisive, Tony Hoffman says, "analytical people respond well to deadlines—but not to ultimatums." Don't give the bank a final take-it-or-leave-it offer even if you've reached your top limit. At that point, break off the negotiations temporarily, saying, "I'll look at some other properties and check back with you Thursday to see if you've thought of any better way of structuring this deal." Or you might say, "If you don't find a buyer for this property in the next few days, you can call me if you want to. Maybe we can talk further if I haven't made a commitment on another property by then."

When you reach a complete deadlock and can't think of any new approach, as a last resort you might try turning sour for a while. One skilled negotiator deliberately becomes more negative than the bank at such times. She bad-mouths the whole proposition, announces there's no way to make it profitable, and spells out why negotiations should be broken off. Her theory—admittedly risky—is that the banker, contrary by nature, will swing over to the opposite side and begin to defend both the deal and the need for her to continue talking.

Your skill as a negotiator can make the difference between profit and loss in real estate situations—whether you're buying or selling or exchanging. It can put you into ventures where your financial stake is low but your profit is high. And it's a skill that improves with practice. So get into negotiations as often as you can, if only for the exercise.

But keep in mind that the best transaction is one in which both parties come out ahead. Usually, in a negotiation to buy or sell property, the final price will be somewhere between the top and bottom prices that both parties had set as their limits. You're better off if the other people finish with the feeling that they've been fairly good negotiators too—because you may want to deal with them again later on.

One veteran real estate investor says, "When we reach a final agreement I always point out what the other party has gotten out of it. I try to show them that they've done well for themselves, so they'll feel good about having dealt with me. I want them to speak well of me around town."

Buying After Foreclosure

So far we've considered techniques for buying (or making advance agreements to buy) before foreclosure. Of course you can also buy distressed property at the foreclosure sale, or afterward.

Buying at a foreclosure sale is an art in itself, worth a separate chapter, so we'll save it for Chapter 10. Then too, there are wide-open public auctions of real estate which may be owned by almost anybody (including a financial institution), and there are special tactics you can use at such auctions. You'll find these in Chapter 11.

Right now let's concentrate on how you can pick up property *after* it has been sold at a foreclosure sale.

Some successful investors buy only at this stage. They do business exclusively with the "Real Estate Owned" (REO) departments of institutional lenders.

Generally they concentrate on smaller institutions, where the REO people get to know them well and can arrange sales without waiting for okays from so many higher-ups. Another reason they go to smaller outfits is that larger ones usually have their own real estate management departments, which are less eager to sell off properties quickly.

Other successful investors start by looking over foreclosed properties, deciding which ones they want, then finding out who owns them. They can find out by calling the trustee, receiver, or title company, or by checking at the office of the County Recorder.

You may want to try some such plan of operation to see whether it suits your tastes and talents. At least it avoids the hassle of ringing doorbells and leaving notes with delinquent debtors. So let's see how to go about post-foreclosure buying from institutions.

Winning Your Way with REO Officers

You start by paying a visit to the head of the REO Department at some financial institution—let's call it Majestic Savings & Loan. You tell him you're interested in buying something from his portfolio.

"Fine," he says. "Here's a list of addresses."

It's not a long list—just three or four properties. And it doesn't include any of his choicest properties. After all, he doesn't know you.

Never mind. Go to work on what he shows you. After you've bought a few things from him he'll be more cooperative. In fact, he may phone you about a foreclosure coming up, and say, "Why don't you go out to see the owner and get a quit-claim deed to the property? Majestic would rather not put it on our books."

When you reach that stage he'll be in your pocket. He'll go to great lengths to help you take property off his hands. He may offer to increase the loan, cut the interest rate, advance money for refurbishing, even grant a moratorium on payments. But don't wait for him to offer. From the beginning, ask for every concession you can think of. He may say yes unexpectedly. All institutional leaders have broad power to help a buyer take over property they want to dump.

But I'm getting ahead of myself. Let's return to your first dealings with the man from Majestic, when he thinks you're an ignoramus and tries to jack up prices on you. Here's a blow-by-blow synopsis of how the haggling might go.

Majestic has a fourplex, we'll say, and you want it. You figure you can resell for $100,000 after brightening it up a bit. You go to the title company, look at the chain of title, and figure out that Majestic was into the property for about $53,000 when it foreclosed.

So can you buy it for $53,000? Nothing near that. The Majestic man knows as well as you do that it can be worth $100,000 so he tries to make you pay almost that much.

He tells you the book value is $96,482.31 (a number he makes up so you'll think he's analyzed the building down to the last doorknob). "I want to get my book out of it," he says. "But to help you buy it I'll give you good terms—only 15 percent down."

He's guessing that you have $15,000 or so in ready cash. If he can get you on the hook for that big a down payment, he thinks you'll keep paying and paying, even after you know you were taken for a sucker. He's seen it happen many times; people keep throwing good money after bad rather than walk away from a mistake.

But not you. The 15 percent is okay but the price tag isn't. So you counter with something like "I might be willing to offer $85,000."

He rocks back as if you'd punched him. "Ridiculous! I can't consider it at all. The committee would laugh me out the door."

So you go to work on him along the lines I sketched earlier: "Have you seen your property lately? Do you realize what problems you've got there? My contractor went out to look at it, and gave me a list of problems that have to be fixed. Here it is. Read it. You can see I'll have to spend $13,000 to repair the place before I can put it up for sale."

Now he realizes you know what you're doing. He can't say much after he studies your contractor's estimate.

When he's absorbed it, you restate your position: "I can offer $85,000 minus the $13,000 for repairs."

The Majestic man doesn't surrender. He keeps shaking his head. But he's been softened up. Now you can follow up with an offer that's hard to resist.

A Way to Buy for No Money Down

You say, "Tell you what. Just advance the $13,000 in increments as I get the work done, and make it a built-in part of the loan for $85,000. On that condition, I can see my way to a 15 percent down payment."

He'll probably accept. If he does, you're buying the fourplex for nothing down, in effect. Your $12,750 down payment (15 percent of $85,000) will be more than offset by Majestic's $13,000 for the repairs you need to make.

On top of that, if you act as your own general contractor and hire the work out, you can probably get it done for less than the $13,000 that a general contractor would charge. Afterward you'll own a beautiful set of apartments worth $100,000 for a total price of about $80,000—and for a net cash outlay of less than $10,000.

However, let's assume that the Majestic officer still doesn't go for your proposition. You can pull another ace out of your sleeve at little or no cost. Here's how.

Practically every bank and S&L has some real dogs in inventory—abandoned wrecks that it can't sell to anybody. You say, "Remember that horrible house you own on Limbo Lane? I'll take it off your hands if you let me have this deal we've been talking about."

This almost always works. Majestic knows they can eventually unload the fourplex elsewhere if you don't take it, but not the Limbo Lane hovel. The REO man knows, too, that Majestic stands to make a profit eventually by cutting its loss on Limbo Lane now. So he may advance all the money you need for refurbishing the house. He may also pay for the title policy and grant a moratorium on installment payments. Ask for all the concessions you can think of.

Three Dynamite Words: "Loan to Facilitate"

As you were reading the last few paragraphs, you may have wondered why Majestic wouldn't just as soon sell you the fourplex with little or no money down, and leave you to pay fix-up costs on your own. It's simpler that way and adds up about the same.

Nevertheless no S&L would want to do it. Here's why. There are state laws that say any financing with less than a 20 percent down payment must be classified as a "loan to facilitate" and must be flagged out as such. When government examiners walk in to check the association's records, they look sharply at these red-flagged "loans to facilitate." If they find too many loans where the down payment is subnormally small, the lender has a lot of explaining to do.

It looks better on the books if there's a substantial down payment, even though the same amount is handed back for repairs. As soon as the property is put in shape, the lender can reappraise it, establish that the buyer now has a 20 percent equity, and reclassify the "loan to facilitate" as a regular loan.

Here's one more example of how your REO friends can help you. Suppose Majestic has a little house in its foreclosure inventory that catches your eye. You estimate it can be worth $58,000 after you make some improvements. Majestic asks $48,000.

Suppose also that you figure the improvements will cost $4,000 if you hire somebody else, or $2,000 if you do them yourself.

Therefore you say to Majestic, "I'd like you to advance four thousand to renovate the property."

If Majestic is aching to sell the house, the REO man might say, "Okay, here's how we'll do it. We'll sell you the house for $48,000 but give you a $4,000 advance to be used as a down payment, and another $4,000 when you finish the improvements, leaving you owing a balance of $44,000." Or he might shape the deal various other ways that come out about the same in the end. Do you see what this means? Without putting up any of your own money, you could conceivably turn a quick profit of several thousand dollars.

Make Sure About Furnishings

In some of your transactions for distressed property, questions may come up about furniture. Suppose you're buying an apartment building with some furnished units. Does this mean you automatically get the furniture? No. Never assume that buying a building makes you the owner of what's inside.

Furniture is personal property, not real estate. Even after foreclosure, the furniture belongs to whoever owned it before. Never mind that the apartments were and are rented furnished—in all likelihood the former owner still legally owns the furniture, and just hasn't bothered to take it out. If you want the furniture, you'll have to buy it from him. Since he almost surely has no further use for it, he'll probably sell for whatever you offer.

Still, you need legal advice in any transaction where furnishings are involved. Your lawyer must make sure who really owns them. And he must distinguish between "fixtures" and "furnishings." Fixtures usually change ownership with the building, while furnishings don't. But which is which? You might assume that draperies, rugs and awnings are furnishings, since they're generally usable anywhere—but suppose the house has a big bay window, and the draperies for it are custom-made. Are they usable elsewhere?

And what about wall-to-wall carpeting? Isn't it "attached" to the house? What about a built-in refrigerator or clothes dryer? Lawsuits come up over such questions. Rather than risk legal trouble, you should insist on a detailed list of what is being sold with the building, item by item, and have the list incorporated in the contract of sale.

You Can Use Land to Acquire Foreclosed Property

As I've said, lenders are sometimes amazingly lenient when they're angling to get rid of foreclosed property. They'll even lend against the security of unimproved land (normally a no-no in the banking world) if you structure the deal properly.

Suppose you own $300,000 worth of land free and clear. Majestic S&L has six houses it doesn't want, worth an average of $50,000 each. If you could persuade Majestic to swap these homes for your land even-up, you'd then be in position to borrow against the homes and raise a good hunk of cash. Later you could dispose of your equities in the homes as you saw fit.

However, Majestic won't even consider a straight exchange. What could it do with your raw land?

And yet, by adding a sweetener that takes no money out of your pocket, you can make the exchange advantageous to both sides. Here's the way to do it.

You tell your REO friend, "Immediately after the exchange I'll buy the land back from Majestic in a separate transaction, for the same $300,000 price, but on liberal terms with 30 percent down." (Sometimes you can even offer to buy the land back for more than your selling price. You'll still come out way ahead, as you'll see.)

Your proposition is almost irresistible to Majestic because:

(1) It immediately reduces the REO inventory by six homes and $300,000.
(2) It can make new 80 percent loans on these homes if it wishes, thereby putting $240,000 back to work earning interest.
(3) The land will be in its REO department only momentarily. Your down payment of $90,000 on the repurchase will be

no problem for you, because you'll be generating $240,000 by taking out loans on your six newly purchased homes.

(4) Majestic will also be earning interest on an additional $210,000 through the purchase-money mortgage or trust deed it will take back from you as buyer of the land.

Is it a good deal for you? Sure. Look at the advantages:

(1) You walk out of Majestic's office with $150,000 (the $240,000 in new loans on the homes, minus your $90,000 down payment to buy back your own land).

(2) You own and control property worth twice as much as you did before ($600,000 instead of $300,000).

(3) If the land goes up in value you'll still profit from its rise. And if the real estate market goes up your six houses will be worth more too.

(4) There is a tax advantage. Your capital gains tax will be much less when you eventually resell your land, because you can now report that its cost to you was $300,000 instead of whatever smaller sum you originally paid. Check with your attorney to be sure you don't run afoul of anti-churning rules.

When you want to exchange land and buy it back, a federally chartered S&L is generally your best bet. State associations must operate under tighter legal limits. The federals can sell land to you for as little as 25 percent down, and can give you as long as 18 years to pay.

How to Buy from a Private Lender

As you probably gathered in reading this far, setting up a deal with an institution is far different from working one out with an individual owner, debtor, or investor. The interplay of personalities plays a bigger part when you buy property from a private lender who has foreclosed on it.

Maybe you'll want to experiment with this kind of negotiating too. There are plenty of opportunities, because people who hold second mortgages often have to foreclose when the borrower stops paying. Usually they don't want the property themselves any more than a bank does. What they want is their money back.

You can make a list of private lenders who've had to foreclose by checking with the County Recorder, or with title companies. Once you've identified some individual as the owner of a particular property acquired at a forced sale, here's how you can proceed.

Call up and chat with him or her on the phone. You can get a pretty good idea by the way the conversation goes and his tone of voice how the owner feels about the property.

For example, you might start by saying, "Mr. Holder, I understand you recently took over a property on Downcast Avenue. Would you be interested in selling it? I'm looking for a house to buy."

Usually he'll say something like "Maybe."

"What's it like?" you ask, and follow up with detailed questions, even if you've already looked at the property closely. Just by chatting with the owner you're building up a pleasant relationship.

Usually he'll tell you it's a highly desirable house. Eventually, of course, he'll suggest that you go and look at it. This is your cue to say, "Yes, I guess I will. Thanks, Mr. Holder."

Next day you call him again: "I looked at the house, Mr. Holder. Have you seen it lately? Well, I'm afraid it isn't as nice as you believed. The tenants let it get into terrible condition. It's the sort of house I've been looking for, but I'd have to spend a bunch to fix it up."

He'll argue a little or a lot, depending on his personality. He'll talk about the good points, real or imaginary, of the house and yard. Let him talk. But keep coming back with details about the bad points—in a friendly, if sorrowful, way. You can wind up the conversation somewhat like this: "I really don't know what to tell you, Mr. Holder. I guess I shouldn't have called you at all. On the other hand, there might be some way to work this out. Let me talk it over with my wife. Then I may call you again."

What have you accomplished? You haven't made a deal, obviously. You haven't even talked price. But now Mr. Holder has started thinking about selling for a more modest price than he originally expected.

Remember that the average person who took a mortgage that turned sour is quite happy just to get his money out of it. Naturally he'd be happy to turn a profit, and at first he hopes to do so. But if someone deflates his notion of the current value of the property, he'll generally snatch at almost any offer.

So when you phone Mr. Holder for the third time, you can suggest a bargain-basement price as a starting point for negotiations. He may startle you by accepting—especially if it's high enough to get his principal out.

Therefore your suggestion shouldn't be a forthright offer. You don't want to be in a position where he can say, "Okay, you've bought yourself a house." You merely ask whether he would sell if you could pay the amount you mention.

From there you go on to discuss the down payment, and other terms and conditions. Since the property is far from desirable (if it were, someone else would probably have bid for it at the foreclosure sale, or sooner) you needn't be liberal in the terms you propose. In truth you're doing Mr. Holder a favor by buying at all, and you have a right to expect an unusually favorable arrangement. Use all your skill as a negotiator.

Make Sure the Ex-Owner Can't Undercut You

A dispossessed owner has a legal right to redeem (buy back) his property—by paying everything due on the mortgage plus costs and interest—during a certain specified period, if it was foreclosed under mortgage law. Depending on state law, this period can vary from seventy-five days in Colorado up to three years in Massachusetts.

So if you buy property from a lender who foreclosed, there may be a cloud on your title. It blocks you from reselling during the redemption period. Who'll buy if you can't prove ownership? How can you guarantee that the dispossessed owner won't claim it again?

"Aw, the ex-owner is broke," you may say. "He owes everybody. There's no chance he'll redeem this property." But you can't be sure. Suppose he inherits money or wins a lottery?

There's one way to make sure he won't buy back the property. Get him to sign a paper waiving his right of redemption (unless this is forbidden by law, as it is in a few states). You can often induce him to do this for a few hundred dollars. It's money well spent for the freedom to resell during the redemption period.

When You Resell, Break Up the Second Mortgage

This is a good place to insert a bit of advice about reselling property. Purchasers may not be able to buy unless you carry back a purchase-money mortgage. But when you do this, give yourself protection in case a purchaser can't keep up the payments. Arrange the transaction in such a way that you can foreclose quickly and economically if you have to. Here's how.

Let's say you're selling for $100,000. The buyer wants to pay $15,000 down, take on a new $60,000 first mortgage (for which you have a commitment from a lender) and give you a $25,000 purchase-money mortgage for the balance. If the down payment is acceptable to you, should you accept the offer?

No. Don't let the $25,000 debt be written up as one large second-mortgage loan. What you need is a $24,000 second and a $1,000 third, even if the total payments, interest charges and everything else will total the same in either case.

The reason: If your debtor defaults, foreclosing a $25,000 mortgage will cost you hundreds of dollars in trustee's fees, deeds, and other charges. You can foreclose a $1,000 third for a fraction of the cost.

Another reason for making two loans instead of one is that a second is generally easier to sell for a good price if there is a third behind it. Somebody considering purchase of the second feels safer because he figures that whoever owns the third will probably take over the payments if there is a default.

Breaking up a big second into an even larger number of small loans gives you a further advantage. If you ever need cash you can sell or hypothecate (put up as collateral for a bank loan) only those notes necessary to raise it, instead of selling or pledging the whole amount of a big second mortgage.

KEY POINTS TO REMEMBER

· Institutional lenders may agree in advance to sell you property after foreclosure at a lower price than the owner demands.

- To buy real estate from a lending institution, make your first approach at the highest possible executive level.
- When negotiating to buy from an institution, be ready with a list of everything that's wrong with the property. Show the REO officer that it may be worth less than he thinks.
- If you offer to buy the worst property on an institution's list, you can get many concessions.
- A down payment of 20 percent or more, with most or all handed back to cover the cost of repairs, helps the lender meet legal requirements. Suggest it.
- You can exchange raw land for foreclosed properties, then buy it back, and still make a handsome profit.
- When a private lender must foreclose, usually he'll be happy just to get his money back.
- When buying, get a dispossessed owner to waive any right to redeem the property.
- When reselling, break up a purchase-money mortgage into several small loans.

__10__

Buying at a Foreclosure Sale

We come now to the third of the three big chances for buying debt-ridden property at a fraction of its worth. Instead of buying from an owner who can't keep up mortgage payments, or buying from a lender before foreclosure, you can buy during an actual foreclosure sale.

This little known way of investing could become a whole career for you if you develop know-how. It offers chances for faster, bigger profits than any other nonspeculative investments.

Before getting into this chapter you may want to look back at Chapter 7 to refresh your memory about the foreclosure laws and how a lender gets some (maybe all) of his money back by forcing the sale of a mortgaged property. To repeat the key point, the legally required preliminary to a foreclosure sale is to advertise (several times, in most states) that the property will be sold by "public auction" at a given time and place. The same advertisement must be posted prominently on the property itself, twenty days before the sale in most states.

Your Clues to the Treasure Hunt

Foreclosure sales are more common now than at any time since the 1930s. In 1982 Tom Randall, a vice president of California's largest trust-deed service company, told the *Wall Street Journal,* "We're setting new records each month." And David Shulman,

137

138

a UCLA economist, told *Money,* "If things are not more normal by 1983 a lot of people could lose their houses."

In most areas there are too many foreclosures for any one person to follow. To pick and choose among them, your first step should be to tune in on a steady stream of advance notices of foreclosure.

There are various ways to find these notices. One is by digging into an odd kind of newspaper that you probably never noticed before: a legal newspaper.

The foreclosure-sale advertisements I mentioned above must be published in a "newspaper of general circulation" in the city, county, or judicial district where the property is located. (A big-space ad for a foreclosure sale means a whopper of an auction where the advertiser wants to attract a crowd of excited and foolish bidders. That's not for you.) What you'll be scanning are small-print ads, cold little announcements without either hard-sell or soft-sell.

Normally they tell five required facts: (1) where the property is located, which means a legal description of the lot, and perhaps a street address which may or may not be correct, since the law doesn't require it; (2) the name of the owner, soon to be the ex-owner; (3) the name of the creditor—usually called the benefi-ciary—who'll get the first and biggest chunk of the proceeds; (4) the location of the "public" place where the property will be auctioned; (5) the date and hour of the auction.

Almost every metropolitan area has a weekly or daily legal newspaper that exists mainly to publish notices required by law. It contains dozens—maybe hundreds—of foreclosure notices (usually called trustee's sales) as well as items about judgments, tax liens, lawsuits, new incorporations, and various other legal proceedings.

This publication is named something like *Legal Advertiser* or *Law Bulletin.* If there's one in your area, a lawyer can tell you how to get it. A subscription generally costs about $5 a month. Just buy the latest issue. You won't want to subscribe until you're a big operator, because a single copy gives enough notices to keep a beginner busy for weeks.

What if there's no legal journal in your area? Probably that's good. It makes your job somewhat harder, but it also means you're in an uncrowded field with little competition. The required notices still have to be published. They'll be scattered among a flock of local-news weeklies or dailies. This is ideal if you want to concentrate on just one or two localities; subscribe to the few newspapers there, turn to the back pages and look at the column headed "Legal Notices." If you want to range a bit farther, hire a clipping service.

Some of the best bargains are hidden in the legal columns of these little papers. That's because a creditor sometimes wants to buy a property for himself, if there's a lot of equity in it. (Equity is the market value minus the money owed on it.) He hopes nobody will come to the sale and bid against him. So instead of putting the notice in the nearby legal paper, he tucks it away in a small weekly at the far edge of the county. Some state laws require only that the "newspaper of general circulation" be in the same county as the property.

Another way of finding out about foreclosures is to stroll into the county courthouse or hall of records, or wherever the County Recorder's office is located. This can be quicker than scanning newspapers, once you learn your way around. Foreclosure notices must be posted publicly there, usually on a bulletin board.

However, some counties don't seem to live up to this law as strictly as others. They may let crafty lawyers post notices on out-of-the-way telephone poles. Or the clerks may "post" them in some big book which is open to public inspection—if the public can find it—in some clerk's office. If notices are hard to locate, don't get discouraged—because most seekers thereabouts *will* get discouraged and leave the field to you. Ask the nearest clerk in sight, "Where can I find foreclosure notices?"

He or she may not know, but will at least refer you to someone else. Clerks seldom know what other departments do. Nevertheless, courthouse people are on the public payroll, paid to help the public, and if you persist you'll find the right place in twenty minutes or so.

Counties have different systems of indexing recorded documents. Some do it by book and page, others by instrument number, still others by reel and image. Get acquainted with whoever handles real estate notices and ask for help in learning how to find what you want. Most clerks, being human, enjoy showing off their expertise. If you approach them with humility and diplomacy, they'll probably teach you all you need to know about finding and using their records. After your first couple of visits, the work will be simple if time-consuming.

In and around big cities there are still other ways to find out about scheduled auctions—easier ways. But remember that the easier it is, the more competitors you'll have. One of the easiest ways is to check the real estate section of your Sunday newspaper. Almost as easy, in some populous areas, is to make contact with a service that specializes in listing default and foreclosure notices. If there's one in your area, many real estate firms probably subscribe to it at a rate of about $25 for four weekly issues. If you scan copies at a friendly realty office, you won't have to read all those newspapers or sift through documents at the courthouse. Additional methods of seeking out foreclosed properties are detailed in John Beck's *Forced Sale Workbook,* available through Impact Publishing Company, 2110 Omega Road, San Ramon, CA 94583.

A Broker Can Be Your Tipster

Very early in your operations as a real estate investor of any kind, you'll begin getting acquainted with real estate agents. Maybe one in fifty will specialize in foreclosures. He or she can help you.

The others probably won't help much because their main interest in foreclosed properties is in trying to sell them for full market value at 6 percent commission. Foreclosed houses are usually problem houses, which brokers don't love. However, if you offer a brokerage firm first crack at listing properties you put up for sale, they'll probably let you check any weekly "recordings service" to which they subscribe.

When you do find a broker smart enough to follow distressed properties closely, cultivate him or her. Soon you can say, "Let's set up a little arrangement. Whenever you tip me off to a bargain and I buy it, whether it's your listing or not, I'll give you three hundred bucks on the side. And when I'm ready to sell or trade it, you'll get another bonus or a listing on the way out."

This should bring you a juicy deal or two. Once you earn a

reputation for working with brokers and never trying to bypass their commission by selling direct, they'll be bird dogs, bringing you more tips than you can handle. One dealer in distressed properties around the San Francisco Bay area, tells Mark Haroldsen, a former student of mine, of being awakened at dawn by a broker who wanted a promise of $4,000 if he made a buy that only the broker could tell him about.

He said, "Okay, if I don't already know about it." He could add $4,000 to his cost estimate in deciding what to bid.

The broker drove him to a mansion that had been for sale at $120,000 with no nibbles. "The bank has foreclosed," the broker said. "You can buy the house at ten o'clock this morning for $30,000. There's a public sale scheduled, but the paper gave the wrong time and place. Only I know that the sale is on for this morning."

Sure enough, he made the only bid, handed the auctioneer a cashier's check for $30,000 and at 10:02 was given a trustee's deed to certify that he owned the mansion, which was easily worth $90,000, and gave the broker a $4,000 check on the way downstairs. A week later he sold the property for $64,000, all cash, and gave his tipster another $100.

Of course it isn't every week that a dealer turns a $30,000 profit on one house. But virtually any foreclosed one-family home can net you $5,000 or $10,000 when you resell. Finding your first property may take a couple of months, but after that, as you learn the ropes and accumulate ready cash, you can soon be acquiring houses every week or two. What other work could pay you $5,000 a week?

How to Pick Promising Auctions

There's work involved in learning how to zero in on a few promising properties among the many being foreclosed. For this you need more facts than you'll find in the legal notices or in the publications that specialize in foreclosure data.

Sometimes, as I warned earlier, the street address of a property won't be shown, since the law requires only the legal description of its location. To convert this to the street address, use map books which are kept at title companies and in many real estate offices. With a bit of blarney and a few small gifts, you can get access to one of these books.

Or, if you're starting out and haven't made contacts yet, you can find out the street address for yourself in the county assessor's office. Ask a clerk to show you how. Basically, the process is to get the assessor's identification number from the office maps. Then you convert this number directly into the street address by using a conversion index.

Before you close the map book, it's a good idea to photocopy part of the map, or make a hand-drawn copy, in order to be sure you find the right property when you go out to look it over. Jot down the nearest cross streets and distance from them.

The address is your first clue to whether a property is a potential buy for you. If it's located in a slum or ghetto or otherwise deteriorating neighborhood, forget it. There are better bargains in newer, growing neighborhoods and in older ones being rehabilitated.

Particularly when you're beginning, your best bet is to concentrate on a promising area as close as possible to your home, in order to save driving time. As you work this territory you'll soon get to know its prices, values, real estate agents, lending institutions. You can become the area's one best-informed bidder for distressed properties.

One shortcut to information about a property in your area, or anywhere in the county, is to phone the law firm mentioned in the foreclosure notice. (An attorney may not be mentioned, but if one is, this is a clue that the property may be worth your attention.) A law firm involved in foreclosure may be glad to give you details about the property's location, appraised value, and any repairs that are needed inside.

Of course you'll never bid on a property without looking at it. The worse it looks (if it's in a good area), the more promising. You can make a fortune by looking for dirty windows. That doesn't mean just ordinarily dirty, but really encrusted, cracked, or broken. They proclaim that the house is abandoned or at least neglected. Other tip-offs to an unwanted property are a weedy front yard, peeling paint, graffiti, unrepaired damage. It won't cost you much to fix up these blemishes and give the house "curb appeal," as realty people say. Someone else's discard can make you a four-figure profit.

Getting a look at the interior may be difficult, because you have no right to go through someone's home just because it's in foreclosure. But you can ring the doorbell with a $10 bill in hand, and if someone answers, you may be able to bargain your way through the door. Still the odds are that the occupants will be too surly to let you in.

If the house is vacant, you may be able to pick up a key from whoever will be conducting the foreclosure sale. This person, known as the trustee or receiver, is usually an employee of a bank or S&L that holds the trust deed.

If you're not lucky enough to get inside, try talking with the neighbors. Sometimes they can tell you plenty. Beyond this, you can only make an educated guess at how much repair work the house will need. Make it a "worst case" guess, with plenty of margin for error. Even so, this is too risky on your first few buys. Get some experience in real estate first.

Always Ask This Question

Let's say you've been inside. You know enough to be sure the property is worth at least $75,000. But only $30,000 is owed on the trust deed. So you go to the auction, bid $30,000 and get the property because nobody bids against you. Have you really snatched a bargain? Maybe. Then again maybe not. Why not? Because one or several mortgages may be ahead of the one you paid off.

Maybe you've bought a second note on a property for which somebody else holds a $50,000 first. To get title, you must pay off the $50,000. If so, that's why no one else bid.

Advertisements in legal papers seldom tell whether a property has been pledged as collateral for several loans, or whether any other mortgages are senior or junior to the one being foreclosed. (If they're junior they'll be wiped out, of course, unless the property happens to sell for more than the amount of the older debt.) Don Scully, president of California Foreclosure Services in San Jose, says third and fourth mortgages are more common than they used to be. He has handled a foreclosure on a house encumbered with nine mortgages. How would you like to buy at foreclosure and then find eight other lenders ready to foreclose on the property?

In short: Never bid at a foreclosure sale until you have a report on the property's loan position.

Sometimes you can buy a preliminary report from a title company for about $50. Do this if you can. It doesn't provide insurance but it screens out most clouded titles. For one thing, it shows whether the debtor really owns the property, or if the owner is his estranged wife who may turn up someday and take her property back.

Some companies won't sell preliminary reports. You'll have to settle for general information they give free (just oral information, nothing in writing) about the deeds recorded against the property. At least this is a beginning.

Anyhow, no preliminary report is enough, because new tax liens or personal liens could be recorded against a property or its owner just before the sale. You can't be sure unless you go and comb the county records.

Usually this is too much time and trouble unless you think you have the inside track on a bargain that seems too good to be true. Here's an alternative. At the auction, before the bidding starts, ask the trustee or receiver, "Can I see a report on the debts recorded against the property?"

Probably he'll have such a report, and will show it. Even this isn't quite enough. Always stipulate, "I'll only bid subject to receiving a title insurance policy to protect my ownership."

If the lender wants to sell, and you're the only bidder, he'll say, "Okay, we'll buy the insurance for you."

But if several bidders are there—or if the lender wants the property himself—he'll announce firmly, "This sale is being made without warranties or covenants of any kind."

Then you're on your own. Normally I'd advise you not to bid.

Steer Clear of Government Resales

If a property was originally bought with the help of a subsidized loan from VA, FHA, or HUD, there probably was only a tiny down payment. Foreclosure means the tenants lived there virtually rent-free for a while, maybe making a few payments but missing quite a few, then wandered off in search of greener fields. They had little to lose. Probably they let their house become a hovel.

Okay so far. Slobs default on conventional mortgages too. But here's the catch. A conventional lender will usually unload a foreclosed house for barely enough to cover the loan plus costs —since he knows the ex-owners are entitled to any surplus. Uncle Sam says, Oh no, "I'll send an appraiser to see how much the house is really worth, and the bids will start near this figure."

As you probably realize by now, in buying a defaulted property, you make money by buying cheap. There must be a wide gap between your bid and the true value. Sure, you expect to pay for refurbishing before you sell. But the rule of thumb is that for every dollar you spend on improvements, plan to get back two to five dollars at resale.

The government doesn't strew bargains around for realty people. If it forecloses a house with a conservative appraised value of $60,000, it may start the bidding at about $57,000.

Furthermore, it may require a buyer to improve the property enough to meet FHA standards. So if you buy a house with just adequate carpeting, too bad. Out comes the carpeting. You put in new FHA-approved carpet with the correct amount of pile per square inch. You make sure it meets the FHA fire resistance standards.

Of course most FHA and VA deals can be bought for a very small down payment with existing mortgages, instead of putting up most of the cash as you must at other foreclosure sales. That's fine for someone who buys the house to live in. But anyone who buys for resale must buy with a sizable equity spread. John V. Kamin, an economist who has studied FHA and VA foreclosure sales, says you'll have to search among hundreds to find one with much profit potential.

You Can Start with a Slim Bankroll

Maybe you're wondering how much cash you'll need to get started in the gold rush for defaulted homes. You can plunge in with $2,000 or less. Here's how.

Just pick out properties being foreclosed by holders of second trust deeds or second mortgages. There are plenty of these. In fact, it's unusual nowadays for a property owner *not* to sign at least two notes against his equity, since that's one of the easiest ways to raise cash. In western and southwestern states, about the only time you don't find a second on a property is when the first mortgage is an FHA or VA loan made within the last few years. Usually these borrowers didn't have enough down payment to satisfy a conventional lender.

The point is that second borrowings are often only $1,500 or $2,000—yet are often foreclosed. Borrowers get in over their heads in times of high unemployment and low profits. When the holder of a second forecloses, and you buy his interest in the property, it doesn't matter that there's a first mortgage or trust deed ahead of you. It's probably an old one at low interest. Just keep making the payments on it.

How to Borrow Cash to Bid With

When you bid you may be asked to show your money. Be prepared. Decide the maximum amount you'll bid, then go to a mortgage lender several days before the auction. Tell him the details about the property you hope to buy and resell. Ask for a letter of commitment—that is, a letter saying he'll lend you a stipulated amount on the property if you get title to it at the foreclosure sale.

He'll probably give you the letter, but with a string attached: You must pay him about 1 percent of the value of the commitment right now. If you don't get the property and take out the loan, he keeps the 1 percent for his trouble. On the other hand, if you do close your deal, this fee will be refunded to you in the form of a credit to your account.

With letter in hand, go to your bank. Use the letter as security for a loan to make the purchase, and the bank will give you a cashier's check to take to the auction.

If you get the property, you pay off the bank with the new mortgage loan promised in the letter of commitment. If you don't, you simply hand back the check to the bank, plus interest or other charges that may be due.

Normally you'll ask for a slightly larger loan and cashier's check than the maximum you plan to bid. This will necessitate a little paper shuffling at the auction, but not much. Naturally you'll start by bidding less than your maximum, if possible. If you make the buy, either with a low bid or at your top limit, the auctioneer will give you a refund for the difference between your check and the amount you must pay.

Sometimes a cautious banker will insist on making out the check jointly to you, the trustee, and the title company so that it can be cashed only with the endorsement of all three parties and used only for the stated purpose. Or he might make the check out to the title company only. In such cases the title company will give you a letter to the trustee, certifying that it is holding the money in trust for you to buy that particular property.

As soon as you begin to dabble in real estate, it will pay you to file financial statements with your banker (whether or not you have any immediate need for loans). Update it about every six months. This helps if you ever need money in a hurry. With a fairly current financial statement on file, the bank will usually advance you money immediately, up to the limits your statement will support.

First Get the Feel of a Few Auctions

Before you start to buy at foreclosure sales, you should go and watch several, just to get used to them. Don't wait to pick out properties you want. That can come later. Just visit auctions at random, without money so you won't be tempted. You can get times and places from a legal paper or courthouse bulletin board or wherever.

Even before you start visiting, you may make an interesting discovery.

Games Insiders Play

Normally the site will be a library or city hall or the front steps of a bank. But you'll notice an occasional sale to be held at some lawyer's office in a tiny town far off the main roads. Sure, the public is welcome. But try to find the office.

Trust-deed sales can be held in any "public" place—which includes a multitude of oddities. One sale was announced for 2 A.M. under a bridge. Another was on a mountaintop. (I'm talking about trust-deed sales.) In most states, mortgage sales must be held in a courtroom.

148

When you see a sale scheduled for an out-of-the-way place, you can easily guess why. The beneficiary (the person or organization that holds the mortgage and is foreclosing) doesn't want bidders at the sale. Why? Because the amount owing on the trust deed is small compared to the value of the property, and the lender wants to become owner. (When a lender is bidder, the amount of the loan doesn't have to be paid in cash.)

Any time there's $25,000 or $50,000 equity in a halfway decent foreclosed property, the beneficiary may try to snap it up. In fact, one big mortgage company forecloses faster and oftener than any other lender in its part of the state, and habitually keeps its foreclosure sales as secret as possible. "More than any other company I know of, I believe they really try to get the properties for the foreclosure profit," says Stuart M. Sherman, who has specialized in buying at foreclosures for eighteen years.

In addition, some officials and clerks in county offices—and some politicians who know their way around—try to profit from inside knowledge of defaults. This is another reason why certain notices are on poles or in back rooms, as I mentioned earlier; somebody in the know wants to grab off a giveaway.

Then too, some people make a business of buying up delinquent notes just so they can foreclose. Because of all these operators, you may discover that the most interesting sales are the ones in the best-hidden announcements. Don't bother to attend for any reason other than to study the peculiar characters there. As a novice you shouldn't try to outbid them.

Best-Kept Secret in Real Estate

This brings me to a more general point. Not just in the situations mentioned above, but in the majority of cases, profits from foreclosed properties are so fat that the whole business of buying them is kept as secret as possible. Few investment books or articles tell much about this murky field. Insiders don't want others crowding in. That's why foreclosure notices are in small print. There might not even *be* many notices, were it not for age-old common laws requiring this legal way of transferring property to be done publicly. Only the laws enable an alert outsider to pierce the veil.

As you go to foreclosure sales, you may begin to notice a few people who attend often. These are professionals. They make a full-time living buying and reselling forfeited property. They come well prepared, with knowledge of a property's value and the status of its title. They also have an accurate idea of the cost of putting it in shape for resale.

Therefore they are tough to compete against. They know each other and seldom bid against each other, because they don't want to push the price up. If several of them are at the same auction, very likely they'll go into a corner and decide who'll buy. Maybe they draw straws. Sometimes they make agreements to take turns buying.

They have tricks to discourage a novice from outbidding them. They may use fronts who keep bidding until the novice drops out, then later rescind their bids on a technicality, so a professional gets the buy at the minimum price. Or they may pay off potential buyers by slipping them a few thousand dollars for not bidding. In some states this is against the law.

These pros only go after the best deals. Except for them, you won't have much competition. The average foreclosure sale attracts four or five bidders, against whom you can use tactics of your own when you feel experienced enough to start bidding.

For example, you may get rid of rivals by telling the trustee (auctioneer) that you want all bidders to show him their cash or cashier's checks. Often they can't do this. Some are shills sent by a foreclosed owner to build the price up as high as they can, since he'll get whatever proceeds are left over when the lender's claim has been paid. Others simply aren't smart enough to come prepared.

When you learn your territory, you may do better than pros do there. They must spend time investigating over a wide area, so they can't help overlooking some of the good buys in your backyard. Knowing the properties, you can spot values quickly without losing too much time investigating unpromising possibilities.

Women are specially suited to this game, either separately or with their partners. They seem to have a keener sense of property values. They understand their particular area almost intuitively. Some of them spend more time than men do in visiting and talking—and thereby gleaning valuable information.

When No Bidders Show Up

One more bit of advice for your warm-up phase, visiting auctions without planning to bid. You may stumble into an auction where only you and the auctioneer are present. This might be a good opportunity, even without money in hand.

The auctioneer will start the proceedings in the usual way, saying, "On behalf of the beneficiary I am authorized to bid x dollars." This bid is usually the total amount of the loan and costs. Next, under normal procedure, he'll say something like "I'll accept further bids in increments of $500."

At this point, since you're the only prospective bidder, the trustee may be willing to answer questions. Ask him about the status of the title, as I advised earlier, and ask whether he'll accept a bid contingent on your receiving a title insurance policy.

Favorable answers mean you can go further. Of course the property may be such a dog that nobody wants it; this could explain the absence of bidders. On the other hand, it could be a bargain that nobody noticed. So you should play for time to investigate it.

If the beneficiary's bid is so low you could easily top it if you wish, you should ask the trustee, "Are you willing to postpone this sale for a few days while I get the money to bid?"

Of course he'll say no if the beneficiary wants to acquire the property. But if the beneficiary doesn't, the trustee probably will grant any reasonable postponement. This gives you time not only to get a letter of commitment and a cashier's check, but to go and see the property. You needn't feel any lingering doubt about the beneficiary's wish to sell; invariably, before a sale, beneficiary always tells trustee whether he wants the property or would rather get rid of it.

When You're Foreclosing

Realty investing takes many forms. If you're active in it, sooner or later you'll probably find yourself holding a delinquent second mortgage and foreclosing on it.

Maybe it's a purchase-money mortgage that you took in order to help someone buy a property you were selling. Maybe you bought paper from a mortgage company. Maybe you bought from some private lender, at a discount, because you knew the property was valuable but the owner had abandoned it.

For whatever reason, you are now in the position of lender or beneficiary. The auctioneer or trustee or receiver, whichever you prefer to call him, is your representative. In effect, he is your employee. You really want the property if you can get it for a reasonable price. How do you arrange to give yourself the best possible chance that this will happen?

Of course you tell your auctioneer privately that you want to buy. "But I may want you to postpone the sale," you say. "If so, I'll pull out my handkerchief."

When you arrive at the sale, if you see other people there— perhaps including professionals—you may decide that opening the bidding would be too risky. The price might go higher than you can pay. So you give the signal. The auctioneer announces that the sale is postponed and rescheduled for such and such a time—maybe three weeks later—at a different place.

Yes, this is legal. In many states a receiver can postpone a sale as many as three times. Of course there must be a new series of advertisements—three in twenty-one days, in California. You hope that your delaying tactics will get rid of the competition.

Several Ways You Can Profit

But we'll assume you run out of postponements and must permit bidding. Other bidders are still with you. What's your best strategy now?

If you are foreclosing on a $30,000 second you bought for $20,000, say, you might think your opening bid should be $30,000. That's what the trustee would suggest. It's what a bank or S&L would do.

But if you do this you'll pay trustee's fees and perhaps other costs based on $30,000. It's much better to tell the trustee to announce that your opening bid is $1,000.

This likewise should be your strategy if no other bidders have appeared. Then the sale would be made at $1,000 and you'd save a bundle in trustee's fees. You'd also take a capital loss of $19,000—the difference between what you paid for the trust deed and what you got at foreclosure. Since you probably owned the trust deed only a few months, your loss would be short term—which is preferable for tax purposes, as you probably know.

However, we're imagining other bidders on the scene. The bidding might go up briskly. So halt it immediately. As soon as others start to bid, announce that you want to see their money.

The nice part about this, in most states, is that you yourself need not produce money. You're a creditor trying to get money back, remember? There's a credit to your account equal to whatever is owed you under the terms of the note you're foreclosing, plus all costs. Only when the bidding goes over that sum is there much chance that you'll need to show cash for the excess.

Another problem for your rivals is that they must produce more cash than just $2,000 or whatever they bid. They must show enough to cover the amount owed you on the note plus costs. Thus your maneuver precludes anyone from picking up a bargain for a few thousand.

Another maneuver you might try, if several properties are to be auctioned on the same day, is to ask the trustee to sell your target property last. Maybe the bidders standing around will run out of money before yours comes up.

But let's say your efforts fail. Competition persists. The house you hoped to buy for $1,000 is bid up to $35,000.

Don't be discouraged. You still can hardly miss making money.

You have two choices, both good. You can stop bidding and let someone buy the house for $35,000. In that case you get all your costs back (assuming they haven't gone above $5,000) plus the $30,000 owed to you on the second. So you're $10,000 ahead —a good return on a $20,000 investment of only a few months. That's extra cash you can use when the next chance comes along.

The other choice, if you're already well-heeled, is to keep bidding and buy the property anyway. Presumably you've studied it, know its value when fixed up, and know what the fixing will cost. So you may outbid the competition and still reap a worthwhile gain.

Now let's return to the scenario where you get the property for $1,000. Why not hold it for more than a year before selling? You're $19,000 out of pocket, but this short-term capital loss will offset other gains you may make during the year. When you finally sell, the profit will be long-term capital gain, so you'll have to pay tax on only about half of it. In effect, you've converted pretax dollars into after-tax dollars because your $19,000 short-term capital loss covers twice that amount in long-term capital gain.

After You Buy a Foreclosed Property

There are other possibilities too. Any time you buy at a small fraction of market value, you can turn around and sell for a fast profit (short-term capital gain) or you can rent after making the place attractive and comfortable. Let's examine these possibilities.

When I speak of reselling I don't necessarily mean at full market value. In general, a property offered below market value is more liquid than the fully priced ones, especially since the speculative boom in houses may have run out of steam. Having bought cheap, you might ask two or four times what you paid and still be so low you'll sell quickly.

Remember, there aren't nearly enough one-family homes to meet the demand. The only reason sales are slow is because owners are trying to get full value or more, while few people can afford to buy at current mortgage-interest rates. There are always eager young people willing to buy a house as is and do their own rehabilitating if the price is right.

If you rent, you'll almost surely have a positive cash flow because you paid so little for the house that your loan amount and payments, if any, can be covered by the rent income. And this income is very likely tax-sheltered. Then too, after you've rented for a few years, resale prices may be higher. Your total return can be handsome.

Here's another factor to think about. In some big states— Illinois, for example—persons who have been foreclosed can redeem the property as much as two years after the sale, if they pay interest to the purchaser. To be safe in those states, you *must* plan on renting during the waiting period. You can check the law in your state by asking a lawyer, or writing to the State Real Estate Commissioner.

Before putting up a "For Rent" sign—and after you rent—make sure your property is maintained well. It should look good in order to attract and keep good tenants. It should be painted, the lawn trimmed, the inside clear. All its fixtures should work. Then you should—no, must—select tenants carefully. And while the house is rented it's still up to you to keep it in good condition. None of this is particularly hard. For guidance, see my book *How to Manage Real Estate Successfully—in Your Spare Time* (available for $24.95 at all quality book stores or by phone order from 1-800-AL Lowry or 805-496-4400).

Dealing in foreclosed properties is no game for the lazy. That's another reason why it's uncrowded. It takes time to learn it. It takes time to look at properties and go to auctions. On the other hand, it's a fast-moving game when you start playing. There's no dickering. Prices are set and purchases made in a few minutes.

And the winnings can be astounding. When owners get over-extended in hard times such as we've seen recently, there are chances to acquire million-dollar properties for a dollar over the mortgage. Yet sometimes there are no bidders, because in hard times few people have faith in an economic recovery. Many fortunes were built on small investments made during depressed times.

Think it over. You may want to take a close look. And then you may decide to join the hunt—and get rich.

KEY POINTS TO REMEMBER

- You can get clues to valuable properties by watching fore-closure-sale notices.
- A good real estate broker may tip you to foreclosure sales in advance. Make it worth his while.
- Never bid on property without inspecting it.
- If property is located in a declining area, forget it. Concentrate on promising locations close to your home.
- Don't bother with FHA or VA foreclosure sales.
- Properties foreclosed by holders of second mortgages are often bargains. Usually the first mortgage is an old one at low interest, which you can afford to keep up.

- When you go to a foreclosure auction, take a cashier's check for slightly more than the maximum you plan to bid.
- When foreclosing, try to arrange to buy back the property itself, starting with a minimum bid. You can resell for less than its market value and still make a good profit.

11

Bargains on the Auction Block

"Come on, folks," pleads the auctioneer. "If you've priced property like this, you know it's worth at least $90,000."

He is a kindly-looking, gray-haired fellow with a resonant voice. He is standing at a small table in front of neat rows of folding chairs. He continues, "You've read the description. You know what the last owner paid. You gonna let it go for forty?" He looks as if he can't believe it. "Who'll say forty-two?"

His floormen are darting between the rows to locate bidders and relay their bids loudly. Heads swivel to follow the action, turning from auctioneer to bidders and back. The price mounts as the auctioneer wheedles and prods. But at last the crowd of about two hundred people stays silent, and he says, "The highest bidder is the lady in blue. If you'll please step over to the office, ma'am, we'll take your check and give you the papers to sign."

He hasn't banged a gavel, and he hasn't cried out the famous last words, "Going once, going twice, gone," because the gavel and the words traditionally denote a final sale. This is a real estate auction, in which the sale occasionally isn't final for various reasons, as we'll see.

For generations auctions have been familiar and exciting spectacles in America. Auctions sell almost anything, from antiques and art objects to zinc plates and zithers. Nearly all our huge tobacco crop is sold by auctioneers. Three-fourths of our livestock change hands at auctions. You can find automobile auctions in any big city almost any weekend.

However, wide-open public auctioning of real estate didn't spread until the 1960s. And the use of auctions to sell whole tracts of new homes originated during the nation's big building slump in the mid-1970s. Even now, most real estate investors are only vaguely aware of the process, and haven't discovered that bargains go on the block every day. Good real estate—and bad —can be bought at bigger discounts in auctions than anywhere else.

Why Real Estate Is Auctioned

Real estate is a durable, comparatively scarce, highly prized form of property. You wouldn't think any owner would part with it for just any little sum an auctioneer might get. But there are several reasons why this happens.

Sometimes the parting is unwilling. As we saw in the previous chapter, owners may borrow against their property, then sink into such dire financial straits that they can't pay what they owe, so the lender forecloses. The law says any foreclosure sale must be by public auction—but there seldom is much competitive bidding, for reasons we've analyzed.

There are other situations, too, in which an owner is parted from his property involuntarily: Tax lien auctions, bankruptcy auctions, sheriff's sales. These aren't quite as secret as some foreclosure sales, so investors needn't do quite as much detective work to find good buys. I'll give you details later in this chapter.

Probate sales—auctioning property after the owner's death— are held occasionally. This chapter will cover them too.

But in addition to all the above, there are auctions arranged deliberately by property owners, often with the help of real estate brokers. Even wealthy owners can get extended beyond their means, and instead of borrowing at stiff interest they sometimes prefer a quick sale at the best price an auction may bring. Then too, a property may languish on the market for some time without getting any nibbles. Putting it up for auction can be a way of attracting qualified buyers—with cash.

Years ago, real estate brokers hated and feared auctioneers as a threat to their business. But the enmity has disappeared because most auctioneers now cater to brokers, handing them the standard 6 percent broker's commission. So if a broker's client needs to unload property in a hurry, when no buyers are in sight, the broker may be truly helpful by lining him up with an auctioneer who is well known among real estate people. The age-old sales device can put money in the pockets of the owner, the broker, and the auctioneer himself. Dozens of real estate auctions nowadays are the result of referrals by real estate brokers.

Just about every kind of real estate you can think of is for sale at auctions. The properties range from cottages to mansions, from barbershops to sawmills and movie studios. If you're interested in land, you can pick up tiny slivers of it, vacant lots, or entire islands or orchards. If you want income-producing real estate you can find one-family houses, apartment buildings, farms, and a wide range of commercial and industrial structures including huge hangars and warehouses.

In 1980, for almost the first time, large numbers of brand-new residential buildings went on the block. Some builders found that auctions were the fastest way to dispose of unsold single houses, and some real estate developers made the same happy discovery about whole subdivisions. Usually, by working out minimum bid prices with professional auctioneering firms, they got returns they could live with. But there were cases where a developer's dream had become a nightmare, and an auction for whatever it would fetch was the only alternative to foreclosure by a financial institution. Larry Kates, partner in Wilshire Equities, a firm that has made millions by sniffing out below-cost buys, has a saying, "Fools build so that investors can buy."

In 1981 the nation's largest home builder, U.S. Home Corporation, resorted to auctioning its homes in nine states. The company, like many builders, had borrowed heavily to finance construction, and the interest payments on its vast inventory of unsold houses were fearsome. The houses sold for only 60 to 70 percent of what U.S. Home had been asking—but businessmen know that in slow times it's better to sell quickly at a loss than to keep capital frozen in inventory.

The biggest firm of real estate auctioneers may be Hudson &

Marshall, of Macon, Georgia. In 1981 it auctioned off more than 600 condominiums and new one-family homes in the Southeast —about three times as many as it sold the year before. Meanwhile, Martin Higgenbotham, a Florida auctioneer, sold 204 houses and apartments, more than doubling his 1980 sales. And in Southern California, in one August weekend alone, 127 condos valued at about $20 million were auctioned off.

By 1983, with new housing sales still stalled by high costs of borrowing, auctions were a fast-spreading rescue operation over most of the nation. What does this mean to you as an investor?

Clearly it means many more chances to build a fortune quickly, without much risk if you do your homework before the auctions. Virtually all auctions are advertised weeks in advance. So you can study the properties, talk to advisers and agents and do some comparison shopping. Any auctioneering company will encourage you and your advisers to inspect, will answer questions long before the auction, and will even seek out answers for you if it doesn't already have them.

When you find properties you want, you won't need time-consuming negotiations or exceptional bargaining skill to get a good buy. Just determine what price you can pay, keep your bidding below that limit, and if someone bids above it, move along to the next potential bargain on your list.

Where to Find Auctions

Auctioneering firms announce their auctions by advertisements in newspapers. Sometimes the ads are just one-paragraph boxes in the classified-advertising pages of the *Wall Street Journal,* or in the real estate sections of metropolitan Sunday papers. Other times—especially if a whole bunch of houses or condos are to be sold—the auctioneer may take a big ad in the business section of a daily paper.

If you have trouble finding auction advertisements, call the advertising manager of any big newspaper near you and ask him where to look.

However, finding the ads is only half the job, because they seldom reveal where the auction will be held. Most real estate auctioneers don't want gawkers and curiosity seekers cluttering up the scene (although Higgenbotham seems to welcome them; he hires a bluegrass band or string combo to attract a crowd, and raises clusters of balloons). Therefore their ads often conclude with a line like "For complete information and to obtain the Auction Fact Sheet, telephone . . ." Or they may merely give the auctioneer's mailing address, assuming that anybody likely to buy real estate at auction will be smart and energetic enough to write to the auction advertiser for information.

As an alternative to watching newspapers, here's a way to start a stream of auction announcements flowing directly to you. Look in the Yellow Pages of big-city phone books in your area. Under "Auctioneers" you'll probably find a dozen or more firms listed. Some firms tell what they specialize in—furniture, restaurant equipment, machinery or whatever—but others give no clue. So you'll have to do some phoning to find out which companies auction the types of property you want. After you identify them, write to them (preferably enclosing a batch of stamped and self-addressed envelopes) asking them to add your name to their mailing list for future auctions.

The Yellow Pages don't list all the real estate auctioneers. Some firms that handle only expensive properties aren't shown there, because they feel they don't need to be.

For example, the two firms that are probably California's biggest—Kennedy-Wilson of Santa Monica and Robert Rouse of Beverly Hills—don't buy Yellow Pages space. But the Los Angeles telephone directories (all areas) list them on the white pages. If you'd like to be notified of their big-bid auctions, a simple request on a business letterhead will start the process. You'll be asked to submit credit information. If you pass the screening, you'll get invitations.

Nine Other Ways to Find Auctions

The less crowded auctions of smaller and shabbier properties—mostly desperation cases—offer you more bargains than you can shake a writ at. For information about them there are at least nine sources.

1. The legal newspapers mentioned in Chapter 10 publish notices of bankruptcies, probate sales, sheriff's sales, and other

kinds of forced-sale auctions. These auctions are seldom conducted by a professional auctioneer whom you can telephone for
details. (The rare exceptions occur mainly in a probate sale
where an executor wants to get as much money as possible for
heirs—of whom he may be one—and a bankruptcy sale where a
conscientious sheriff considers it his duty to get the maximum for
creditors as well as debtor.) Usually a forced-sale auction is arranged by a court officer who knows little, and cares less, about
the property. On the other hand you probably won't run into the
secretiveness that cloaks foreclosure sales when a creditor or
some other insider hopes to be the sole bidder. So these announcements generally schedule auctions at convenient times
and places and give somewhat more detail than you're likely to
find in foreclosure-sale advertisements.

2. Tax-lien auctions—sales of property on which taxes
haven't been paid—are usually advertised in a local newspaper
as well as the legal paper. Back-tax bargains in farmland or raw
acreage are available all over the country, many for as little as
$100 per acre.

3. In every county—and usually each city as well—there is an
office that arranges the tax-foreclosure sales. Usually the office
is tucked away in some far corner of the county courthouse or
city hall. You can drop in at this office and ask for its current
brochure on surplus city-owned or county-owned real estate.
Usually all the properties in the brochure are put up for auction
once a year, or once a quarter.

4. The federal government also auctions off big and little properties seized from people who default on payments to one of
Uncle Sam's myriad real estate programs or to the Internal Revenue Service. Phone the nearest federal office and ask for an
application blank, which, when you fill it in and return it, will get
you included on the notification list for whatever categories you
want.

5. After owners fall five years behind in paying property taxes,
the county may deed their property to the state, which means
that the county tax collector is legally required to try to sell the
property at public auction. In some counties there are so many
tax-deeded properties that auctions are held every three months.
Lists of these properties are published in local newspapers, but

only at intervals, so you may miss seeing them. A better way to keep informed is to write to county tax collectors, enclosing a stamped return envelope, and ask them to add you to their mailing list of prospective buyers of tax-sale properties. Most counties send out mailings about their auctions although the law doesn't require it. In counties that don't keep mailing lists, the tax collector will at least tell you approximately when and where the next auction will be advertised, and will probably suggest that you phone at about that time for further facts.

6. Sometimes people or companies owe more bills than they can pay, and are surrounded by an impatient army of creditors, all with outstretched palms. To liquidate the debtor's property—that is, turn it into cash which will be divided among them—the creditors can file a petition for "involuntary bankruptcy" with the clerk of the nearest U.S. District Court. (Bankruptcy is a federal case, governed by the laws set down in the Federal Bankruptcy Act.) Or the debtor himself can stop the siege by petitioning the court for "voluntary bankruptcy." Either kind of petition sets in motion the machinery for tabulating a debtor's assets, placing them under strict supervision, and possibly liquidating them (usually by auction) if a court-appointed referee decides this should be done. The referee meets with the creditors and calls on them to elect a Trustee in Bankruptcy—usually a lawyer who specializes in bankruptcy law—to be custodian of all the bankrupt's assets. If the creditors don't want to elect a trustee, the referee appoints one. At any given time the same lawyer may be acting as a Trustee in Bankruptcy for a dozen or more different bankrupts. And he'll be glad to put you on the mailing list for his auctions if you send him a supply of self-addressed stamped envelopes. He wants the auctions to pull in as much money for the creditors as possible, so he welcomes potential bidders. Ask a district court clerk or a bankruptcy lawyer for names of trustees.

7. Many civil lawsuits end with a plaintiff winning a judgment against a defendant. Usually, this means the loser is ordered to pay a sizable sum of money to the winner or winners. However, the unhappy defendant sometimes won't or can't pay. In that case a sheriff or marshall may seize some of his property and sell it publicly to satisfy the judgment. If the property is real estate,

the lawman may padlock the buildings and post a notice that the property will be sold on a certain date. You can find out about these sales (a) from a bulletin board in the county courthouse, and (b) from whichever newspaper of general circulation the sheriff uses to advertise his sales, or possibly (c) from mailings sent by the sheriff's office. Sheriffs are legally required to advertise their sales on bulletin boards and in a newspaper, and if you have trouble locating them, just phone the sheriff's office and ask where to look.

As for mailing notices of sheriff's sales on request, most sheriffs do this as good public relations. Sheriffs are elected, remember. Usually you need only send a supply of self-addressed envelopes; the average sheriff will provide postage as a public service. In fact, if you call his office and ask whether any sales are scheduled soon, you can probably get full information over the phone. And in most states the law provides that you can even phone in a bid, or send it by mail, to the sheriff's office before an auction. Of course the bid will then be publicly announced at the auction itself.

8. When a property owner dies, the executor of his or her will sometimes arranges to sell the property. He can do this either by a private sale—to his next-door neighbor, to a business crony, or to any stranger who happens along—or by a public sale, which often takes place in a courtroom.

But before there can be any kind of sale, the law says a dead person's property must be appraised, and any offer to buy must be at least 90 percent of that value. So you won't find really fantastic bargains in probate court. However, many of these appraisals are surprisingly low, because nobody is showing the appraiser through the house and pointing out its good features. Then too, it may be appraised many months before the sale (a year is the maximum the law allows) and market values may have gone up in the meantime.

Anyhow, whether the property is sold privately or by auction, the highest bid must be approved by the probate court. The judge gives his okay during what is called a confirmation hearing. Usually he confirms several probate property sales during the same court session. Here's where you come in. During the session anyone can make a higher bid in open court. This is known as an "overbid." Usually there's little competitive bidding in confirmation hearings. So it may pay you to watch for announcements in legal newspapers, or at the bulletin board of a court building where confirmation hearings are held. But let me remind you again: As with all other property up for auction, always inspect probate properties in advance and decide on the maximum you'll pay. Typically these aren't problem properties, so if the bidding becomes hectic in court you might get carried away and bid too high.

9. Every big bank has a trust department. The trust officers handle investments for wealthy widows, invalids, and others who for some reason can't or don't want to look after their investments. When one of these people dies, the trust officer may need to liquidate real estate in settling the estate. Therefore if you're interested in this type of investment, it's a good idea to get acquainted with bank trust officers, then call them periodically to ask if they're getting ready to put any property up for bids. After a while they may get in the habit of calling you.

The Calendar and the Weather Can Help You

In deciding which auctions will give you the best chances to whisk away big bargains, the two most important factors to watch are the time of year and the weather.

The three or four weeks starting about December 10 can be a great time to bid. People tend to feel pinched for cash around then. They also tend to be busy with holiday festivities. So there's a good chance you may be the only bidder at some auctions.

Another good time is the first three weeks of April. The Ides of April are tax time, remember, with accompanying pains in the bank account for many would-be bidders.

Budget problems can be severe for families with children (especially children in college or private school) at the start of the school year in September. And for these same people, late June marks the start of another expensive and hectic time because of school graduations and vacations.

Therefore, if you can be well stocked with cash in December, April, June or September, and can arrange your affairs so you have leisure time to look at properties and attend auctions, such times can be richly profitable for you. Auctions will be sparsely attended and bids will be appreciably lower.

As for weather—the worse it is, the better for you, if you can stand the discomfort. Rain, snow, freezes and heat waves keep many bidders away from auctions. So grit your teeth and go treasure-hunting when weaker types stay home.

Check Before You Bid

Most auction properties are problem properties, neglected by their past owners. So this is a good time to elaborate on what I said in Chapter 10 about looking closely at a property before bidding.

First find out if the auction requires a minimum opening bid. Then, even if you can't get inside, a little inquiry in the neighborhood will probably establish a consensus on what the place is worth.

Next, if you think you've found a bargain, you may want to pay an appraiser or some other expert to make sure. Remember, you're not getting the warranties you could get when buying from a private owner, nor do you have any chance to insert escape clauses in the contract of sale, like stipulating that your purchase is subject to various contingencies.

Finally, unless the auctioneer will guarantee title, you'd better hire a lawyer or a title-insurance company to make a title search. This search—a check of local records in the office of the town or county clerk—is your best way of making fairly sure you'll have a clear right to improve, sell or exchange the property once you buy it. The search may turn up building restrictions that would prevent you from adding a garage or a porch or some other improvement you were planning. There may be unpaid taxes; liens filed by a contractor who did some work on the property and never got paid; pending lawsuits that would involve the property; easements that would give someone else the right to drive through the property or run a sewer pipe across it.

There may also be hidden "defects in title," as lawyers call them, that would only come to light in searching far back through the register of deeds. Maybe the property you plan to buy was transferred years ago by a forged deed. Maybe a deed was signed by a minor who couldn't legally do so. Maybe a deed was delivered after the signer had died and the property should have passed to his heirs. Maybe the resident of the property you want to buy, who has now been declared bankrupt or lost a damage suit, is an imposter who moved into the house after the real owner died or disappeared and that owner's descendants could come back and take the property away from you. Such surprises do happen now and then.

In one well-known case a mansion was sold at auction by three brothers and a sister, heirs of a millionaire who left no will. Years later another sister, who had been living in South America, returned and claimed her rightful share of the estate—which of course included the mansion. Papers that had been filed in probate court were fraudulent because they didn't include her among the heirs. Luckily the investor who bought the mansion at auction had also bought title insurance. So he simply notified the insurance company, which cleared the title by buying a deed from her to the investor at no expense to him. If this investor hadn't protected himself with title insurance, he would have had to pay the sister for her fifth of the property and then tried to find the four other heirs to sue them for fraud.

Title insurance may cost $300 or $400. Only once in a thousand times will a buyer benefit from it. But in that one case it can prevent the loss of a property. And if you plan to borrow on property, you'll find that lenders insist on it.

Buy Only What You Can "Steal"

Some astute investors, after checking a property and figuring what it's worth to them, go a step further. They subtract 10 or 20 or 25 percent from that price, and bid no higher. Their philosophy is, "If I can't steal a property, I don't want it."

Bidders like this have paid less than $15,000 for corner buildings in areas that soon were revitalized, and sold the buildings for three or four times that much. Tony Hoffman, whom I mentioned earlier, got his start in real estate by buying a decrepit Victorian mansion at auction, converting it into a triplex, and selling it six months later at a $40,000 profit. Harvey Rosen, of Los Angeles, did even better in 1972 on his first venture: he netted $100,000 in 45 days by buying and reselling an apartment building in Claremont. In April 1981 a bidder at a Phoenix auction got a new three-bedroom condo for $120,460; the asking price since January 1980 had been $185,320. In Salt Lake City last year a four-bedroom house was on the market for four months at $92,000—then went for $58,000 at auction.

Buying empty land at auction can be even more profitable, but more risky too, especially if you buy a parcel too small to build on. Yet the price is sometimes so low—$10, say—that the possible profit is worth the small gamble; an owner of adjacent land may be glad to pay $1,000 for it later.

At a tax auction in Queens, New York, a bold bargain-hunter bought a small slice of land for $1,000 and held it ten years, waiting for something to happen. Then he got $165,000 for the sliver from David Muss, chairman of a big New York real estate firm, who needed the land to complete the purchase of a tract for a shopping center.

Let Leverage Help You

Leveraging, as you probably know, is the magical art of making a little money act like a bundle. In other words, you use cash for only a small fraction of the purchase price; you borrow (or "finance," as money men prefer to call it) the rest. Thereby you multiply your purchasing power, and incidentally reap handsome tax benefits.

When builders or real estate developers stage auctions, they often set up attractive financing by assuming the bank's cost of extending a mortgage at below-market rates. In some recent auctions buyers have been offered 11.5 percent, for the first three years of the loan. Beginning with the fourth year, however, the rate would float up or down between 11 percent and 18.5 percent depending on the prevailing rate each year.

The packet of advance information you receive from an auctioneer should contain all the financial facts you'll need. If the expected sales price is much higher than existing mortgages against the property, the auctioneers should also include a commitment from a lender. (It will be contingent on the lender's approval of you as the mortgagor.)

Although the foreclosure auctions I described in Chapter 10

are usually all-cash deals, other kinds of distress-sale auctions generally require only 5 to 20 percent down as a deposit that binds the successful bid for about thirty days. A personal check may or may not be acceptable. (One warning: your deposit isn't refundable in most states unless you fail to qualify for a mortgage or your bid is found unacceptable for some other reason. So you'll have great difficulty backing out if you change your mind.)

An institutional auctioner of default properties, such as a bank, governmental agency, or sheriff, is interested primarily in cash sales. So you'll need to be sure about your financing; otherwise you may become one of the victims of foreclosure yourself. If you know the potential financing sources, you should be able to get short-term financing in order to meet the strict time requirement of the default sale, then refinance with a conventional mortgage. If you've bought right, your cash flow or profit from resale will be high enough to make the cost of borrowing worthwhile.

You Can Bid and Win Without Attending

Because there are so many auctions of various kinds, if you begin scanning the field systematically you may soon find more good prospects than you can cover personally. But you can bid at most of them without being present.

One way is to have someone else attend and bid for you. Your attorney or a trusted friend can be your stand-in. Of course you must be specific and emphatic about your bidding limit.

Another way is to submit an absentee bid before the auction date. Many auctioneers let you do this. They'll keep your bid confidential until the auction opens.

One good thing about absentee bidding is that it protects you against auction fever that might tempt you to bid unwisely if you were in the midst of the hurly-burly. In sending a sealed bid you're competing against other bidders, of course, but you can do it scientifically. One useful technique is to make your bid an uneven number. Try to figure out what competitors are likely to bid (experience will help you with this). Then bid just a few dollars over this amount, if the property is worth it to you. Most people who use sealed bids think in round numbers—$5,000 or $5,500 or something like that. Therefore your bid should be an odd sum like $5,005 or $5,502. Those few extra dollars definitely improve your chance of submitting the top bid. On the other hand, if it's not worth quite that much to you, send in an offer of $4,951 or $5,498. You might just get the property.

Auctions Are Adventures

Today's real estate auctions vary in atmosphere. Some are as hushed as a rare-book sale. Others are raucous. The more you attend, the faster you'll adjust to whatever scene you encounter.

Gamson & Flans, a Los Angeles firm that has been notably successful ever since it opened in 1979, operates with quiet elegance. The two partners are evasive about their sales methods, saying they don't want to enlighten their competitors. But they evidently try to get property sold before the date of the auction.

They say they encourage a "buyer to make his bid and the seller to accept it or counter it" in advance. On auction day, only what's left over is offered through the traditional bidding process, without much urging by the auctioneer. Nevertheless Gamson & Flans generated an estimated $60 million worth of dwelling sales in 1980.

A Kennedy-Wilson show, on the other hand, is meant to be fun, the partners say. Bidders are carefully screened before receiving a card that entitles them to bid, but when they arrive at the auction they are beguiled by a Dixieland band for an hour's pre-auction warm-up. Scantily clad waitresses circulate with free drinks poured by a bevy of bartenders. Altogether close to a hundred employees are on hand before and during the bidding.

Winning Strategy for Auctions

Auctioneers are human. Don't antagonize them. They dislike an active bidder who repeatedly starts the bidding at a ridiculously low price. I've seen an auctioneer's assistant call such a troublesome character to one side and give him a talking-to. Sometimes an auctioneer will even hold up the bidder to sarcasm and scorn in front of everybody, ridiculing him over the public address system.

When you're at an auction, always wait for others to make the opening bids. If you want a property, you can join in after the fast action has slowed down.

Canny bidders sometimes use a technique called a shut-out bid. For example, if you know a property is a good buy at $9,000 and the bidding is around $6,750 with increases of only $50 or $100, your first bid might be a sudden jump to $8,000. This can shock those who've been actively bidding. It knocks out their hopes of buying for around $7,000 or $7,500, say. It also may stun others who were waiting to enter the bidding at about that level. An auction is no place for slow deciders. Before any of them recover from the shock, the auctioneer may close the bidding and you may win for less than you'd otherwise have had to pay.

This shut-out tactic works especially well during the last half or quarter of a long auction, when bidders are feeling less buoyant than in the early going. Pick your spots and try it.

How to Spot Phony Auctions

There's no way a beginner can be sure, in advance, which auctions will be real bargain bonanzas. But there are a few tip-offs to those that definitely won't.

If an auction advertisement describes the property in glowing terms, beware! Such an advertisement may use phrases like "A first-time price reduction of $70,000 off the previous asking price has been approved for the auction of these luxurious residences." The savings may turn out to be largely illusory. Sellers often inflate the asking price a month before an auction to encourage higher bidding. To be sure you'd get a bargain you'd need to know the price history of the house or apartment you're considering, and how the pre-auction price compared with asking prices on similar properties in the area. Local real estate agents probably can tell you.

If no minimum bid is required on a house or apartment you're considering, or if the minimum is much below recent prices thereabouts, this is, of course, a favorable sign. But it's not a sure indication, because the usual auction procedure allows a seller to reject all bids if he says they're too low. (However, if he's using a professional auctioneer, the fact that he'll have to pay the auctioneer's fee and expenses anyway may discourage him from refusing to sell.)

Talk to others at an auction. Ask questions about the auction company. Find out from those who have attended similar sales if the company seems to get high prices for most properties it sells.

Another unfavorable indicator is when an auctioneer uses high-pressure, fast-talking, overenthusiastic techniques to stir up the bidding. Sometimes he himself has a financial interest in what he's auctioning.

Watch for Shills

"Shill" is an old American slang term for an assistant to a gambler or swindler or pitchman. One of my dictionaries says the word came originally from "shillaber," an obsolete word that means a decoy.

Anyhow, his job is to lure the unwary into buying inferior merchandise, either by his own bidding or by making fake purchases of it. At real estate auctions, as far as I know, a shill almost never buys anything, probably because legal restrictions might put him and the auctioneer in danger of prosecution for fraud if the purchase turned out to be a pretense. But shills do bid enthusiastically.

They generally speak up when there are no bids, or bidding is slow. Also, if there's only one bidder, they may bid against him to keep him raising the ante. Some auctioneers even have ways of signaling their shills to bid. It could be a physical signal, such as tugging at an earlobe. Or it could be a code phrase such as "Come on, folks," or "That's ridiculous."

Shills are hard to spot. But you can develop a sense for them after a few auctions. If you notice someone who bids often but never ends up as the buyer, you've probably identified a shill. Try your best not to bid against a shill. Don't enter the competition if a suspected shill becomes active. An auctioneer will probably stop signaling his shill to bid against you if you suddenly stop bidding whenever he makes a bid.

Maybe You Can Buy When the Auction Is Over

It's important to be sure you understand the rules of any auction at which you hope to make a buy. Often the rules allow buying after an auction sale ends, and this gives you one more chance to grab a giveaway.

Sometimes an investor who dropped out of the bidding has second thoughts about the worth of the property, or finds he'll have more money available than he thought he would. Others, who may have been absent from the auction, may hear what the winning bid was and realize they could still get a bargain by bidding slightly higher. Remember that a seller usually can reject the top bid submitted at the auction if he chooses.

Gerard Nierenberg, a well-known lawyer who sometimes handles real estate negotiations, tells of one big auction where this principle enabled an associate to buy a surplus aircraft plant owned by the government.

The General Service Administration had put the plant up for auction. Nierenberg and his associate decided to bid $375,000 for the building and equipment. In his book *The Art of Negotiating,* Nierenberg tells what happened:

"A hundred or more people arrived at the auction but Fred, by intuition, was able to point out a group of three men and say, 'There's our competition.' He was absolutely right. Brokers and bidders in an audience behave differently. We started with a bid of $100,000 and they countered with $125,000. We bid $150,000. When they had bid up to $225,000 Fred was silent and we left the auction. I was puzzled; our final bid was supposed to be $375,000. But Fred explained that he read on the offering circular that if the government did not feel the price was high enough, they could reject it. Since we were the second highest bidder, the auctioneer would naturally contact us, tell us that the bid of $225,000 had been rejected, and ask if we would care to make another offer. We could then counter with a higher price and ask the government for certain valuable concessions, such as taking a portion of the price in a mortgage. Within seven days this occurred, just as if Fred had written the script."

Of course the average reader of this book isn't likely to be buying surplus aircraft plants, but you can sometimes use Fred's strategy by letting the bidding stop at a miserably low level. Whenever you decide you're willing to pay more than the winning bid at an auction, don't wait for the auctioneer to seek you out even if you were second highest. Get in touch with him as soon as you can. If the highest bid was subject to refusal, you're in a position similar to someone who makes an offer through a real estate broker. Your bid may simply be accepted or turned down. Or the seller may send back a counter-offer suggesting a change in terms. Even though the seller has already told the auctioneer his rock-bottom price, this procedure gives him one last chance to sell below that if he must. Whether he will or not depends on how badly he needs the money.

At an auction itself, once a bid is accepted, things don't happen much differently than at a conventional sale; they just happen faster. Ordinarily you'll be led to an office where an auctioneer's assistant puts your bid—your offer, that is—into written form as a standard purchase agreement or sale agreement. The auctioneer takes this document and your check (probably 5 or 10 percent of your bid) and presents it to the seller. If your bid at least equals the minimum price the seller specified to the auctioneer, the seller is expected to sign the contract. If your bid is below the stated minimum, the seller still has the choices of accepting it, rejecting, or making some kind of counter-offer to you. In the third (and most likely) case, you'll then be in a position to continue negotiating—although sometimes the seller makes the same counter-offer to the second and third highest bidders.

When and How to Sell at Auction

Now let's suppose you own some real estate that has been on the market for some time but seems to be dead in the water. If you're in a hurry to sell, maybe you should put it up for auction.

Before you decide to do this, think about the gamble you're taking. You'll have to pay the auctioneer's fee and expenses regardless. And if the bid is far below what you want, your only chance of getting more is through a counter-offer to the top bidders.

The big advantage of selling at auction is that it usually means a quick sale. "It's the only method where the seller can be guaranteed that buyers will be present," says Melvin A. Giller, president of Nationwide Auction Company. You can almost count on a sale within twenty minutes, at a price above your absolute minimum, but probably well below market value.

You're also likely to get much more of the selling price in cash than you could otherwise. People who go to auctions are experienced real estate investors with big bankrolls. They're ready to write a check whenever a good deal turns up.

If you go ahead, you'll naturally want to find an auctioneer who is good in this field. You can't afford to pick blindly from the phone book. Ask your bank's trust officer for recommendations. Then get in touch with the firms he suggests, and ask them for names of property owners who have been clients. Get the clients' opinion of the service they received.

Make sure your chosen auctioneer has a strong marketing program. Study his promotional material and procedures—his advertising, brochures, publicity, and his way of staging auctions. The more razzle-dazzle his methods, the bigger his bill will be, but maybe he'll get you a bigger price. You'll have to decide by comparing his record with competitors' records.

An auctioneer's fee is negotiable. A typical fee is 5 or 6 percent of selling price—or of the highest bid if you reject it. (Keep in mind that in this situation, by prearrangement, the highest bid might come from a shill, to jack up the auctioneer's commission.) In addition the auctioneer will show you his budget for promotional expenses, and expect you to pay these in advance.

In your early screening of auctioneers, ask about their charges. And get a sample of the Auction Agreement each one uses. Have your attorney review it. Typically the promotion program will cost ½ to 1½ percent of your property's appraised value. When you pick an auctioneer, you and he will work out financial details, including any financing to be offered to bidders. If it seems necessary, either you or the auctioneer will try to get a commitment for new financing.

We live in changing times. There are changes in the way real estate is bought, and in the way it is marketed. Today homes are probably not bought with the idea that they'll be lived in for a lifetime or for generations. Turnover is faster each year, and auctions speed the turnover.

Auctions are the bargain basements of the real estate business. They offer enticing vistas if you care to study them. Why not take a look?

KEY POINTS TO REMEMBER

· Try to get mailings from agencies and individuals responsible for auctioning real estate.
· The best times to bid at auctions are the last part of December, first part of April, start and finish of the school year, and whenever the weather is bad.
· Make sure the title is clear before buying.
· Be ready with cash for 20 percent of your bid.
· Wait until the fast bidding has slowed down. Sometimes you can win with a sudden shut-out bid.
· Don't bother with heavily advertised auctions, or any at which an auctioneer uses shills or high pressure.
· Whenever you're willing to pay more than the winning bid at an auction, get in touch with the auctioneer after the sale. He may accept your higher bid.

12

How to Fend Off Foreclosure

"It's cliffhanging time for me," I was told recently by an investor whom I'll call Rory Splotz. "It's like the dam has broken, the woods are afire, and the enemy is surrounding us, buddy. In a word, desperate."

Rory's real estate investments—heavily leveraged—had thrived for several years. Now suddenly he was bogged in red ink. Some electric ranges had burned out. Some plumbing had burst. Burglars, vandals, serious family illness, and an embezzling stockbroker had obliterated most of his liquid assets. So he missed payments on mortgages, insurance, and taxes. Soon he was hit by default notices.

Then the foreclosure warnings began to arrive.

Foreclosure: a New Growth Industry

Rory's plight was not unique. In 1979 and 1980 homeowners by the multitude had mortgaged themselves to the roof, taking calculated risks that time would escalate their equities and bring down mortgage rates. But by 1982 the outlook for interest rates remained cloudy, and property values slumped. Consequently the resale market was stagnant in most parts of the country. When balloon payments fell due on second and third mortgages written in the inflationary mid-1970s, people like Rory Splotz found they couldn't refinance and couldn't sell out at profitable prices.

So scurrying for money turned into a race to the courthouse—mainly for hard-pressed homeowners who had refinanced their houses to pay other bills, but occasionally for rash investors like Rory who hadn't heeded (or didn't know about) my oft-given advice to "arrange for monthly payments that you *know* you can meet," and to "be sure the income from a property will cover the payments on the debt," and to "always keep an adequate financial reserve," and so on. Of course, even a prudent investor may get squeezed by an unforeseeable series of major personal misfortunes. All anyone can do in a hurricane is hunker down.

Anyhow, by autumn of 1981 there were laments like "Mortgage delinquencies are rising to serious levels," from the U.S. League for Savings, a trade organization of savings and loan associations. Defaults in various areas were nearly double those of a year earlier. In August 1982 the *Wall Street Journal* headlined a major report, "Bad Real-Estate Loans Grow at Many Banks; 1983 Outlook Is Grim," on the same day that a bankruptcy lawyer, writing in the *Los Angeles Times,* remarked, "Three years of recession and high interest have seen the annual consumer-bankruptcy number jump from just under 200,000 in 1979 to more than 400,000 in 1981. . . . Business bankruptcies have increased as fast as consumer cases."

Long-Term Survival Strategy for Investors

Obviously Rory isn't the only investor hanging by his fingernails. Later in this chapter I'll analyze the self-rescue techniques I suggested to him, on the chance that some readers of this book may need similar advice.

But first you should be aware of precautions you can take long before lenders grow uneasy about you. "In time of peace, think of war" was a maxim of the great city-state of Venice, which lasted more than a thousand years. Its ancient principle is still good for modern investors. In time of prosperity, make connections that can help in time of need. And as you invest, arrange your ventures to stay off that treadmill of debt called "negative cash flow."

Here are steps Rory might have taken several years ago to

fortify his position. You may want to consider taking them now, just in case:

1. MAKE FRIENDS BEFORE YOU NEED THEM. A network of contacts is invaluable to an investor. The way to build such a network is by getting into circulation and lending a helping hand wherever possible. Analyze local civic organizations such as Rotary, the Chamber of Commerce, political clubs, special-interest associations, and ethnic groups. Make every effort to join those where successful people cluster. Give some time and money to become solidly established in them. Often you can volunteer for a fund-raising drive or a political campaign and form strong friendships.

Become a steady customer of a popular local barber who hears all the gossip; much of the gossip is about real estate these days. Strike up acquaintances with a few local street cops, detectives, and clerks around the courthouse or city hall. They hear all the rumors and know what is happening with everybody in town. Also they're aware of which lawyers fight hard for clients. Cultivate a few of these younger, hungrier lawyers if you can; they know how to help people in financial trouble.

Get to know some of the most active real estate agents, attorneys specializing in realty matters, accountants and other money people. Try to win their confidence and respect by steering a little business their way, lunching with them occasionally, passing along information you pick up through your network. Stockbrokers and mortgage brokers often are close to wealthy investors who have surplus funds to invest; someday you might want to tap some of those funds.

2. GET LENDERS' DOORS OPEN EARLY. The best time to talk to bankers and S&L people is when you don't need to borrow. Through your other friends, try to get introductions to several loan officers, and to branch managers and higher-ups whenever possible. Ask their advice about investments you're considering. Let them know about properties you've bought and sold. Casually mention that you "may want to do some borrowing in a year or two." Make a point of dropping in often to make deposits or to cash checks, and pausing to exchange a few words with your

friends behind the big desks. You might even borrow money you don't need and repay it quickly to build up your credit rating. Money men lend more easily to customers they know personally. "Bankers aren't evenhanded any more than other prudent business men are evenhanded," says A. A. Milligan, past president of the American Bankers Association. "Different people are treated differently. A banker who is evenhanded is a fool and an automaton."

3. Don't put many eggs in one basket. Spread your investments. Buy inexpensive properties in several promising neighborhoods. Even though these cheaper properties may take more maintenance and may bring you undesirable tenants occasionally, they're much easier to keep rented—probably because lower- and middle-income people are more likely to be renters than are the high-bracket types.

4. Build a reserve to cover negative cash flow. Just as banks and businesses set up a "reserve against losses," you should make yourself set aside at least one-fifth of your investment capital to cover any monthly deficits. For example, you've owned a property for several years; you decide to refinance or sell it and use the proceeds to expand into several properties. You get $50,000. Instead of using it all to buy other houses, just use $40,000. Put the reserve $10,000 to work in a money fund (if interest rates are attractive enough at the time) or in a second mortgage. There are plenty of hard-money lenders who handle a lot of small, short-term amortized loans. You might even learn how to buy discounted notes and thus boost your effective yield to 20 percent or better.

5. Watch your tax payments. You can lose your property automatically by not paying real estate taxes when they're due. A mortgage holder must notify you if he intends to foreclose, but unpaid real estate taxes are considered "automatic liens"— which means that tax authorities don't have to inform you that they have a lien against you. They can sell your property to make up for unpaid taxes even though you didn't know you were behind in payments. Usually they send routine notices of taxes due, but if one of these goes astray in the mail the error doesn't excuse

you. You are still expected to know when taxes are due, and how much you owe. The only way to guard against this calamity is to check regularly at your city hall to see whether any taxes relating to your property are on record as unpaid.

Renters Can Help Protect You

6. OFFER A LEASE OPTION. If you buy a one-family house with little or no money down, the loan payments plus taxes, insurance, and operating costs will probably add up to considerably more than you can hope to collect in rent. For example, let's say your purchase price is $70,000 but your debt service and other expenses are $700 per month. Similar houses nearby are renting for $500. So you face a negative cash flow of $200. What to do?

Place a newspaper ad, "Rent with Option To Buy." In order to get a renter enthused about this idea you must project what the property will be worth in three years. Maybe you project appreciation of 10 percent a year because rental units are scarce, nearby property is being upgraded, and employment in the area is increasing. Nevertheless you reduce this to 8 percent to be ultraconservative. If the property appreciates only 8 percent a year it will be worth more than $88,000 in three years.

So you offer a lease agreement with an option to buy within three years for $88,000. The tenant is to pay $500 per month rent, plus $200 per month for the option.

"What happens to my $200 per month if I don't exercise the option?" an applicant will probably ask. "Will you refund it? And will you credit it against the purchase price if I do exercise the option?"

This is a point for negotiation. Naturally you'd like to keep the $200 with no strings. The tenant would like to get it back either way.

Maybe you can compromise at a credit equal to $100 per month if the tenant buys, but no refund if he doesn't. Options aren't normally refundable if unused. If they were, option buyers would be risking nothing.

Sellers Can Help Protect You

7. LINK YOUR PAYMENTS TO THE NET OPERATING INCOME. This can be done by what is called a performance clause.

Brokers' financial figures (based, of course, on what the sellers say) tend to be too rosy. The net monthly income may be smaller than they predict. To protect yourself against monthly losses you can try to negotiate a performance clause with the seller. For example, if he's willing to accept a sizable note secured by a trust deed, the agreement might stipulate that payments on the second note won't be more than 95 percent of the net operating income minus the payment on the first mortgage.

8. GET THE SELLER TO CARRY A "REVERSE WRAP." Sometimes you may buy an investment property where the cash flow before debt service is projected to be low the first year, higher the second year, still higher the third, and so on. To stay in the black during the precarious early years, you can ask the seller to carry a wrap-around mortgage with payments equaling the monthly cash flow before debt service. For a complete understanding of wrap-around mortgages see my book *How You Can Become Financially Independent by Investing in Real Estate*.

If your payments are less than the sum needed to pay the interest, the mortgage carried by the seller is called a reverse wrap. This means that his equity is increasing each month, until your cash flow before debt service exceeds the amount of the monthly interest.

9. STRETCH THE AMORTIZATION PERIOD. Maybe a seller refuses to carry your note for more than five years. If you still want to buy his property without accepting a negative cash flow, you can keep down the size of your payments by negotiating an agreement that your payments will be based on a 40-year amortization schedule, even though the balance will be due and payable after five years.

Assuming a 12 percent interest rate, here's a comparison of your payments on a $50,000 loan under the two schedules:

AMORTIZATION PERIOD	MONTHLY PAYMENTS
5 years	$1112.22
40 years	$ 504.25

Of course the lower monthly payments bind you to produce a lump sum, or balloon payment, of about $49,600 when the five years are up. So you'd better be sure you know where that sum will come from.

Lenders Can Help Protect You

10. BORROW TO PAY OFF A DISCOUNTED NOTE. Cash you get by borrowing is, of course, exempt from income tax. You can sometimes wangle a discount on an existing loan by offering an immediate payoff.

One of my students, Jan Stimach, faced negative cash flow when she started making deferred repairs in an office building she'd bought. She went to the junior lender on her property and pointed out that the interest rate was sharply below current rates, so he could make more by reinvesting the money at current rates. "If I pay you in full, will you give me a 15 percent discount on what I owe?" she asked. He figured it out and found that this would be to his advantage. So she borrowed enough to pay off the discounted note and get rid of those painful monthly payments.

11. NEGOTIATE A MORATORIUM ON PAYMENTS. Sometimes you can convince lenders that letting you postpone payments is the best way to keep you solvent. For instance, suppose you can't raise rents in your apartment house until you make various improvements. You'll need cash to pay for the renovation and make up for the lower rents. Rather than see you swept under by negative cash flow, the average lender will agree to let you defer debt payments (or make only part payments) during the months when you're diverting money into improvements that will enhance the property's value.

Quick Ways to Boost Cash Flow

12. RENT TO SINGLES. Rather than renting to a standard family, you can rent to a group of singles who'll pay more total rent than a family. Just place an ad which says in effect "Singles Welcome," and set the rent higher. Singles tend to be troublesome, but you may prefer to face the possibility of trouble rather than the certainty of negative cash flow.

HOW TO FEND OFF FORECLOSURE

13. SPLIT UP A PROPERTY. A fourplex or triplex usually brings higher total rent than one big house of the same size. If your house is too small to convert, you may still add more rent-paying tenants by converting a garage, attic, or basement into a separate apartment for a single. This works best when you can rent the single to someone related to the family, such as a mother-in-law or a grown son or daughter. This is illegal in some communities if the neighborhood is zoned for single-family homes, but I find that authorities seldom enforce the prohibition if the extra residents don't bother neighbors.

If They're Rich, How Come They Owe So Much?

Readers of *Los Angeles* magazine are primarily "upscale" types —young Southern Californians with plenty of income, often heavily invested in real estate. So it's interesting that this magazine's September 1982 issue contained a sixteen-page special section featuring problems of readers who found themselves in "that confusing state of being unable to cope economically on an income that's at least three times the national average." As the section pointed out, Southern California housing foreclosures had tripled in the preceding twelve months, and the Los Angeles bankruptcy court became the busiest in the nation. "One major personal-bankruptcy firm in Southern California reported that 90 percent of its clients are seeking protection from mortgage-related commitments," the magazine noted.

The magazine analyzes problems of one couple whom it calls Ross and Sue Dempster of Chatsworth. They owned five properties and expected realty investments to make them millionaires. "It seemed that buying real estate was never going to be a problem because I was always going to be making more money," said Ross, who in 1979 was earning $45,000 a year as a commissioned lumber salesman. That was the year they paid $60,000 down (of which $25,000 was borrowed on a second trust deed) and moved into a $168,000 house.

Sue was earning $12,600 a year as an escrow officer. The couple counted on her salary to cover a good part of their $1,132 monthly mortgage payments. Sue was laid off. The monthly commissions to Ross kept dwindling along with the housing market. In 1981 the Dempsters' income had dropped to $33,000.

In addition to the payments on the mortgage, they had to pay $350 a month on the second trust deed; $150 monthly on a Palm Springs condo in which they shared ownership; $465 monthly on the mortgage of a house in Yorba Linda which they'd bought as an investment and rented out. (The rent was $365, so the negative cash flow on this investment was $100 a month.)

Their net outgo on just three properties was $1,732 each month or almost $21,000 a year. Most of Ross' income of $33,000 went for living expenses plus other fixed charges such as utilities and car payments. Now they've cut up their credit cards but still owe $2,500 on them.

A financial planner, asked to comment on the Dempsters' position, said: "This is the typical scenario of the two-income couple. The mistake was living up to both incomes. It's all right to have your fringe and excess expenses paid by the second income. But the basics, like mortgages, should be paid from primary income. They got overleveraged. To their credit, they are willing to bite the bullet."

The bullet they bit was the Yorba Linda house, which they sold for $129,000. But after expenses the transaction brought them only $5,500 cash, of which they spent $2,000 to put up a barn on their two-acre property. Ross calculates "it increased the value of our property by $20,000." Well, maybe.

The buyer of the Yorba Linda house now pays $1,250 monthly to the Dempsters. They in turn pay $800 monthly to their original lender, leaving $450 each month as additional income. So their net cash flow is still negative. And in three years the Yorba Linda buyer must make a $40,000 balloon payment. Let's hope he can do it.

Still, the Dempsters aren't worried about losing any property through foreclosure. They figure their net worth is $293,000— and that they can sell the Yorba Linda trust deed for 80 percent of its face value if need be. They'll probably pull through all right if the lumber commissions don't shrink much further.

Now let's come back to Rory Splotz, who is in far worse shape.

Rory has eight negative cash flows. He started in real estate by buying a $60,000 house for 10 percent down. He rented it for

$400 a month. This wasn't a gilt-edged investment because the payments on his first and second mortgages came to $515, leaving him on the wrong side of the ledger by $115 every month.

However, within two years Rory had raised the rent to $625, the market value of his $60,000 house was up to $80,000, and his tax deductions for interest and depreciation left him feeling rich.

"I can buy seven more houses," he said. "What am I waiting for?"

He refinanced his original property for $64,000 and used the $20,000 cash which remained after paying off the old mortgage. He bought seven houses for no money down, paying about $10,000 for closing costs and keeping his other $10,000 in reserve to soak up the negative cash flows he foresaw.

The homes he bought cost an average of $80,000 each. Here's how he set up the purchases:

$64,000 first mortgage from S&L
  8,000 second mortgage from mortgage broker
  <u>8,000</u> third mortgage carried by seller
$80,000 purchase price

On each house, Rory's payments are roughly as follows:

$ 760 monthly on the first mortgage
 100 monthly on the second mortgage
 <u>150</u> monthly for taxes and insurance
$1010 monthly outgo
<u>− 700</u> monthly rental income
$ 310 negative flow

Rory makes no payments on the third mortgages. He persuaded all seven sellers to accept a so-called "straight note," which doesn't require payments of either principal or interest during the term of the note. Instead Rory is to pay the entire principal and all accrued interest at the end of a three-year term.

He thought he could get long-term conventional financing after three years to retire the second and third mortgages. But with such financing nearing extinction, Rory is wondering where he'll get the $91,000 or so in lump sums he'll need when these mortgages expire.

Meanwhile, the negative cash flow on the seven properties adds up to $2,170 per month. That's not all. His first property is also devouring cash again, at the rate of about $200 a month, because he refinanced and got a new mortgage at higher interest. So his net outgo is about $2,370 per month or $28,440 a year. His $10,000 reserve is gone.

Rory earns a fairly good salary, about $30,000 a year. But living expenses use up most of it. Because of the recession, he didn't get a bonus and raise he'd counted on. So now, with all those extra bills for repairs and medical costs, he's deep in debt.

Will he wind up as a distressed seller like those we read about earlier?

Will he lose some or all of his properties through foreclosure sales, tax lien auctions, sheriff's sales or bankruptcy auctions?

Eleventh-Hour Survival Tactics

I think Rory can survive. If you should get into a similar fix, you could survive too, by choosing among the tactics I've suggested to Rory. Here they are:

1. TELL YOUR LENDERS THE FACTS. This should be your first step—before you're late with a single payment. "Creditors are sympathetic," says Stan Benson, president of the nonprofit Consumer Credit Counselors, "unless they send you a friendly reminder and don't hear a thing from you."

Offer partial payments if you can. Explain when you intend to pay more—but don't make any commitment you're not sure you can keep. When lenders conclude you're conning them, they'll turn hostile.

People who took second or third mortgages in order to sell their property to you won't want to foreclose and take it back. Very likely they sold to escape the negative cash flow. Some holders of seconds and thirds have accepted partial payments for years rather than assume the payments on the other loans. If you're trying to resell a property, keep your lenders updated about every prospect. If you're working on other self-rescue plans (such as I'll explain in a moment) tell your creditors these plans in detail, and phone every few days with a progress report.

This works just as well with banks and S&Ls as it does with private lenders. These institutions probably don't want your property. In fact, they're increasingly willing to help delinquent borrowers; only one-fifth of all delinquent mortgages ended in foreclosure in 1981, according to the Mortgage Bankers Association of America.

In some cases a mortgagee will accept payment of interest only until your financial picture gets brighter. In other cases the payments you've missed can be rescheduled. Occasionally a bank refinances an entire loan over a longer period to allow for smaller monthly payments. Some banks will even arrange for another lender to bail you out. All because they don't want your loan classified as "nonperforming"—which usually forces them to set aside money to cover the possible loss.

2. SEND AN INTERMEDIARY if you've already made Rory's blunder of ignoring inquiries from lenders. Have your spokesman take along your up-to-date financial statement as evidence of your newfound frankness.

In fact, even if you haven't yet received the first "friendly reminder," you may be better off using a go-between. Most of us aren't very good at negotiating for ourselves from positions of weakness. Three centuries ago Sir Francis Bacon wrote an essay, *Of Negotiating,* in which he advised, "It is generally better to deal by the mediation of a third person than by a man's self. Use bold men for expostulation, fair-spoken men for persuasion."

When you think about it, the advantages of having someone mediate for you are obvious. He's more relaxed and detached than you are, so he can talk intelligently to you and to your creditors. He can negotiate without committing you, so you needn't put all your cards on the table. He can say things about you that you couldn't.

Your best intermediary is usually a lawyer, because banks may fear that unless they are lenient the lawyer will advise you to file for protection of the bankruptcy laws. (More about that later.) Try to get an attorney who is thoroughly familiar with the laws

188

on foreclosure and bankruptcy. Finding a good one takes more than browsing through the Yellow Pages. The American Bar Association suggests the referral services sponsored by many local bar associations. For a modest fee (typically $15 to $20) a lawyer recommended by a bar association will spend as much as an hour on your problem, perhaps referring you to a specialist. The ABA also suggests trying the clinics run by the nation's 157 accredited law schools. Ask a law school if it offers diagnostic advice. Asking for a referral can come later.

For less expensive negotiators, try nonprofit groups like the Family Service Association of America, which has 300 agencies in the U.S. and Canada, of which more than a hundred will counsel debtors at no charge; and the 172 credit-counseling services affiliated with the National Foundation for Consumer Credit, 1819 H Street N. W., Washington, D.C. 20006.

Now how about your wealthy connections, if you've made some?

Of course they won't go and negotiate for you. But they can put in a friendly word, and often this carries weight. If a top executive of a bank or S&L gets a call from an important customer inquiring about your case, he's bound to be impressed—and he'll probably call his lending officer to ask about you. The lending officer will be impressed too.

Bring In Partners

Wealthy people can also help more directly, if they have confidence in you. They can become your co-investors and co-owners.

3. FORM A LIMITED PARTNERSHIP with a few well-heeled doctors, lawyers, merchants or anyone else who has a large taxable income but little time to find investments. If necessary you can offer them 100 percent of the tax write-offs—all the deductions for interest on your properties, for taxes on your properties, for depreciation of your properties. Stipulate that when you sell these properties you'll share the profits 50–50, or whatever ratio is agreed on. All you ask is that they put in enough cash to cover your negative cash flow and to meet your balloon payments, if these come due before you sell.

This is a sweet deal for them. If we use the figures on the Splotz properties as an example, it would mean that your limited partners would invest $28,440 this year, divided among them. Their shared write-off for depreciation on the eight houses would presumably be at least $34,000—for a direct cash savings of $17,000 if they're in the 50 percent bracket. They could also deduct Rory's negative cash flow, since it goes for interest and operating expenses. Without stopping to itemize all their tax breaks, you can see that Uncle Sam would actually put a bundle of tax-free cash in their pockets for investing in Rory's money-losing properties. And they stand to reap a good capital gain when the properties are sold.

Of course Rory, as the general partner, must still do the work of managing the properties, and potentially can lose more than he's invested, if someone sues him. Meanwhile he's making no money from his investments, and he'll take only half the profits (maybe less) when he sells. But he's certainly better off than he was without partners. Now he won't lose the properties through foreclosure.

4. OFFER AN EQUITY-SHARING DEAL. You can skip ahead right now to Chapter 18 if you wish and read my whole chapter about such deals. The basic idea is that you offer a partner partial ownership of your property—which of course means a share in the profit when the property is sold—in exchange for enough money to cover negative cash flow or to pay off debts.

Similarly, you can offer a tenant a percentage of the profits when the house is resold, if the tenant will put up money now to help you with debts. Or the tenant can buy an option on purchase of the house, as I explained earlier in this chapter.

Attract Some Buyers

5. SELL A PROPERTY FOR ZERO DOWN. Sounds crazy? It's actually very smart—providing you bring in a buyer who'll put up collateral and will also cover your negative cash flow. The collateral makes the sale secure, so the buyer won't walk away and leave you stuck for the mortgage payments.

For example, suppose you decide to sell a house like Rory's original investment, on which you owe $64,000. Since the house is worth $80,000, your equity is $16,000. If you sell for no money down, you give the buyer a $16,000 second mortgage, and he assumes the $64,000 in existing debt (still possible, as I write, with state-chartered savings and loan associations).

To protect yourself, you can insist on a "blanket mortgage" covering not only your house but also some property owned by the buyer. This property could be another building with equity worth as much or more than yours—or it could be other belongings like an automobile, boat, jewelry, stocks, bonds, or anything else of appraisable value.

 A blanket mortgage is a loan secured by several pieces of property. If the borrower defaults, he forfeits them all. Therefore when you sell a property for no money down and take back a blanket mortgage, you can be fairly confident that the buyer won't stop paying you, since it would cost him other assets as well as your house.

The proposition may not sound attractive to a buyer—until he remembers he's acquiring a property for zero down. Assuming that he's in a strong cash position so he can cover the negative cash flow, he'll come out ahead at tax time because of the good depreciation and write-offs. Then too, if he sells the house when the market turns up again, he'll have a healthy capital gain. It's a sound investment. Why should he mind pledging other property as security?

Incidentally, you don't really need a blanket mortgage. You can tie up the buyer's other property just as well by taking a first or second mortgage on it.

6. SACRIFICE ONE PROPERTY TO SAVE OTHERS. As you read my previous suggestion you may have wondered, "Why not sell in the normal way, for cash down?" The answer is that in any market few cash buyers want property that shows a negative cash flow.

Still, if your price is low enough, you will attract bargain-hunters. You'll probably have to dump at a loss (which will give you a tax deduction, though not a very attractive one) but it may be a good move if it brings you enough money to save your other properties. It's a way of buying time, of hanging on until the market cycle turns.

Will the Market Keep Getting Worse?

I'd like to pause here momentarily and talk about economic trends. In times of business recession, of slumping prices and tight money, it's natural to wonder whether times will ever get better. The historical fact is that bad times have always been followed by good times. For a little reassurance, read these comments made by supposedly well-informed writers of newspaper editorials during depressed years in the past:

> "All is darkness and despair. As a nation we are at the bottom of the hill." *Detroit Free Press,* 1837.
>
> "Nothing in this country is safe, solvent or reliable." *Philadelphia Gazette,* 1857.
>
> "Collapse is a grim reality. The days of the Republic are numbered." *New York World,* 1873.
>
> "On every hand there is depression, wreck and ruin. We can't go much further." *New Orleans Picayune,* 1893.
>
> "The old ship of state is sinking." *Wall Street Journal,* 1907.

7. Borrow on your other assets. This is another way of buying time. Whether you use it depends on how badly you want to hold onto your property, and how soon you expect your income to increase.

You may be surprised how much money you can raise. Have you thought of borrowing on your insurance policy? Could you pawn your jewelry, sell your stamp collection, thin down your household belongings through a garage sale? Will your friends, relatives, or boss advance money if they realize you're hard-pressed?

If you own stocks, you can borrow on them by turning them over to a broker as security for a margin account—which means you'll still collect dividends on the stocks, while the broker lends you a percentage of their value and lets the interest charges mount up indefinitely without asking for payments. Bank overdrafts and credit-card cash advances are other temporary sources of quick capital.

If a Second Mortgage Is Due

Maybe you've been covering negative cash flow each month, but a second or third mortgage will soon expire, so that the principal will be due. How can you pay? Most of my previous suggestions are possibilities. Here are others.

8. GET AN EXTENSION BY OFFERING HIGHER INTEREST. If the mortgages are owed to the original sellers of the properties, they may not feel any urgent need for the big lump-sum payment, and will have to find some other place to reinvest it. Maybe you can solve this problem for them. Offer to increase the interest rate you're paying by 3 percent if they'll extend the term of the mortgage for three to five more years. (This suggestion assumes, of course, that you can handle the bigger monthly payments, and the balloon payment is your main problem.)

9. OFFER A ONE-TIME FEE FOR AN EXTENSION. Keep in mind that the lender's alternative is to take back a property he sold because he didn't want it.

10. OFFER A SHARED-APPRECIATION MORTGAGE. You continue paying the same interest, but contract to pay the lender a percentage of the profits when you sell the property.

If All Else Fails

Now let's assume the worst. You've completely run out of money. The banks and/or private lenders are screaming, "Put up the money or, by God, give us the keys!" Foreclosure notices are posted. Still, you can fight for your property.

11. STUDY THE FORECLOSURE LAWS IN YOUR STATE. Retain one of those tough, hard-fighting lawyers I mentioned earlier, if you can scrape up enough cash (or other inducements, like a share in the property if he saves it) to get him interested.

In recent years the legislatures have passed laws to protect unfortunate borrowers from unduly tough lenders. In some states

the court calendars are crowded and judicial foreclosure proceedings may take months. After the actual foreclosure sale, you may still have one or two years (three in Massachusetts) to redeem your property. Spread word that you plan to do so; it can discourage bidders at the foreclosure sale, since title will be clouded.

12. STUDY YOUR FORECLOSURE NOTICE. If there's any factual error, you or your lawyer can force the lender to withdraw the notice and start over. For example, if you made a payment in May but the notice states you didn't, this is grounds for stopping the proceedings. Even if you don't spot any error, you can still demand an itemization of amounts due. If the lender doesn't provide it, or if he has made a mistake in itemizing, this too is cause to stop the foreclosure sale.

13. LOOK FOR GROUNDS FOR AN INJUNCTION. Such as undue pressure or fraud when you bought the property or got the loan. Maybe the seller or lender told you the property could be divided into apartments when it was strictly zoned for one-family homes. By asking a judge for an injunction, you may stall the foreclosure until a court hearing is scheduled.

14. CONSIDER BANKRUPTCY. Consult an attorney well-versed in bankruptcy proceedings. (The American Bar Association, at its 1982 meeting, held a seminar entitled "Bankruptcy in the 80s: Our Biggest Growth Industry.") Even if you can't find or can't afford a good bankruptcy lawyer, you can learn enough to scare your tormentors. Two New York publishers, Herbert Denenberg and Crown, have published books on do-it-yourself bankruptcy. You might also want to look for a book I've read called *Strategies for the Harassed Bill Payer,* by George Belden.

Under various conditions, a lender can't seize property while a borrower is in bankruptcy. The lender can't get either his money or his property, and can't even get enough control of the property to rent it for income. That's why some lenders will actually pay you not to declare yourself bankrupt, and others will extend your mortgages.

15. PROTECT YOUR CREDIT BY GIVING THE PROPERTY BACK. This is a sort of farewell gesture, to be considered only when you've

tried everything else, and are sure to lose your property. Bankruptcy could ruin your credit rating, preventing you from borrowing again. To dodge this stigma and wipe out your debt to the carryback seller, you can give him a "deed in lieu of foreclosure," sometimes called a quit-claim deed.

This is attractive to the seller, especially when he knows it will take at least four months to complete foreclosure. During this time you can legally refuse to make monthly payments on the loan. Four months without loan payments, plus the fees necessary to push through the foreclosure, can cause painful cash-flow problems for the seller, especially if he is a private lender. Therefore he might be glad to pay you a good sum for a quit-claim deed.

For you, it erases your debt and saves your credit, so you can go forth and borrow again. For some reason this solution is especially common in Canada—perhaps because bankruptcy carries a heavy stigma there. According to John J. Tonner, regional senior bankruptcy officer of Canada's federal Consumer and Corporate Affairs Agency, "More people are walking away from their homes than are actually going bankrupt. They just sign quit-claim deeds for $1. They don't fight."

If Foreclosure Comes

16. SEE IF THE FORECLOSURE SALE CAN BE SET ASIDE. Attend the sale with a friend as witness and with a tape machine to record the proceedings. If anything is done wrong, such as refusing to recognize a bidder, the sale can be set aside. Ask your lawyer about various errors to watch for.

17. APPROACH THE BANK'S REAL ESTATE OWNED DEPARTMENT after your redemption rights have expired and see if you can be reinstated as owner. If the bank is saddled with a flock of foreclosed properties it can't sell and can't rent, it just might let you move back in with much lower payments and obligations, since other liens and judgments have been wiped out.

KEY POINTS TO REMEMBER

· Cultivate a network of informants about what's happening in local real estate.

- Structure your investments to avoid negative cash flow, and hold at least one-fifth of your capital to cover it if it occurs.
- Check regularly to see if any taxes on your property are recorded as unpaid.
- When you buy rental property, ask the seller for a performance clause or a "reverse wrap." Or try to have your payments scaled as if the amortization period were much longer than it actually is.
- Sometimes you can reduce a debt by offering to pay the principal in full, then borrowing to get the necessary lump sum.
- Sometimes you can convince a lender that letting you defer payments is the best way to keep you solvent. Have a go-between tell him the facts.
- Consider renting to a group who will pay more total rent than one family.
- Try to recruit wealthy people as your co-owners.
- Consider selling your property for no money down, if the buyer will put up security and also cover your negative cash flow.
- Consider borrowing on other assets or selling the least productive ones.
- If the principal is due and you can't pay, try for an extension by making the terms more attractive to the lender.
- If you get a foreclosure notice, study it closely for factual errors that may invalidate it, and review the circumstances for anything that would entitle you to make a fight in court.
- If you declare bankruptcy you may prevent a lender from taking your property.
- To avoid the stigma of bankruptcy, consider deeding the property back to the lender.
- After foreclosure, a lender may be willing to reinstate you as owner.

_13_

Negotiating with
Tricky Sellers

Jerry Nierenberg faced the heaviest loss of his career as a real estate investor.

A trust company had sold him a half-ruined apartment building, literally at a fire-sale price because a fire had left little but a gutted shell. Since he was the sole bidder, and the company was under pressure from city authorities to remove the walls as a safety hazard, it had grudgingly accepted Nierenberg's all-cash offer. But it knew the land itself was worth almost twice Nierenberg's bid. The building's foundation and salvaged materials were valuable too, but the company couldn't cash in on them because it had no expertise in selling scrap or junk.

The unhappy trust company lawyer drew up a thirty-page contract of sale and thrust it at Nierenberg with a warning, "Don't dot an 'i' or cross a 't.' Sign it this afternoon or the deal is off." Nierenberg, who is a practicing attorney, read it and signed.

That was on Friday. On Saturday, by an amazing coincidence, a second fire swept the ruins and totally demolished them. There would be almost no materials left to salvage.

The title closing, formally transferring ownership to Nierenberg, was scheduled for Monday. He spent Sunday studying the contract and delving into law books. He knew that the streets around this property were closed because of the wreckage and unsanitary conditions, which the city would order corrected immediately. This would cost a lot of money.

He also knew that under certain unlikely circumstances—such as the second fire—a trick clause in the contract entitled the company to force him to take possession immediately instead of several weeks later as originally agreed. Thus he would have to pay taxes, insurance, and management expenses that he hadn't figured on.

Sure enough, on Monday the company made this demand. But there was more. "Remember," the company lawyer triumphantly told Nierenberg, "in this contract you waived the statutory protection." He was referring to a statute that makes the seller pay for a fire loss before the title closing. Because Nierenberg had waived its protection, the loss would be his.

But his Sunday of legal research had prepared him. "You're correct," he said. "We waived our statutory rights. But that means we have only the right that existed under common law before the statute was passed."

Under common law, a fire loss before title closing was usually the buyer's loss—but the courts had made many exceptions. Nierenberg showed the trust company a court decision that applied to this situation: when a building was sold with the land, and the building was damaged by fire, the loss would be the seller's. The seller must deliver exactly what he contracted to sell or there must be an adjustment in price.

"Now, that wonderful contract you drew up made it extremely clear what we were buying," Nierenberg continued. "Not once but four times it stated we were buying a partially damaged building. Now the building is totally destroyed. We are entitled to a partially damaged building or an adjustment in price. We'll take over the property immediately to save you trouble and expense —but we'll adjust the price downward by $100,000."

The attorney blustered about canceling the sale and suing him.

But Nierenberg had considered this possibility. He knew that if the dispute went into litigation, it wouldn't come to trial for at least two years. During that time the trust company would have to pay $50,000 in taxes on the property, and would lose about the same amount in interest in the money Nierenberg stood ready to pay. So even if the company won the case, it would be out of pocket at least $100,000.

In the hectic haggling that ensued, Nierenberg gave back half of his $100,000 reduction in price (as he had planned all along, for the sake of a quick settlement). Thereupon the papers were signed and the closing went through. Nierenberg and his associates became legal owners of land worth more than twice what they paid—plus some piles of rubble that were far less costly to remove than the original shell would have been.

Pitfalls in Purchase Agreements

In the first part of the book I discussed ways to buy real estate at such low prices that your profit is built into the transaction. One of the principles I've mentioned repeatedly is to know just what you're buying. But even if you've looked closely at property, and even if the price is far below market, plenty can go awry unless a buyer is alert.

Whether the seller is an owner in financial trouble, or an institution, a broker, or someone selling at auction, there are ways to bamboozle a buyer. In this chapter I'll show you what to look out for.

Jerry Nierenberg's narrow escape from disaster in the burned-building purchase shows the importance of understanding whatever documents you sign in a real estate transaction. His legal knowledge protected him. Before you sign any purchase agreement or contract of sale or letter of intent or whatever it's called, ask your lawyer to study it—unless you yourself are an attorney.

Virtually the only exception might be a standard printed form sold at stationery stores. Don't put your faith in forms printed by auction firms, lending institutions, or other business organizations. Their "standard contract" could be full of dynamite.

For example, one large S&L's printed mortgage agreement contains fine print stipulating that if a monthly payment is late—or early!—by so much as one day, the entire balance becomes due immediately. I've known the S&L to foreclose and seize a property whose mortgage fell afoul of this clause.

No, the only printed form you can feel fairly safe in signing (providing you've read and understood every word) is one that you can quickly identify by a couple of lines either at an upper corner or at the bottom. They will say something like "Julius Blumberg, Inc., Law Blank Publishers—80 Exchange Place, New York City." That is, you should look for an imprint signifying that the contract was printed by some company specializing in blank legal forms.

If there's a typewritten purchase agreement, or if a printed form is crammed with typed inserts, you can bet that the seller's lawyer was the author of the typewritten material. He's under no obligation to tell you what it means or implies. Very likely he tucked in some cute contingency clauses (like the waiver of statutory protection that almost trapped Nierenberg) which you may or may not feel you can live with. Even if you're willing to accept them, be sure to place a time limit on the contingency. Your attorney can help you with the wording. If you would like to have a set of the forms I use, send $5 to cover the cost of handling to The Lowry Group, 3390 Duesenberg Drive, Westlake Village, CA 91362.

Can You Prove What They Said?

You and the seller may agree orally on certain points not covered in the document. But in real estate any oral agreement "isn't worth the paper it's printed on," as Sam Goldwyn supposedly said. Get it in writing. Otherwise the seller may say later, "Naw, you misunderstood."

Of course you can sue if he agreed in front of witnesses that the dishwasher in his apartment building or the furniture in the lobby were included in the selling price, only to remove them before you arrived. But courts are slow and lawsuits are expensive. You may save yourself money and irritation if you make sure the contract itemizes all furnishings, appliances, fixtures, shrubs and other property included in the buy.

Even in good faith a seller can be wrong about what he tells you. For example, you may ask, "What happens if this building gets badly damaged after you vacate but before I take possession?" and he may answer, "No problem. My homeowner's insurance would pay for it." But most homeowner policies lapse if there is any change in title to the property. And some courts have held that a new buyer becomes owner the minute the purchase agreement is signed. Probably you can protect yourself by having the seller's insurance policies amended to protect both parties. One phone call to the insurance company may take care of this.

A better protection would be to make sure the agreement says the premises will be turned over "in the same condition as they are now, reasonable wear and tear excepted." Then if there's a fire or flood or vandalism or other unpleasantness, you won't be the loser.

Your lawyer will want to add certain clauses to the contract if they're not in it. Everything that the seller has promised to do to remedy defects should be written into the contract. A sentence should state, "The plumbing, electrical work, and heating are in working order." Don't be embarrassed about the contract getting too long. Paper is cheap.

Does this sound like too much fuss, especially if you and the seller get along like great pals? Well, I should warn you that when somebody wants to trick you, he usually sweet-talks you. He praises your brains and your business sense. He encourages you to tell him all about your kids, and murmurs admiringly as you brag.

If somebody tells you what a good deal he's giving you, and slaps you on the back saying, "I'm only doing it because we can trust each other," look out. His hand on your back may be feeling for a place to stab you.

Let me tell you what happened once when a buyer and seller agreed they didn't need a lawyer at closing. Together they drew up a deed by filling in the blanks on a standard form. It was a simple, straightforward transaction. The buyer paid the money, took the deed, and locked it in his safe as the seller warned him to be sure to do. This buyer didn't know that unless a deed is recorded with the County Clerk, there's no proof of ownership. So the "gentleman's agreement" became quite ungentle. The seller turned around and sold the house again.

The law says that the first deed filed owns the house. The second buyer found a clear title when his attorney filed his deed. What could the first buyer do with his deed afterward? I guess he might use it as proof of fraud, if he could only find the seller and sue him.

I've known shady brokers who sold two or three different customers the same property. They figured they could stall lawsuits for years, then skip town. Never buy a property without checking title first. And when you receive a deed, go straight to the County Clerk and get it recorded.

Beware of Binders

You come across an apartment building whose absentee owner has let it go to seed. He owes money all over town. You seek him out, and after hard bargaining he agrees to sell for a price that assures you a handsome profit on resale.

Over a round of celebratory drinks, the owner asks you for a "binder" to seal the deal. This is a piece of paper saying that the seller agrees to sell, and the buyer agrees to buy, at the agreed-on price. It also states the buyer is putting up a deposit he'll lose if he doesn't go through with the deal. This deposit money is sometimes called "binder money" or "earnest money" or "good faith money."

Don't put a binder on the building. Binders don't bind. They're just good-faith gestures, favored by laymen but not by lawyers. The seller can usually back out if he wants to, binder or no binder. And you'll have trouble getting your deposit back. He may just say, "See you in court."

On the other hand, the seller or his agent may bind *you* inflexibly if they word the binder shrewdly. Something like the following would be enforceable: "This first day of April, 1982, Fred Ripp, the seller, agrees to sell, and Joseph Bungle, the buyer, agrees to buy, the house and lot at No. 711 Shady Lane, for $92,500, and herewith tenders $1,000 as evidence of his good faith. The aforesaid sum of $1,000 may be retained by the seller if the buyer does not make the purchase. (Signed) Fred Ripp, Joseph Bungle."

Those scribbled lines could make you the defendant in a lawsuit for big money. Suppose you find you can't obtain financing for the purchase? Suppose a crowd of creditors hold liens against the property? Suppose an earthquake shakes it down tomorrow? You'd still be committed to pay the stipulated purchase price, even though you haven't signed an actual contract of sale. A binder can be a form of contract, with terms that must be met just as if it were the most formal of documents.

So what do you do when a seller says, "You're going to put up a binder, aren't you?"

You can say, "If you mean a deposit, sure. I'll put it in escrow as soon as you're ready. And I'll have my lawyer draft a contract of sale tomorrow."

At this point he may say, "I need the deposit money right now."

This is a danger signal. Alarms should go off in your head. Normally a deposit is left with either the buyer's or seller's lawyer, or put in escrow.

The minute you give the seller any significant sum, you're losing part of your control over the situation. With your money in his pocket, he may start demanding changes in the terms. Or he may disappear.

Not only in real estate deals, but also in any transaction, you'd better think hard before you write a sizable check not counterbalanced by some enforceable commitment from the other party. Advance payment is the hook in nearly every get-rich-quick scheme, investment swindle, confidence game, ransom extortion, and home-repair rip-off ever invented.

You probably are safe enough in placing a deposit with an established financial institution or auction firm. But if you feel the smallest doubt about the integrity of someone who is selling you real estate, check with your attorney before handing over more than a nominal deposit directly to him.

Keep an Exit Open

And of course you must make the seller sign a detailed receipt, with a proviso permitting you to withdraw from the deal. Get it worded something like this:

"This deposit is returnable immediately if inspection, investigation, contract terms, survey, or title search reveal facts unacceptable to the buyer or his attorney." For his part, the seller may want to note on the receipt that it is "subject to approval by my attorney," or "subject to execution of sales contract." Fair enough.

Even in the simple act of writing your check, be careful. The seller might want you to put a notation on it like "part payment for the property at 711 Shady Lane," which—in the opinion of some eccentric judges—could constitute a written commitment to buy. Make sure your check carries no notations of what it is for, except an identification of the property and a statement that a contract of sale is to be drawn later.

In any case, argue with a seller who wants your deposit paid to him. Explain the risk this involves for you. Maybe you can talk him out of it. Maybe not, if he urgently needs your money (perhaps as a deposit on a house he hopes to buy). In that case, rather than let a good deal fall through, you may want to offer to pay the deposit in return for some concession on his part, such as better terms or a lower price. As long as your money is dangling before him, you're in the driver's seat.

Incidentally, if you happen to discover that you've been cheated shortly after giving the seller a check, you may be able to stop payment even if it's a certified check. Most people don't know this—so your fraudulent seller may not hurry to cash your certified check.

A certified check just means that there is, and will continue to be, enough money in the account of the issuer to make good the check. It isn't quite like cash or a bank cashier's check.

If you need to stop payment, hand-deliver a letter to the bank instructing them to do so. This works most of the time. However, a bank may refuse to honor your stop-payment order if it chooses. Or it may demand that you post a bond equal to double the amount of the check, to protect itself in case the payee sues. Posting the bond is worthwhile if you can spare the money— because by blocking the crooked seller from getting his/her money, you're in a strategic spot to force a settlement.

The Delaying Game

Sometimes, after lengthy negotiations and what you think is a full agreement, a seller may suddenly balk. With pen poised to sign, he may say, "I don't want to rush into this. Give me a few days to think it over."

Delay is a classic tactic in negotiations. Remember when the

United States was trying to negotiate peace terms with the North Vietnamese? They quibbled about the shape of the bargaining table, raised other bizarre objections, stalled week after week. Meanwhile the bargaining position of the United States, which was under mounting pressure from its citizens to end the war, steadily weakened. Twenty years earlier, the Koreans played the same game against us in armistice negotiations at Panmunjom.

Sellers of real estate sometimes secretly prefer not to close a deal, for various reasons such as:

They want time to hunt for other prospective buyers.

They want to use your offer to extract better terms from someone else.

They think the passing of time will weaken your negotiating position.

They hope their seeming reluctance will make you willing to pay more. Many buyers feel an emotional need to end the tension of negotiation as soon as possible.

They hope delay will pressure the broker to take a smaller commission.

One shrewd and greedy owner of a California beachfront home agreed to sell it to a New Yorker who wanted to occupy it during the summer. Closing the contract was scheduled to take place just before the summer season. But at the agreed date, the seller suddenly refused to convey title. He gave the excuse of inability to find a decent place to move into. "I'll have to stay in a hotel, which will cost me a ton of money," he told the New Yorker. "Give me a few more months—unless you can pay me an extra $5,000 for hotel expenses."

The New Yorker badly wanted to spend the summer at the beach. He realized that if he took the seller to court, months or years might pass before he got justice. He reluctantly paid the seller an extra $2,500 to do what he had already promised to do —move out immediately.

This seller had played the delaying game boldly because he had discovered how desperately the buyer wanted to take possession immediately. The man from New York had made two damaging mistakes early in the negotiations. He let the seller know that time was important to him, and he let the seller schedule transfer of title for a date so late that the buyer would be running out of time.

How to Discourage Stalling

Bring a written offer with you—at least in blank form—to the very first meeting with a prospective seller. Any friendly real estate office can probably give you some kind of a blank purchase agreement. Or you can buy them at most business stationery stores. If you're alone in the hinterlands, order a pad of them from Professional Publishing Corporation, 122 Paul Drive, San Rafael, CA 94903. Ask for their Form 101, Residential Purchase Agreement and Deposit Receipt. I believe it's legal in every state, and it's easy to use.

Don't try to buy property by phone, because the phone doesn't transmit signatures. Making a telephone offer merely gives the seller a chance to fish for more without committing himself. Even if he says, "Okay, you just bought yourself a house," he's still free to stall later.

Some tricky sellers try to victimize a buyer even after they've signed all the papers. They simply delay moving out of the building they've sold. This may save them from paying rent elsewhere, or give them time for completing purchase of something else. Or, as in the case I mentioned of the greedy beachfront-property seller, they just want to squeeze a buyer who needs the property right away.

Protect yourself by legal precautions. The contract should specify a rent the seller will pay you for each day he stays past the promised date of vacating. A good attorney will insist that an adequate sum be put in escrow to cover this.

After signing the contract, a seller may still stall by putting off the date for final transfer of ownership. The law in most states allows postponement unless your contract says "time is of the essence." So you may want to put these magic words into your purchase agreement, specifying the exact date and hour and place of the scheduled title closing.

However, this clause can be a boomerang, if for any reason you can't hand over a check for the stipulated amount on the specified closing date. Including "time is of the essence" entitles the seller to insert some stipulation that you must pay a penalty for each day you delay. Or, if he finds a more generous buyer after signing with you, he may use your delay to nullify the whole contract. So you'd better make very sure of your financing before you set an inflexible date for formal completion of the transaction.

The Third-Party Stall

Sometimes you'll be negotiating with a married couple who jointly own property. Don't discuss terms until both husband and wife (or all the owners, whoever they are) can be present. Otherwise one owner can stall indefinitely by saying he/she can't decide alone.

Of course there may be times when you *can't* get everyone together, such as when you're dealing with a group of heirs to an estate. In that case you can insist that somebody be empowered to negotiate for the whole group.

Francis Greenburger, a notably successful real estate investor, tells a story on himself that illustrates this point. Negotiating with an owner named Harvey, he got him close to signing. "I think your offer is realistic," Harvey said, "but my partner Burt is from another era, and he may be reluctant. He's out of town."

"I can't offer any more," Greenburger said. "If he won't accept this, let's forget it." He waited ten days. Finally Harvey phoned to say that Burt was still away but he, Harvey, was prepared to do the deal at $185,000 and explain it to Burt when he returned.

One hundred eighty-five thousand dollars was $5,000 more than Greenburger had offered. But he had grown impatient, and he gave in. However, when the contract of sale came through, he noticed that only Harvey's name appeared. So he called Harvey's lawyer to ask about Burt.

The attorney, a veteran of many realty transactions, chuckled. "There isn't any Burt," he admitted. "Burt only exists in Harvey's mind." The phantom had pressured Greenburger into paying an extra $5,000.

Even before you start negotiations, you can discourage stalling by making it clear that you don't much care whether you get the property, because there are other properties you may buy instead. You want the sellers to realize that they need you more than you need them.

Once into negotiations, push for an immediate decision. After hours of bargaining, if somebody stands up and says, "We'll think it over," they'll be harder to deal with next day.

Try to forestall such a move by suggesting action the moment you think they're near the point of selling. You can say something like, "I'll phone the bank and ask them to set up the escrow," or you can simply sign the purchase agreement and hand it over, saying "I've marked the place where you sign."

If they insist on thinking it over anyhow, hand them your written offer and announce that it must be accepted within forty-eight hours (or maybe that very day, depending on the situation) or it will be permanently withdrawn. Remind them that you're looking at other properties. I like to specify the precise time my offer expires, such as ". . . at 4:30 P.M. on December 19, 1982."

If the deadline passes, cancel the offer and let them call you. Since you know they're under pressure to sell, you can hang tough. Get up and walk out of any face-to-face argument. If this kills the sale, plenty of other properties are available at giveaway prices nowadays.

On the other hand, if the prospective seller does call back, you may end up buying this property for even less than you previously offered. You might invoke a phantom of your own if you feel like it, mentioning an associate who is "angry about the delay."

A moment ago I mentioned the special difficulty of dealing with a group of owners. This always arises when you make an offer to the REO (Real Estate Owned) executive of a bank or S&L. His institution doesn't want the property, but his job is to dump it for the best price possible. So one of his stalling tactics is to say that he'll have to see whether "the committee" or "the president" will let him sell for the price you offer. He'll usually come back and report they want more. "Take it or leave it; no use arguing with me because I don't have the final say" is his attitude. (Brokers often use the same runaround. They carry your offer to the owners and return with a higher demand.)

You needn't sit still for this. Tell the spokesman your offer is final, and set a deadline just as you do in negotiating with an individual. But in this situation you can sometimes go a step further.

Underlings in financial institutions often stall because of personal timidity or indecision. If you have a connection higher up in the organization, don't hesitate to break off negotiations and take your offer directly to the superior. Likewise if you're dealing with a dilatory real estate agent, you can sometimes go over his head to a top executive of the realty firm. The higher you go in any organization, the better the treatment you'll probably receive. The average administrator is more flexible about rules than his subordinates.

Occasionally you can get rid of a phantom third party merely by gentle ridicule. A seller doesn't like to look ridiculous.

> Three doctors from a Midwest city used this ploy every time I represented them in the purchase or sale of a property, and I was supposedly their good friend.
>
> They had an attorney who would always be the one to go through since he "always had their consent," yet whenever I obtained an agreement from him on the phone, one of the doctors would always come back to me in a few days saying, "Tom didn't check with me. I will only sell for . . . ," and he would try to push the price up.
>
> It's a great cat-and-mouse game and can only be won by passing the middle man and dealing directly with the real decision maker, even twitting him, if need be, for using the middle man as a gambit.

Look Out for Lowballing

"Lowballing" is a term well known among car dealers and industrial salesmen. It means offering to sell at a deceptively low price. Once the customer accepts this price and feels mentally committed to the transaction—maybe even signs something—the game begins.

Having eliminated other bidders and landed a contract that establishes him as sole supplier, a contractor may delay deliveries and keep pleading specification changes or technical troubles to justify cost overruns. This is one reason the U.S. Government's costs are usually much larger than budgeted; having ordered a large supply of a specific aircraft or missile or gadget, it can't turn elsewhere when the supplier says he must shut down his production line unless he gets a higher price.

Automobile salesmen have a hundred excuses for changing the price after shaking hands on a deal. These include veto by higher authority, overlooked extras, mistakes in the sales contract, misunderstandings, errors in transcribing, legal delays and missing-man games.

In real estate, tricky sellers lowball in various ways. An example: simply demand more at the very last minute, gambling that the buyer wants the property so much—or has invested so much time in negotiating—that he won't balk at a fractional increase.

Greenburger's book *How to Ask For More and Get it* (Doubleday) tells of a seller who tried this but went too far:

> I said I could only begin serious negotiations if the seller agreed at the outset that the price we were talking about was $10,000 less than he had advertised. He . . . invited me to begin negotiations. Once everything else was out of the way and I had gotten major concessions from him (move-in date, preclosing repairs, agreement to install a new well pump, appliances to be included in the purchase price) he attempted to restore the original asking price. I laughed and left.

That is a good way to counter a crude attempt to repudiate an understanding. Laugh and walk out. It worked in the case Greenburger described; the seller phoned later to accept the original deal. It will often work for you too.

Lowballers often probe to find out what your real top price is by starting low, then asking more, mentioning that of course the price doesn't include the refrigerators or the carpeting or what have you. This maneuver is so old that it was the basis of a comedy skit I saw as a boy. A customer asks an optometrist the price of a pair of glasses. The optometrist says, "$10." The customer looks pleased, so he adds, "For the frames." The customer still doesn't protest, so he follows with "The lenses are $5." As the customer reaches for his wallet, he adds "—each."

My advice in dealing with anyone this tricky is to drop him at the first sign of bad faith. You'd have trouble with him even after the closing; you'd run into breaches of contract, legal delays, absenteeism, insults, endless confusion, falsified records, nonpayment of court judgments. Recently, President Reagan thought he had sold his California home only to find that the price had been altered in the purchase agreement after it was signed!

Telephone Tactics

As I said earlier, it's futile to try to make a deal by phone. But what if the seller suddenly phones—from far away, perhaps—to demand a change in a deal already made?

Probably he isn't calling on the spur of the moment. Very likely he weighed the alternatives—letter, telegram, use of an intermediary, face-to-face confrontation, or doing nothing—and chose to telephone as his best chance to get what he wants from you.

If so, he has prepared carefully. He's sitting in a quiet place, safe from distraction. In front of him are his notes and a blank pad for further notes. In his hand is a sharp pencil. At his side is a computer. Attached to the telephone, possibly, is a tape recorder to take down every word you say. No doubt he has figured out your probable objections and decided what to say in rebuttal. In short, he's all set. He's laying for you.

And how about you? You're caught by surprise. Maybe you're at a cluttered desk, or in the middle of a meal. Your records of the agreement aren't at hand. In such a fix, how can you make the conversation work for you rather than against you? Here are suggestions.

1. LISTEN CAREFULLY AND SAY LITTLE. Let the other person do most of the talking. Take full notes. If he asks questions, answer with your own questions like "Why do you ask that?" or "What do you mean?" or "Why should I?"

Try just saying nothing. Your prolonged silence—especially during a long-distance call—may push the other party into talking compulsively, from nervousness, or from the mounting phone charges. Often he'll say more than he intended—and maybe reveal unsuspected weaknesses in his own position. Since he wants to change the agreement, you can watch for ways to change it to your own advantage.

2. DON'T SAY YES OR NO. Don't argue. As soon as you fully understand his position, make some excuse for breaking off the

conversation. You can say the equivalent of "I'm due some-where else right now. I have to go. What time would it be con-venient for me to call back?"

3. GIVE YOURSELF TIME to think over the position—perhaps talk it over with your attorney and/or some other expert. When you decide exactly what your response should be, you can either write a letter or have your adviser write a letter or have your adviser make a call-back to continue probing by phone. Very rarely should you yourself talk further with the seller by phone.

4. DON'T TAKE FURTHER CALLS from the seller. Impatiently awaiting word from you, he may phone again before you've de-cided what you're going to do. At that point you have several choices. You can say (a) "Please put your proposition in writing and send it to me so I'll be sure I understand it"; or (b) "You caught me at a bad time. There's someone with me. And I'll need to get my data together before we talk further"; or (c) if the other party is really insistent and keeps bothering you, just break off. Of course I'd never recommend being so rude as to hang up on another person, but if you break the connection while you your-self are in mid-sentence, he'll think you got disconnected by mistake. When he calls back, let him get a busy signal, by care-fully leaving your phone off the hook, and he'll figure the line is out of order. From then on you can resort to the expedient of having someone else answer your phone until you've decided how to deal with this pest.

5. DON'T LET THE OTHER SIDE DRAFT ANY CHANGES you're will-ing to make in the original agreement. You or your attorney should write them. Perhaps the seller has sent a draft, at your request or on his own. Use it only as a starting point. Type up a new memo of understanding, or sales contract, or whatever you need. Send two copies, both with your signature, to the seller. He signs one copy and sends it back to you, keeping the other for his files.

Whatever document you send will probably start out, "Pur-suant to our telephone conversation on such-and-such a date . . ." or "As per our discussion on the telephone, we have agreed that . . ."

In any complicated real estate transaction, you're better off doing the writing (with your attorney's help) than letting the other person (or his attorney) do it. The advantages to you are important. You're in control, determining when an agreement will be drafted, the form it will take, and when it will take effect. Nothing should happen until you make it happen.

And of course you don't have to comb a document for trick phrases when you and your lawyer are the authors.

The Seller Who Dangles a Dirty Profit

Suppose you can't quite get together with a seller and his broker. Later he calls you suggesting you come to see him privately, when his broker won't be present. What then?

I've known instances when a broker rips off a seller. More often the seller tries to do the ripping. A temptation always exists for buyer and seller to go behind the broker and divide his commission between them—especially when the commission would amount to many thousands of dollars, all for a "mere" introduction.

Maybe you as buyer can get a better price this way. But it's unfair to the broker. He'll never work with you again. And he might decide to sue for his commission, if it's big enough to justify the trouble. While states vary as to exactly when a broker is entitled to a commission, they generally agree that when a broker procures a buyer willing and able to buy at or near the seller's asking price, then the broker should get paid. This may be true even if the deal later breaks down, especially if the seller is at fault. And some courts have held a buyer, too, is liable to brokerage commissions when he conspired to cut out the broker.

If a seller is devious enough to cheat his broker, he may well try to cheat you too. My advice is to forget about his property. You'll sleep better.

Highballing Could Bilk You

Another seller's trick is to start by asking a deceptively high price. Sometimes the price is not only far above what he's willing to take, but far above market value. He figures that when he brings it down near market value, pleading illness or some other emergency to try to force a quick decision, you'll think it must be a bargain.

You must determine how much you're willing to pay by how much return you'll get on your investment. Once you determine that, make an offer about one-fifth less than your top price. The asking price shouldn't figure in your analysis at all. It becomes a factor only when you try to find out the seller's true bottom price and offer no more than that.

One way to get a sense of this is to know what he paid for the property and when. A real estate firm may be able to tell you. If not, you can find out by consulting the local Hall of Records or Registry of Deeds. Either the purchase price will be listed, or the tax stamps on the recorded deed will enable you to compute the price. But bear in mind that a really crafty seller may have used an extra bunch of tax stamps, with an eye to fooling buyers about the actual price.

Remember too that if the seller bought the property "subject to mortgage(s)," the result of your tax-stamp calculations will give you only the previous owner's equity in the property.

If your figuring indicates that the owner bought this property for much less than he says he did, be especially skeptical of all his other claims.

Sellers of income property may claim that it is producing more revenue than it really is. For example, you may be shown the rent roll of a commercial building, indicating that nine tenants pay $6–$8 per square foot and three pay $12. You'd better find out who the high-paying tenants are. One might be the building owner, and the others might be in cahoots with the seller.

A seller who falsifies current and future income can cost you tens of thousands of dollars, because you take gross revenue into account in figuring your offering price. Here's how it might work out. Suppose the seller shows that ten tenants each pay $400 a month for a total of $48,000 a year. Then it sounds like a bargain at six times the gross, or $288,000. But what if the owner had prepared to sell the building by raising the rents from $350 to $400? Then six times the true gross would be $252,000—and you might pay $36,000 too much. (Of course this is a simplified example. You'd also look at other factors, if you're smart, in deciding how much to offer.)

This kind of highballing might make it impossible for you to raise the rents any further—especially if they were close to market before the increase. This deceitful owner we're talking about may have persuaded the tenants to go along with the increase by offering them a free month's rent or a delay in the effective date of the raise. (Notice that one month's moratorium in rent payments means the actual increase in rents was only $17, not $50. If you try to jump rents above that, tenants may move.)

Study the Seller

If you're negotiating with an individual owner, find out as much as you can about this situation. Is he having trouble selling the property? How long has it been on the market without moving? Is he under pressure to unload it quickly? Has the asking price been dropped? What are comparable properties selling for?

By investigating a seller's previous transactions, you can get an idea of what sort of person you're negotiating with. You may find out how much—or little—profit he was satisfied to take, and how long he held out for it, and whether he tried lowballing or highballing or other games.

It's also useful to know the recent history of the property you're considering. Roy Cohn, an attorney famed for toughness in negotiations, tells of a case in which a man named Ulich wanted a vacant lot on a lakefront. He hired a broker to find such a lot for him. The broker found it—but secretly sold it to a friend, then had his friend sell it to Ulich at a fat profit. When Ulich (or Cohn) discovered this, he sued the broker. A court made the broker and friend disgorge their profits and reimburse Ulich.

Many homeowners use crude methods to set their asking price. They may put it at $99,000 because a friend a mile away got $99,000 and his home wasn't as nice as theirs. The truth may be that the friend started by asking $99,000 but finally settled for $90,450. When friends ask him what the house sold for, he says, "I got what I wanted." So the rumor spreads that he got $99,000.

Another crude way of arriving at a price is to rely on what real estate people say the house is worth. Realtors hungry for listings will always talk high price, so as not to offend the owner and risk losing the listing.

In preparing to bargain with a stubborn seller, it's well to arm yourself with a detailed list of what similar properties sold for, preferably nearby. If he's merely stubborn rather than tricky, your data can be more persuasive than anything else you might say. It's a way of teaching him the property's current market value without criticizing him or his property. Your list should cover at least three comparable sales.

To compile such a list you might start with real estate agents. By now you've probably cultivated a few friends in the business, and they can draw on their files, or on multiple listing sources, for the information you need.

If they can't produce, drive around and look for "Sold" signs. If you see a resident walking the dog or tinkering with the car, ask if he remembers any houses being sold in the last six months.

Another way of getting useful information is to chat with owners, managers, or neighbors of property near the building you're considering. You probably won't have to pump them. Just introduce yourself and explain that you're negotiating to buy a nearby property. Point it out to them. Gossiping comes naturally. They may tell you things about the property and its problems that will help you avoid a mistake. Such information might be very hard to extract from the owner or from other sources.

This brings us to the whole broad subject of defects that you can't detect by quick inspection. The next chapter takes up these hidden problems.

KEY POINTS TO REMEMBER

· Get a good lawyer and have him help you understand any documents you sign in a real estate transaction.
· Never rely on oral agreements. Get them in writing.
· Before you pay any sizable deposit or sign any paper drafted by a seller, insist on some enforceable commitment from him. You're in the driver's seat until he has your money.
· You can stop payment on a certified check.
· Take precautions to discourage sellers from last-minute changes or stalling. Make them realize they need you more than you need them. If they try to disavow an understanding, laugh and walk out.

- Don't negotiate with a group of sellers unless they are all present or have empowered someone to negotiate for them.
- If someone phones you in an attempt to change an understanding or a contract, say as little as possible. Answer questions with questions. Then make an excuse to break off, and don't take follow-up calls. Consult your attorney about any proposed changes.
- If a seller is trying to cheat his broker, drop him. He'll try to cheat you too.
- Investigate how much a seller paid for his property and when. If he says he paid much more, look out.
- Sellers of income property may show figures indicating deceptively high income. Investigate carefully.
- Learn as much as you can about a seller and his situation. Find out the sale prices of comparable properties.

_14_

What Hasn't the Seller Told You?

Real estate people have been going through a period of slow sales. Many homes built within the last year or two have languished on the market, and resale activity in older properties has been halved. Real estate agents have left the business in droves (16,000 of them quit in California alone during one recent twelve-month period). Developers and subdividers are selling for whatever they can get, merely to cut their losses. Tens of thousands of construction workers have lost their jobs. And the savings and loan industry, which usually has supplied ready credit to home buyers, has lately been begging the government for financial help.

Obviously these conditions are excellent for buyers with ready cash. When property is hard to sell, prices drop. But a lower price doesn't always betoken good value. Owners and brokers who are desperate may be tempted to conceal whatever facts about a property which would make it less desirable.

Caveat Emptor Isn't Quite Dead

For many centuries, dating back to the Roman Empire, the Latin words *caveat emptor* ("let the buyer beware") were intoned reverently by courts and legislatures to deny a buyer legal remedies if he bought faulty merchandise. Buyers were supposed to take whatever they purchased "as is." If they got cheated, that was a risk they took; they should have examined their purchase more carefully beforehand. Sellers and agents had no duty to disclose facts, although they might be liable for outright lies.

But in recent years the wrath of consumers forced the states, Congress and the courts to realize that even if we are careful, we can't protect ourselves against hidden defects. It took a while for this realization to extend into the buying and selling of real estate. Arkansas Supreme Court Justice George Smith observed ruefully in 1970: "One who bought something as simple as a kitchen mop was entitled to get his money back if the article was not of merchantable quality. But the purchaser of a home ordinarily had no remedy even if the foundation proved so defective that the structure collapsed."

Finally, in 1975 the Wyoming Supreme Court led the way in a revolution against *caveat emptor* in real estate. It handed down a decision that said: "The ordinary home buyer is not in a position, by skill or training, to discover defects lurking in the plumbing, the electrical wiring, the structure itself, all of which is usually not open for inspection. . . . It ought to be an implicit understanding of the parties, when an agreed price is paid, that the house is reasonably fit for habitation."

Dozens of other states followed Wyoming in dumping *caveat emptor* in favor of a new legal doctrine known as an "implied warranty." The doctrine assumes that a seller makes certain warranties similar to those that come with consumer goods. The warranty doesn't come printed on a card attached to your house. It doesn't have to. The general rule now is that a seller and his agent are expected to disclose defects known to them if a buyer can't see these for himself.

When Is a Warranty Implied?

If you buy a new home that turns out to be a lemon, the builder may still try to brush you off with the old *caveat emptor* dodge. "Let the buyer beware" was the law for so long that many real estate people probably think it still is. So a builder may hand you the sales contract or deed on your house and drawl, "Show me this warranty you mentioned. I don't see it written down anywhere."

You can reply with calm confidence, "You're right, it's not written. It doesn't have to be. That's why it's called an *implied* warranty. State laws now make you responsible for what you sell, whether you write any warranty or not."

By 1980 this principle was fairly well established. The protection came none too soon, because shoddy building is more common lately. "Inspectors say they are regularly seeing glaring defects in brand-new homes," the *Wall Street Journal* reported in 1978. "A few years ago the Department of Housing and Urban Development inspected a test sample of new homes and found 24 percent defective."

If you find things wrong in or around a new house you've bought, notify the builder immediately. Phone him, then confirm your call in a letter sent via certified mail, return receipt requested. If you delay needlessly, you'll weaken your chances of suing successfully—and the builder, realizing this, may be less willing to settle out of court.

It's a breach of implied warranty if a builder picks a bad site— over an underground spring, for example, or on ground that slides or crumbles—or if he doesn't provide enough drainage. This usually holds true even if a resident discovers the fault a year or more after buying. In one Indiana case a builder was held liable for breach of warranty when the basement walls cracked three years after the house had been built.

In these days, when hundreds of tract houses are being unloaded at giveaway prices, the implied warranty gives you a little protection, but not so much that you can depend on it blindly. You can't overlook a nonworking furnace or a big hole in the roof, then claim you were cheated. You're expected to be aware of observable defects if the seller doesn't hinder you from investigating and inspecting.

Furthermore, you'd better know something about the builder. An implied warranty may not help you if he declares bankruptcy or disappears. Look into his reputation. Talk to people who have lived in his houses for several years.

When You Buy a Used House

You needn't necessarily let a builder off the hook just because you're not the first buyer of the property. Tricky developers sometimes sell to a dummy purchaser who then resells. They think the dummy insulates them from responsibility to the second buyer, but courts often see through this. Builders can be held liable to subsequent purchasers "for a reasonable time."

How much time is reasonable? There's no fixed rule. The decision in a case might depend on what the judge ate for breakfast. The time limit varies according to the type of defect; a few states have stretched it to ten years in some cases.

However, as a general rule of thumb, you'd better figure that two years is about the longest you can hold a builder responsible for slipshod work or inferior materials. After that, your target will usually be the owner who sells to you, or his agent.

When a seller warns you, "This property comes 'as is,' " look out! Protect yourself by taking two steps.

(1) Ask the seller for a full, written disclosure of the condition of the house. If he claims he can't be expected to know everything about its condition, say goodby and move on to the next prospective buy on your list.

If he does draw up the disclosure and you decide to buy, then find later that he left a major defect off the list, you'll have strong grounds for a lawsuit. He'll probably give you a rebate rather than go to the expense of a court fight.

(2) Make your sales agreement dependent on receiving satisfactory reports from qualified tradesmen. This is especially important when you buy a questionable property.

For example, maybe the seller admits in writing that the roof is old and "might leak." Now you know the risk you're taking. So you make the contract of sale subject to assurance from a certified or licensed roofing contractor that the roof is watertight and won't need to be replaced for at least two more years. Or you may ask for expert assurance that roof repairs and replacements will cost no more than $3,000. Then if the bill comes to $6,000 because the walls supporting the roof have dry rot and need to be replaced before a new roof can be installed, you can cancel your agreement to buy the property.

Clauses like this are often called escape clauses. They give you some protection against unforeseen major expenses.

Still, courts have held that a written disclosure needn't enumerate the many little flaws that you should be able to see for yourself. In California the judicial rule is, "An 'as is' provision, generally speaking, means that the buyer takes the property in the condition visible or observable by him."

Always Take a Close Look

I've said this before, several times, but it's worth saying again—inspect carefully before you buy, especially if the seller is someone who might move out of the state as soon as he gets your money.

Check all the plumbing, light switches, appliances. Thump the walls and see how they sound. Look for minor trouble spots that sellers seldom mention, like flaking or mildewed areas of wall that are carefully hidden by furniture. Move the furniture. Look behind drapes, paintings, and other wall decorations. Examine the floor under the rugs. Check the basement for clues to water damage, such as fresh paint or cement. If a ceiling has just been replastered, maybe it was done because the roof leaks. Keep in mind, too, that real estate salesmen empty out closets to make them look larger, and unclutter rooms for the same purpose.

You probably won't want to rely on your own eyes if you're buying an apartment building or a big old house. Instead you can hire a professional house inspector. (To find one, look under "Inspections" in the classified phone book.) But he won't break through a wall to see how the inside looks, and he probably won't pull off switchplates or sockets to study the wiring. Nevertheless he'll tend to be an alarmist. If he doesn't find things wrong, how can he justify his fee?

Therefore you needn't pass up an investment because an inspector warns of minor blemishes or farfetched contingencies. Use his report to extract concessions from the seller during negotiations. If the seller denies some flaws reported by an inspector, get that denial in writing as part of the contract of sale.

Structural Soundness Isn't Enough

The seller's written disclosure or warranty should cover you against termites, structural defects, malfunctioning appliances and other major problems that might make a building uninhabitable. But this isn't enough when you buy property as an investment rather than a place for you to live.

Maybe some wiring, plumbing, roofing or whatever works okay but was illegally installed. Bringing it up to code could be costly. Ask your attorney to make sure that the seller gives written assurance that the premises aren't in violation of building or zoning laws.

Zoning obviously can make a difference in the value of a property. Your attorney should make sure that the property matches the zone. Don't take the seller's word for this, nor his warranty. Conceivably he doesn't know that his fifth bachelor's unit (a converted garage) is illegal because the area is zoned for a maximum of four units.

So much for the basics. Now let's look at other invisible factors that might make a property a poor investment even when it seems to be priced as a steal.

How Is the Political Climate?

We all know the old saying that the three most important factors in real estate investment are location, location, and location. But we sometimes forget that local political conditions can make a location good or bad.

If a new shopping center is soon to be built nearby, a location may soon become better than it looks now. Contrariwise, a good building in a good neighborhood at the right price may still be a bad buy if the town council intends to assess the cost of a sewer program that will cost property owners a bundle. An alert lawyer in town will know what's brewing, and will tell you, if you retain him before buying.

Or suppose you figure that you make a little house chic by certain inexpensive improvements such as a fence and garden. You might find out that a local fence committee and/or garden club have power to forbid changes that don't meet their esthetic and decorative standards (as is the case in at least three towns I know of). Local dignitaries might make you spend much more on improvements than you'd intended to.

Likewise, if you buy an apartment building for the purpose of converting it to condominiums, and a renters' league is about to win an election on a platform of preventing conversions, how much of a bargain are you getting?

In short, local politics can be important to you. Before buying property in an area you don't know well, make friends with someone who is attuned to the local grapevine—a banker, lawyer, realtor, or maybe the town's most popular barber—and learn all you can about the zoning board, the town council, and other reigning bureaucrats.

Is the Seller Stretching the Facts?

A seller's minor misrepresentations may not be enough to justify a lawsuit, or to make him give back any of your money, but they still can cost you dearly.

He may say that all the units are one-bedroom units. Or that his commercial property has parking for sixty-seven automobiles. But when you try to refinance the property you may find that lenders appraise the units as bachelor apartments, or that the parking lot holds only forty-six cars. It could make a drastic difference in the loan value of your property. Get his statements in writing, and check them for yourself.

He may show you sheets of figures indicating that his building's operating expenses are attractively low. The numbers may be right—but incomplete. For example, they may not include a management fee because the seller is operating the building himself. If you'll need to hire a manager, this cost must be added to the true operating expense. The bank will factor it in when it calculates the maximum supportable mortgage.

And what about those low insurance premiums? Is the building underinsured? What does the policy cover? Take the policy to your insurance man. Ask him if you'll need to budget more for adequate coverage.

With today's high energy costs, and higher bills predicted for the future, you'd better double-check the data on utility costs. Verify the owner's claims with the gas and electric companies. Also ask regulatory commissions whether utility companies are scheduled to boost their rates. And if any residents have long-term leases, see whether these provide for passing along increased utility or fuel costs to the lessee.

224

Probe for Tax Traps

The tax assessment on the property is important too. A seller may try to conceal a high assessment. Or he may show you last year's tax bill even though he knows it will be higher this year. To be sure you know all you should, you'll probably have to go to the tax assessor's office.

Ask the assessment office for a tax card or listing sheet. It will show not only how much the property was assessed, but when. The date is important. If it hasn't been assessed in some years, there may be a bigger tax bite coming. Ask the assessor if property in your area is scheduled for reassessment soon.

As a result of taxpayers' "revolts" at the polls in some states, these states have recently passed laws holding down the amount an assessment can be raised each year. But sometimes the law doesn't apply if the property is sold, so the authorities may use your purchase price as the basis for boosting your tax more than they could otherwise. Ask the assessor if a sale to you may trigger a reassessment.

And while you're in the office, check the listing of the property against the owner's description. If the tax card says the property is 17,000 square feet but the owner says he's selling you a 23,000-square-foot building, this probably means he has made an addition that hasn't been recorded and therefore hasn't been assessed. Or it could mean assessors made a mistake, and will raise your tax when they correct it.

Are the Boundaries Right?

The contract of sale is supposed to describe the property exactly. But is the seller's description correct? Are the avocado trees out back really on your land, as the seller says they are? And how about the driveway and fence? If they encroach on someone else's property by even a foot, you might have trouble. Here are precautions you can take:

(1) Make the seller identify the boundary lines and spell them out in your written agreement.

(2) Get a copy of the seller's deed and check the boundaries by following the legal description.

(3) Get a copy of the plot plan from the seller. Study it to make sure that improvements, trees, walkways and the like are really inside the boundaries.

(4) If this checking raises any doubt in your mind, commission your own survey. You can make the sales agreement contingent on a surveyor's confirmation of the information given to you.

Are There Other Claims on the Property?

If important money is involved, it's prudent to have your lawyer check for outstanding liens on the property and for easements or other use rights that might affect it.

Maybe the seller—or some previous seller—gave an easement that will allow a neighbor or a contractor to run a sewer pipe across your chosen spot for a swimming pool. Maybe you plan to add a garage to the house, but an old easement to the telephone company could block this. Remember, once an easement is granted by a property owner, it can't be revoked unless both parties are willing. The easement still applies even though it isn't mentioned again in any later deed. It is said to "run with the land."

Before You Buy—and After

By investigating in advance along the lines I've suggested in this and the previous chapter, you may uncover some problems. Unless they convince you that the would-be seller is a downright shyster, they needn't discourage you from continuing to negotiate with him. Point out the problems tactfully, so he can save face by rectifying his "oversights." You can use them to get him to adjust the terms.

Remember, every dollar you save in purchasing goes to the bottom line of your return on investment. A 1 percent cut in your purchase price might add as much to your profit as a 6 or 8 percent raise in your eventual resale price.

Despite all precautions, you may be fooled occasionally. If so, think carefully about your chances of getting some money back, or even of canceling the transaction. Study the warranties you got from the seller. Even if they don't cover the trouble you've found, you may be able to approach him in such a way that he'd rather settle with you than fight you with the consequent damage to his business reputation.

A book that gives many excellent tips for pressuring sellers to give you your rights (without the expense of litigation, or even hiring an attorney) is *Super-Threats*, by John M. Striker and Andrew O. Shapiro (Rawson).

KEY POINTS TO REMEMBER

· Desperate sellers are tempted to deceive. Inspect carefully. Get statements in writing.
· New buildings carry an implied warranty, enforceable in court. Act promptly if you find something wrong.
· Ask the seller for written disclosure of the condition of a used house.
· Protect yourself with escape clauses in a sales agreement.
· Before buying in an unfamiliar area, investigate political conditions there. Be sure about taxes on the property.
· In case of trouble, approach the seller in such a way that he'd rather settle than fight.

__15__

Rent Control: How to Fight It, How to Thrive Despite It

Many investors in rental property think that if rent control comes to their community, local apartment owners must either (a) stop paying on the mortgages and look for jobs in the nearest fast-food joint; (b) touch a match to the property; (c) jump out a window.

Which isn't necessarily so.

Oh, sure, I know that in New York City, the first big city to impose controls, most owners chose either (a) or (b) and a few went so far as (c).

But I also know that other owners made big profits in that same city, year after year, by buying multifamily dwellings. (I'll tell you their success secrets later in this chapter.)

I know further that astute investors in rental housing are still prospering under various types of rent control in more than five hundred cities including Boston, Philadelphia, Washington, Baltimore, New Orleans, El Paso, and Los Angeles.

The national magazine *Money* knows all this too. Its October 1981 issue reported: "If you do decide to invest in real estate . . . veteran investors favor apartment houses. For small investors, the best buys can be two- or four-unit apartment buildings, which often cost $95,000 or less."

When I appear in television interviews I'm often asked a question phrased somewhat as Howard Ruff recently phrased it to me: "Is rent control a serious threat to real estate investment?"

My answer, if condensed, might begin "No, but—" or "No, if—"

My fuller answer might begin, "It depends on who does the investing, and how they do it."

In past decades, many ignorant absentee owners of rental property prospered despite themselves because rents and/or property values rose fast enough to absorb their mistakes. Today, for such people, rent control may indeed pose a serious threat.

In other words, rent control can choke off the easy profits for goofups, at least until the economy bounces back or the controls are eased. Right now I'm inclined to agree with Joel Pashcow of Integrated Resources, a real estate investment company in New York City, when he says, "We're going through a shakeout that could lead to widespread losses."

The shakeout isn't due solely to controls. There are other factors too. You know them as well as I do. Interest rates are so high the numbers sound more like collar sizes than mortgage costs. Property values are no longer soaring in most areas. Even without rent controls, many properties' operating costs have grown faster than their rental income.

In short, times are tough. But as I teach in my seminars, the best time to buy is when few buyers are around, and owners want desperately to sell.

Wherever rent controls are clamped down, owners of low-rent multiple dwellings think they see floods of red ink ahead—and often the floods do come. Why? Because their properties are badly managed, and they themselves don't realize this or don't know what to do about it. They wish they could sell, but usually don't even try, because they think no one would buy. All of which means that rent-controlled cities are bursting at the seams with opportunities for hard-nosed bargain hunters.

When you start dickering to buy, you'll need to understand why rent-controlled apartment owners feel almost as panicky as the hard-pressed homeowners I described in earlier chapters. To see how the future looks to them, you should know something about the past. Let me sketch some broad background for you.

Why Controls Came

Throughout most of history, being a landlord was handsomely profitable. In this country, starting around 1875, an investor usually paid someone to build an apartment house, borrowed 90 percent of its cost by signing one or more long-term mortgages, then hired a manager or an agent to operate it—and sat back to watch the cash roll in.

The manager or agent rented the apartments, collected the rents, paid the bills, maybe hired a janitor to stoke the furnace and sweep the halls. The manager lived rent free in the building, so didn't expect much pay. In some buildings a "superintendent" doubled as both manager and janitor.

Under this relaxed arrangement, the cash flow depended mainly on the manager's performance. If he or she rented apartments to people who didn't pay, or did serious damage, or caused other tenants to leave, the property ceased to be a money machine—because mortgage payments and most of the expenses stayed the same no matter how much or little rent came in.

Unless at least 85 percent of the rental units produced cash every month, the profit usually vanished. And if the manager slacked off on necessary maintenance, the owner eventually faced a costly crisis of clogged pipes, a blown boiler, leaking roofs.

But the bright side of this picture was that whenever a manager could get the residents to pay 10 percent more rent, with all his costs unchanged, the "leverage"—the fact that only 10 percent of the money spent for the building had come out of the owner's pocket—could double the profits, and give a big boost to the eventual selling price.

Consequently, numerous owners and managers raised rents whenever they dared. Yet tenants did comparatively well through the 1960s and 1970s because rental housing was fairly abundant and owners who overcharged found themselves with too many vacancies.

Even in the 1970s, while tenant complaints grew louder and rent-control movements swelled, rents didn't rise as fast as the inflation rate. But trouble was coming.

Investors had begun backing away from constructing new multifamily dwellings because they saw that the costs of building these were rising faster than the costs of building single-family homes. And maintenance costs rose faster still because house owners did much of their own maintenance while apartment dwellers didn't. Apartment buildings' savings on heat and hot water were gobbled up by the need to hire managers and maintenance people, to buy electricity for the elevator and the lights in the halls and lobby, to maintain the public areas, replace the dishwashers in the apartments, pay the costs of painting and redecorating vacant apartments for new tenants, absorb the losses from vacancies and delinquencies. Since the taxing authorities perceived apartment owners as plutocrats, apartment buildings almost everywhere were assessed a higher proportion of their value in taxes than were private homes. Investors said to each other, "Hey, let's buy houses."

And this is what happened. Many investors got rid of their apartment buildings and started buying single-family houses and renting those instead. Others simply began to lose interest in their rental properties as they saw their profits being steadily eroded by increasing costs. They started cutting back on maintenance and their properties began to deteriorate.

At the same time millions of middle-class renters began moving to the suburbs and buying their own homes. The empty apartments in the cities were filled by low-income people who could not afford their own homes and could not afford to pay much rent. This made it even harder for apartment owners to maintain their properties and still show a profit. Investors were also reluctant to put money into constructing new apartments because projected rents were just not high enough to justify the expense. It was easier and more profitable to build single-family houses for those who could afford to pay good prices to get away from apartment living.

For these and other reasons, new apartments have accounted for less than 10 percent of America's housing starts ever since the middle 1950s. Insurance companies, which had invested heavily in multifamily housing right after World War II, pulled out.

"Slum clearance" and "urban renewal" programs tore down whole neighborhoods. In their place arose huge cheaply built public-housing blocks which became notorious as "slums with hot running water." The urban poor, who were expected to benefit from these programs, turned out to suffer more than ever. The demolitions (plus other ground-clearing for freeways and the like) led to a net loss of hundreds of thousands of housing units. I've seen estimates that the number of new dwelling units constructed were less than one-fourth of the number demolished.

That's how we got our horrendous housing shortage—first in New York, later elsewhere.

With 70 percent of all New Yorkers living in rented apartments, there were plenty of applicants for the few vacancies. The baby boom squeezed housing tighter. When the shortage made even the dingiest rooms rentable, landlords found that money saved on services or on maintenance dropped right into profits. Rent control prevented them from raising their rents to profitable levels, but it could not force landlords to spend money that they did not have. As profits went down for landlords, the quality of life went down for tenants. While the good landlords struggled to survive and keep up their properties in spite of rising costs and fixed rents, the unscrupulous landlords, the slumlords, got rich. They milked their buildings for all they could and made no repairs or improvements. City inspectors would hit them with notices of code violations and threaten to fine them or put them in jail, but there were too many of them and the city did not have the resources to go after them and force them to clean up their act.

Those few who did get caught often chose to abandon their buildings rather than make repairs. They would simply stop paying their property taxes and mortgage payments but would continue to collect rents as long as they could. When their buildings were finally foreclosed or taken over for nonpayment of taxes, they would just walk away, often leaving behind uninhabitable shells. This led to more pressure to protect tenants from greedy rapacious landlords and eliminated any chance of getting rent controls phased out. What had started as a temporary emergency measure during World War II had become a permanent feature in the New York City housing scene. The voters of New York—80 percent of them renters—decided to punish all landlords for the sins of a few, and as a result the city's housing stock and its tax base both began to go rapidly downhill.

What Controls Did

New York-style rent control was a subsidy to all tenants, whether needy or not, at the expense of all owners, whether greedy or not. Frank Kristof of the Urban Development Corporation estimates that New York's rent control has transferred $22 billion from owners to tenants in the years since World War II.

As inflation heated up, property owners in New York had to pay more and more for utilities and maintenance and repairs and every other operating expense. But their rental income was frozen. So in many cases they decided to abandon their property—but first, of course, to take as much out as they could.

Just as rising rents made hate on one side, rent control made hate on the other. Landlords stopped paying taxes, shunned maintenance, defaulted on mortgages. According to Louis Winnick of the Ford Foundation, some owners deliberately rented to criminals (who paid extra under the table) and unruly welfare families (welfare paid the rent) to get even with longtime tenants who they felt had been "robbing" them through the rent-control law in past years. The rent control law allowed automatic 15 percent rent increases whenever an apartment became vacant, as opposed to an average increase of only 5 to 7 percent a year when the old tenants remained. Therefore, by driving long-term tenants out in favor of transients, landlords could not only get even for rent control, but they could get around it and increase their profits. Needless to say this only made the basic problem of rent control worse; the good landlords were made to suffer while the slumlords were rewarded. This made it more impractical than ever for honest landlords to stay in the rental business. Many of them just gave up and turned their buildings over to the city or to anyone who would buy them. Other landlords found other ways to get out from under the rent-control burden.

Throughout the 1960s there was an average of over thirty fires a night in the South Bronx and other ghetto areas as landlords with criminal instincts had their buildings "torched"—often by cooperative tenants eager to make a fast hundred dollars—and then collected on the fire insurance. In the years from 1965 to 1968, some 100,000 housing units in New York were destroyed or abandoned.

You might think this vast shortage would stimulate builders, especially since new construction was exempt from rent ceilings. But it didn't work that way in New York or other rent-controlled areas. Few investors wanted to put money into new apartment buildings, especially in years when the cost of borrowing was high.

If the market value of an apartment house is to keep pace with inflation (and when it doesn't, it isn't a good investment) then rents must keep rising; and the costs of running apartment houses, concentrated as they are in service trades and energy bills, have risen faster than the inflation rate. In New York only a few thousand rental units were built or rehabilitated, and these were so heavily subsidized by real estate tax exemptions that the city paid more of the cost than the developers did.

The city government had to admit that rent control, despite its popularity with millions of renters, was a fearful failure. It hired a large corporation to make a systematic study of its housing problems.

Summarizing afterward, the report stated:

> The pervasive problem was that most owners of the controlled housing were not getting enough revenue to maintain their buildings properly and still earn a reasonable return on capital. . . .
>
> We recommended raising ceiling rents to cover standard full costs, much in the pattern of public utility rate-setting; a program of direct rent assistance to low-income families to offset the rent increases . . . and a special program addressed to persistently substandard buildings.
>
> It was a long, hard selling job. Finally, in May 1970, the mayor sent his proposal for rent-control reform to the city council. We were pleased to have it described in the press as close to our ideas. The city council enacted the reforms in June.

Why Controls Spread

It has been said in recent years that nobody lives in big cities except the very rich and the very poor. That isn't strictly true— there always are swarms of young people in the metropolis to seek their fortunes, and some older people would rather stay in the city despite its drawbacks. But there is too much truth in the saying for the cities' good. High rents (plus other troubles like bad schools and crime-ridden streets) have driven away the bulk of the middle class.

Middle-class people want to own homes. The 1960s and 1970s were banner decades for home construction—yet the supply of new homes didn't grow as fast as the home-buying market. The market grew even more than the size of the population because of late marriages and high divorce rates, which meant smaller but more numerous households.

These smaller households, in many cases, preferred to live in apartments. But renters were far worse off than house-seekers. By 1980 inflation had nearly halted construction of middle-income rental housing in many areas. Vacancy rates sank to all-time lows—around 4.5 percent nationally, but only 2 percent in Baltimore and Chicago, and below 1 percent in Los Angeles, San Francisco, and New York.

In big-city ghettos some people were living in autos and renting kitchen and bathroom privileges from nearby tenements. Meanwhile scarce two-bedroom apartments in chic parts of San Francisco and Chicago often rented for $950 a month or more (up 20 percent, in some cases, from a year earlier).

When apartments are scarce, rents rise. Inflation has added its own boost. People will pay more for groceries and clothes and entertainment in inflationary times, but they have learned to resist rent increases. They begin organizing, and demanding that laws be passed to protect them.

This is especially true of the militant younger generation, forced into apartments because they can't find houses for sale on terms they can afford. About 40 million Americans will try to buy their first home during the 1980s, but most will probably fail to do so, because mortgage rates are not expected to drop much below 13 percent in this decade. Even if inflation cools, banks will be painfully cautious about cutting long-term loan rates in uncertain economic times.

Youth's demands are more desperate than you might think. On September 5, 1979, ten years after Woodstock, about three thousand youngish people grabbed sleeping bags and small grills and camped as long as six days in line waiting to apply for sixty low-interest loans offered by Louisiana's First Homestead and Savings Association. The rate was 7.6 percent. Applications for $3,400,000 in loans were taken in the first thirty minutes. If such an offer were made in 1982, I suppose applicants could have filled the Superdome.

With so many people resentful about the housing bind, it's no wonder that they have forced five hundred municipal governments to clamp lids on rents. The trend seems likely to spread, at least for a few years, until the resulting dilapidation reverses it. I think we're seeing another example of Santayana's maxim, "Those who cannot remember the past are condemned to repeat it." Rent-control movements are unaware of its disastrous failures in New York, Miami, Berkeley, and elsewhere. Their demands are incessant. Recently Henry Schechter of the AFL–CIO said in an interview that he was getting a dozen calls a week from lawyers for municipalities all over the country, asking him for tips on writing rent-control ordinances.

Property owners, seeing this threat looming ahead, might be expected to use prudence in setting rents. Probably most do. Still, in many cities they have been playing catch-up after a decade when rent rises lagged behind the overall rate of inflation and behind heating, utility and maintenance costs in particular. Sometimes the owner of a low- or middle-income rental complex sees no way to stay out of the red except by converting to a condominium, upgrading to luxury rentals, or abandoning the building. Naturally his tenants don't want him to do any of these. They may take him to court merely for raising rents enough to cover his costs—and courts are suddenly sympathetic to middle-income tenants.

What to Do When Controls Are Proposed

It's possible to turn public opinion around. Five weeks before election day in Palo Alto, California (where many Stanford students live in rented apartments), a poll showed a strong majority in favor of a proposed charter amendment that would freeze rents. But on election day it lost, 14,900 to 5,700.

Another reversal occurred in Berkeley. An earlier rent-control law had been thrown out by the State Supreme Court. Some 63 percent of Berkeley voters were renters and had elected a radical city council. The council planned to reinstate rent control through a charter amendment that would roll back rents to the level of a year earlier. About 60 percent of the voters favored the amendment, according to a poll two months before the election. Nevertheless every candidate backing the amendment was defeated, and the amendment itself got only 13,000 votes while about 22,000 voted against it.

How were these turnarounds accomplished? By educational campaigns and intelligent teamwork. Of course, money was needed too, and real estate people can usually raise it, but their money was spent unwisely in some other losing campaigns.

The money in Berkeley and Palo Alto was spent to hire a political consulting firm (an astute, experienced one) and to buy advertising. The consulting firm taught the coalition of apartment owners how to recruit hundreds of their friends to ring doorbells and to telephone voters; other volunteers organized neighborhood coffee meetings to discuss the issue; still others stuffed envelopes in the campaign office.

They presented the arguments against rent control clearly, calmly, and convincingly. The League of Women Voters saw the merit in their arguments, and threw its considerable influence behind them. So did the student newspapers on both university campuses. Even the black community swung over to oppose the rent control propositions; every black city council member, and the powerful Berkeley Black Council, publicly endorsed the stand of the property owners.

The arguments you can use against rent control are readily available from realty research groups, so I needn't dwell on them here. But it's worth mentioning that some observers with no ax to grind have recently come out with statements against rent control.

For example, an interesting new book entitled *Miller's Court*, by Harvard Law School professor Arthur Miller, shows that legislation often produces very different effects than legislators intended. Rent controls, he says, were supposed to be easy ways to improve the position of tenants, but the result was fewer rentals. "The reforms instituted to secure decent housing for tenants in the long run may be responsible for denying them housing altogether," Professor Miller concludes. "Sometimes in law, as in life, it seems you just can't win."

Another new book, *The United States in the 1980's,* contains a chapter by John McClaughry, who served four years in the Vermont legislature and was a member of President Carter's National Commission on Neighborhoods. His chapter on Neighborhood Revitalization has this to say:

> A large number of otherwise knowledgeable people seem to believe that rent control leads to desirably low rents for tenants, with few or no adverse effects upon "greedy landlords." But the evidence is . . . that rent control accelerates urban decay and abandonment, assists the wrong people, misallocates housing space, creates housing shortages, depresses the construction industry, aggravates municipal fiscal problems, and produces heightened social conflicts that defeat efforts for rational accommodation of competing interests.

Another dispassionate observer, usually liberal-leaning nowadays, is the *Los Angeles Times.* Commenting on rent control in Los Angeles, it editorialized in April 1982:

> Housing is a commodity; rent control is a selective form of price control. Shelter is an important commodity, to be sure, but there is no more justification for letting government set its price than there is for letting government decide what umbrellas should cost.
>
> The city's rent ordinance was enacted in 1978 when inflation was climbing toward double digits and vacancies were scarce. Imposing controls was an emotional, political and probably inevitable act under these circumstances.
>
> There is no question that limiting returns on investment also limited the construction of new rental units. Existing housing has been allowed to deteriorate as landlords have postponed painting and repairs.

So, with so many people in agreement that rent control does not work, why is it still a political issue? Why hasn't it died out? Because it *is* a political issue and a very emotional one. In most cities the majority of voters are renters. If they can be convinced that rent control will save them money, then naturally they will vote for it. More important, they will vote for any candidates who claim to support rent control and against those who oppose it. Radical politicians and would-be politicians have caught on to this and turned the rent-control issue into something larger: the opening round in their projected class struggle between the haves (landlords) and the have-nots (renters). The fact that many, if not most, landlords are just working people trying to make an honest living, while many tenants are wealthy, is beside the point. Landlords make a convenient target, especially in hard times. California is a prime example. City after city has been hit with a well-organized campaign financed by a well-known husband-and-wife team, who hit on rent control as a useful tool for their own political ambitions. Petitions are circulated, hysteria is whipped up about housing shortages and poor people being unable to pay their rent, and soon a rent-control initiative goes on the ballot.

But you can't have an effective rent-control law—one that will really stick it to the landlords—unless you have "progressive" city leaders to enforce it. So, in almost every case, several candidates supported by this couple appear on the ballot, with rent control as their main campaign promise. This way they attract many voters who might have little sympathy with their overall plan to create a socialist society, but see rent control as an apolitical bread-and-butter issue.

This pattern has been repeated over and over again in California. Within the last five years there have been rent-control elections in at least twenty different cities, and every time the radicals lose they come back and try again. When they win, they try to expand their power base. They attempt to branch out and use their new-found support to win other elections and put their candidates into office. But more important, they try to spread rent control to the surrounding communities that have not yet seen the light.

The people who are now pushing rent control are, for the most part, not the well-meaning liberals of the 40s and 50s who really thought that rent control would help tenants and felt that it could be fairly administered so as to allow landlords a reasonable return on their investment. All too often today's rent-control advocates have no desire to be fair. They see rent control as a weapon to use against property owners to drive them out of business so the tenants can gain leverage concerning the property. They are well organized, dedicated and determined, but they can be beaten. I am going to show you how. I said at the beginning of this chapter that you can make money in spite of rent control, and that is still true. If your area already has rent control, you can live with it and you can even profit from it. I will give you some ideas on that in a minute. If, however, your area does not have rent control, then you want to do all you can to make sure that you never get it. To do this, you must be organized.

My wife and I were involved in an anti-rent-control campaign recently. We helped to defeat the rent-control proposal by better than a two-to-one margin, but it was not easy. It took hard work and careful planning. Many investors buy property out of town, hire a management company, and then forget about the property. I don't believe in doing things this way. My wife and I own property all over the country, and, while we obviously don't manage it all ourselves, we do stay involved and keep ourselves aware of anything that could affect our property values. Rent control falls into this category, so when there was a rent-control election last year in Oakland, California, we got involved. We are both busy with other things, and Oakland is about a four-hour drive from our home, but we manned phones and helped get the vote out. It was a hard fight, but it was worth it.

Rent control had been on the ballot before. In 1980, rent control was voted down almost two to one. But it is a juicy issue in these hard times, and the radicals behind it were not about to give up. They had been defeated by a two-to-one margin right next door in Berkeley in 1978, but the people of Berkeley got complacent and so two years later the radicals were able to squeeze it through by a bare majority. Once they had rent control on the books—at first as a one-year temporary measure—they held two more elections to strengthen the rent-control law and make it even more anti-landlord than it was originally. One provision they rammed through called for an elected rent-control board, since the radicals did not have a majority of the City Council and had failed in their efforts to stack the appointed board with anti-landlord activists. Landlords may sit on the board, but only as nonvoting members, in order to avoid any conflict of interest. Tenant members of the board, of course, have full voting rights. They decided that it was time to try once again to spread the disease to Oakland.

All the early polls showed that they would win overwhelmingly. Oakland is at least 60 percent renters, and everyone was sure that they would simply vote for what they were told was in their best interest. But when the election was over, the proposal wasn't just defeated—it was virtually laughed out of town. It lost by more than a two-to-one margin this time—a larger margin than two years before. I talked to Douglas Seiler, a young real estate broker (one of the organizers of the anti-rent-control campaign) to find out what other communities could do.

Here are some of his suggestions:

First of all, be aware that there is a push for rent control before it gets on the ballot. Someone has to go out and get signatures from voters, and you can have your people follow them around to make sure that people get both sides of the story before they sign any petitions. You don't want to get into arguments or shouting matches—leave those tactics to the other side—but you do want to make sure that people know what they are signing. It is easier and cheaper to keep the measure off the ballot than to fight it at election time.

You should also be lobbying your City Council and/or state and county officials, trying to get them on your side. Try to get them to come out against rent control in public statements. This worked very well in Oakland, where the mayor and most of the council appealed to renters and homeowners to see beyond the rhetoric.

As soon as you know that signatures are being gathered to get rent control on the ballot, start organizing right away. Be aware that it will take at least four weeks just to get your campaign headquarters set up and get the phones installed, etc. Attend any public hearings and get your side out in force to make your opinions heard in a dignified but forceful manner.

Get the support of the Chamber of Commerce, the Board of Realtors and anyone else who cares about the community and what rent control will do. If people think that only the landlords are opposed to rent control, then they will not be very sympathetic. You must make people aware of the real issues. Homeowners in particular should be made aware that rent control is eventually going to mean higher property taxes and lower property values, as well as a reduction in city services, once the tax base is eroded. Local teachers and school officials should be made aware of the inevitable effect on the local schools. All the voters should be aware of what rent control will really cost. There will be salaries for the rent-control board, the cost of inevitable lawsuits against the rent-control law, and the cost of efforts to enforce it. Have facts and statistics available as to what rent control has done to various cities around the world.

Avoid dealing with the media whenever possible. They like spectacular stories that grab people's attention. Therefore the good landlords who take care of their properties and get along with their tenants do not interest them. They would rather focus on the bad landlord because he makes a more interesting story. If you must deal with the media, then have *one* designated spokesman.

Hire a political consultant to help you run your campaign. A good professional can be worth his weight in gold, but don't waste time or money on expensive surveys or polls. Just get out there into the community and fight it at a grass-roots level. Walk the streets. Knock on doors. Set up a phone bank and call all the registered voters. Send out mailings. Solicit donations and/or volunteer help from any individuals or groups who want to see rent control defeated. *Remember, this is not a battle between landlords and tenants. Do not let the other side get away with characterizing it that way. Tenants have the most to lose if rent control gets in.* Save your signs for the last two or three weeks of the campaign and then be prepared to replace them frequently, because they will get torn down. Warn volunteers that their cars may be vandalized if they have anti-rent control stickers on them. Make use of any incidents that do happen and get full publicity value out of them.

Finally, when the election comes, *get out the vote.* Have poll watchers at every precinct with lists of all those who said they would vote against rent control. If they don't show up by midday, then contact them, get them to the polls. Have rides available for those who may need them and call back any voters who had said that they were undecided, see if you can sway them, and get them to vote.

And finally, when it is all over and you have won . . . realize that it is not over, and the radicals will probably be back for another try sooner or later. In Oakland they could barely wait for the election results before they announced that next time they would try to elect their own people to the City Council and pass rent control by decree. But Doug Seiler and the other responsible people of Oakland have risen to the challenge and are sponsoring their own candidates for the city council. It has been said that the price of liberty is eternal vigilance, and that means that those of us who want to preserve private-property rights in this country have got to stay on our toes and guard against those who want to take those rights away. But even if you lose the fight—*don't panic*. Rent control is like a headache: it is annoying, but you can learn to live with it if you have to. As a matter of fact, you can even profit from the mistakes of others.

What to Do if Rent Control Comes

As I said at the start of this chapter, there's no need to despair if a rent-control ordinance is passed.

You can still make money by owning, or buying, controlled properties.

In fact, rent control might even turn out to be your best friend, for two reasons: (a) panicky owners will dump properties on the market at prices that almost guarantee a profit to a good manager; (b) very few tenants will stop paying or move out, thus virtually eliminating the pesky nonproducing apartments that hurt your cash flow.

"Even during the Great Depression," says the Research Institute of America, "people had to live somewhere. They may not have bought so much, and that's why a lot of businesses folded and plants shut down. But they sure needed a place to live, and that's why they continued paying their rent."

As soon as a rent-control law is passed, your first step should be to read every word of it several times. Be sure you know exactly what it permits and forbids. Even the toughest ordinances permit rents to be raised under certain conditions.

For example, your local law may say you can raise the rent if an occupant moves out. If so, consider offering someone $500 or $1,000 as a cash reward for moving.

Also, the law may say you can apply for permission to raise the rent after improving the property. That's your cue to pick up a few of the worst, most decrepit buildings in the area—at sacrifice prices, of course—and make basic repairs. This should justify raising their rents enough to net you a fine return.

Likewise, the law may exempt buildings containing less than five units. This is a common exception, but many owners don't study the wording closely enough to see it. They may be eager to sell their duplexes and fourplexes, and you may be the only bidder.

Or maybe the law will let you convert a big old single-family mansion, or a nonresidential building such as a factory loft of an abandoned fire station, into rental properties. This can be a bonanza. New Yorkers of all races and creeds have found it so. In Greenwich Village and Brooklyn Heights, then Chelsea, more recently Bay Ridge and the middle West Side, they have been rehabilitating tumbledown shacks and rat-infested tenements, and converting old industrial buildings or even streetcars into new dwellings.

Many lower-income families pay for their home, in effect, by the work they do around a three-family or four-family building where they occupy one of the flats and rent out the others. (The bar associations have a story about a lawyer who got a plumbing bill. "Fifty dollars an hour!" he screamed. "I'm a lawyer, and I don't make fifty dollars an hour!" The plumber answered, "Neither did I, when I was a lawyer.") You may not be a handyman yourself, but if you invest in a fourplex that needs a lot of work, you can probably find a blue-collar family that will gladly do the work in return for a rent-free apartment. With the wages of skilled workers as high as they are, this could be the key to a nice profit for you.

For instance, in Auburn, a city in central New York State, one investor has achieved financial independence by meeting the local demand for rental housing. He buys older mansions—usually at tax auctions—and converts them into small apartment houses.

Almost every rent-controlled city has whole districts where investors are creating attractive apartments in grimy depressed areas and renting them quickly at luxury rates: the North End in

Boston, Society Hill in Philadelphia, Mount Pleasant in Washington, North Beach in San Francisco, North Hollywood in Los Angeles, and so on all over America.

At my seminars I often tell about a group of New York rabbis who bought buildings worth $700,000 for only $300,000 because the owners saw no way to make money on them. The rabbis had learned all the municipal rules and regulations and exceptions. So they raised the rent of tenants in qualifying units whose pay had been raised, as allowed by law. Or they bought out tenants and rented the vacancies at higher rates. Or they added furniture, rewired buildings, renovated kitchens—increasing values to the point where tenants as well as officials agreed the apartments were worth more rent. For each apartment they owned, some clause enabled them to get higher revenues. In this way the rabbis rescued their temples from near-bankruptcy.

The New York Council of Churches tried to do somewhat the same thing on a larger scale, building and managing moderate-income housing. But building is still risky. They learned some lessons by experience that you may want to keep in mind if you undertake any sizable project in a big city. As quoted by Martin Mayer in his book *The Builders,* Enoch Williams of the Council said, "In one project we took over from contractors, Con Ed hadn't got the electricity meters in on time, or never got them in; anyway, they'd never billed the contractor. You take over, and you get a three-year back bill for $75,000. They bill on 'constant demand'—they charge you for what they have to have available at maximum load. You go to the Public Service Commission, they say, 'Well, they were three years late—we'll give you three years to pay.' There's an $18,000 monthly rent roll on the building, no way we can pay an extra $25,000 a year back bills. You know what happens: we didn't pay the mortgage."

Sloppy management is the cause of most losses in apartment investing. With a good manager, owners could usually net a profit on a sizable building even during the tightest years of control in New York, where the average real estate tax pulls out not one but more than three months' rent. Jack Rosenfield, who worked his way through law school by helping out in his family's real estate business, told Mayer happily of earnings from "the standard old six-story, sixty-unit elevator apartment, which a good super can run by himself.''

But good supers are hard to find in the old cities of the East and Midwest where the typical superintendent had three rooms in the basement, was drunk half the time, and came up and sloshed out the halls occasionally. Absentee owners didn't know the difference, or didn't care. So today in these cities people think it's beneath them to manage an apartment building unless they have a big desk, a swivel chair, and someone else to do all the manual labor. So look first at management when you're thinking investment. The best buy is a badly managed property, provided you can replace the manager with someone intelligent who can do rudimentary plumbing and painting.

Of course, if you want to live in a property of twenty units or less and manage it yourself, and you're willing to work, you can quickly convert a money loser into a winner. Just by cutting waste and keeping the property maintained, you can improve the profit margin dramatically without raising anyone's rent. Apartment management is a science; for a complete guide to the principles see my book *How to Manage Real Estate Successfully— in Your Spare Time.* And if a property's expenses outrun its income, you'll find some quick cures in Chapter 12 of the book you're reading right now. Just turn to the section "Quick Ways to Boost Cash Flow."

Another way to prosper under rent control is to find a firm that is efficient at managing many small rental properties. Merely by purchasing supplies in big quantities and keeping repair people on call at reasonable prices, they can save you more than they charge.

"Rental housing is still a solid business here," says seventy-four-year-old Lex Marsh of Charlotte, North Carolina. "It's easy to find resident managers. They don't have to collect rent or do the bookkeeping because we have a central office that does all that. We have maintenance crews that keep everything clean. For managers we pick out a retired or semi-retired couple, or maybe a tenant who's been with us three or four years and wants some part-time work and will take care of up to 100 apartments. A project manager shows and rents apartments, acts as clearing house for service calls, and does the liaison with tenants." Mr.

Marsh owns 2,000 rental units and is building more on a corner of the 85-acre property where he lives.

Don't Fight City Hall

Besides good management, good relations with the municipal authorities are important under rent control. Before you tackle these authorities personally, join some organization—an apartment association, perhaps—that deals with them. You can learn a lot by listening to the organization, and the organization may help if you have a problem.

But don't expect the organization to do all the work. As soon as you feel fairly well informed, go down to City Hall and meet the people who run the rent controls. When they're convinced that you're not a profiteer, they'll be willing to consider your problems.

The first step is to build a reputation for cooperativeness. Obey the regulations scrupulously. If they make life hard for you, keep your temper. It will go even harder with you if you pop off at administrators. From then on they'll make a point of looking over your shoulder constantly, ready to pounce on every "unjustified" act, but not in the least worried about whether their delays or denials of rent-increase applications may put you out of business.

From your very first contact with them, be friendly and conciliatory. Get them talking about their problems, and show that you understand even if you don't entirely agree. Make it clear that you're determined to do a good job for your tenants, to live up to the letter and spirit of the law, but also to keep yourself afloat financially if you can.

Gradually you'll come to understand how these regulators think and work—and they'll come to understand you. Then they'll be more likely to rule in your favor when borderline questions arise. Most regulations are flexible enough to be interpreted in different ways for different people. Even when City Hall rules against you, it can loosen the ruling a little when the dust has settled—especially if you're perceived as a friend who sympathizes with the need to keep rents reasonable.

Show Them the Figures

As a matter of fact, in most cities under rent control the rules and the administrators are much more reasonable than the gloom-and-doom prophets think they're going to be. Usually the city government is just trying to keep rental increases within a range of about 7 percent per year, while doing everything it can to encourage new construction and new investment.

When you need an increase, document your case thoroughly. Get together your bills for operating and maintenance costs and/or for capital improvements. If you take the trouble to prove that costs have squeezed you badly, you're likely to get a favorable ruling.

It's a new ball game under rent control, and the game is well worth playing. You'll be part of a real estate revolution in the making. We're in the worst housing market in four decades, but you can thrive in it and help improve housing at the same time.

KEY POINTS TO REMEMBER

- Rent control is an invitation to astute bargain hunters. Panicky owners will dump property.
- Educational campaigns and teamwork can often get controls voted down. Try for a broad-based campaign. Keep it truthful and impersonal.
- Even the toughest rent-control districts let rents go up under certain conditions. Read the law closely.
- Investigate upgrading property to raise rent.
- Eliminating mismanagement is often the key to profit.
- Cultivate good relations with local authorities.

16

How to Liquidate in a Buyers' Market

Do you want to cash out?

Many real estate investors never do. Some keep acquiring income property year after year, improving and perhaps exchanging it, or living on the rentals. Others simply hold property and watch it grow in value, occasionally converting part of it to cash by borrowing against their equities.

Save This Chapter Till You Need It

Others make occasional sales, waiting until a good offer turns up and until they see a profitable reinvestment. During the early 1980s they've been mostly waiting.

Still others are traders, buying to resell at a profit as quickly as they can, and using their profits to buy more. If you're one of these—and if you've structured your investments soundly, without too much debt—you've probably been buying but not selling during the economic downturn, since you can afford to hold out for good prices. Have you ever sold for less than you paid? That's rare in real estate, although it happens often to owners of merchandise, commodities, stocks and bonds.

On the other hand you may be a trader who prefers (or needs) quick resales despite the slow market. This chapter shows you

248

how to keep on selling. But my advice is not to push hard just now, for you may find yourself accepting smaller profits than you'll get later when mortgage rates sink back to earth. As soon as rates do come down significantly (maybe it will have happened by the time this book is in your hands), there'll no longer be a buyers' market. Buyers will be out in swarms, and real estate will be climbing again because of the chronic housing shortage. So unless you're in a real hurry, just put this chapter aside for reading when and if there's a sale you urgently need to make.

A few nontraders may also want to know, right now, how to dispose of property. They may have a variety of reasons. Some manage their property personally; maybe you're one of these, and maybe you've tired of the work involved. Or maybe you don't manage property, but just want to take your profits and ride off into the sunset. Or perhaps some personal problem calls for a bundle of cash.

If you're in such a category, read on. Otherwise skip this chapter unless and until the need arises.

A Time for Hanging On?

Would-be sellers like you should understand that the game has changed. In 1979 investors would have been foolish to hang on to cash that was depreciating, instead of buying something that would rise with inflation. But in the disinflation that some economists currently predict, it may be smart to hold cash equivalents such as stocks and Treasury bills. That's why timid investors who previously were buying the ultimate "tangible" investment —real estate—have kept their pockets buttoned lately. So your market has narrowed. And your competition has widened, because builders and condo converters are selling at a loss.

Most real estate people began feeling glum when mortgage interest rates soared in 1979 and 1980, and by 1982 their prevailing mood was downright despairing. "Some home builders seem to be giving away money to move houses," reported *Forbes,* a leading financial monthly. *Money* magazine warned, "If you have already invested in . . . homes or other properties, you are well advised to hang on and wait for better times before selling." *Los Angeles* magazine put it more dramatically:

Survival is the word of the year in real estate, the word that's on the minds of buyers, sellers, agents, brokers. . . . Many marginal Realtors got flushed out of the business, a lot of sellers had to reduce their asking prices, and condo developers turned to auctions to unload properties whose carrying costs were killing them.

They call this fiasco a buyers' market. And so it is—*if* you can qualify for the financing. And if you do qualify, you're a member of an increasingly select group, for there's a whole new world of financing to survive, too.

Now let's consider an open letter from a past president of the National Association of Home Builders. It's especially noteworthy for a reason I'll explain in a moment.

The life blood of our business—the supply of mortgage money —is receding rapidly. Without it we cannot operate.

Don't assume that the tight money situation is temporary— because it may well get tighter.

In simple terms, we are being priced out of the money market.

The upward shift in interest rates is undeniably a deliberate government fiscal policy—an effort to dampen inflationary tendencies.

The government and fiscal authorities must face the financial facts of life as they affect housing. They must do so now—not a month or six months from now.

In an election year, candidates for public office will be very interested in your view of the situation, your problems and plans. Tell them.

The above letter was dated August 30, 1956—yes, 1956. The president was Joseph B. Haverstick, whose appeal might have been written in 1982.

The point is that tight money comes and goes. Upswings don't last forever. The paper prices for real estate slowed their climb —and in many cases turned down—between 1979 and 1982. Why? Not because of any glut in the market, but because eager buyers balked at sky-high interest rates or couldn't even qualify for real estate loans.

With buyers forced out of the market, owners were forced to

cut prices in order to sell. Many did. Despite bankruptcies and unemployment and the scary mortgage terms, nearly 2,000,000 used homes changed hands between September 1982 and September 1983. Selling real estate is never impossible. So if you need to liquidate, don't approach your problem in a defeatist mood.

Any talk you hear about a "crash" in real estate prices is foolishness. Sure, asking prices are softer. But when the haggling stops and sales agreements are signed, average selling prices haven't dropped much, if at all. The worst report I've seen comes from metropolitan Washington, where single-family homes were rising in resale value at 20 to 25 percent in the late 1970s. What happened there? Prices "went absolutely flat" in 1980, according to the capital city's chief property assessor, George B. Altoft. Hardly a crash.

The next worst report is from California, another area that saw double-digit price jumps each year in the go-go 1970s. According to the California Association of Realtors, yearly price increases of 6 to 8 percent are more common in the 1980s.

Nancy R. Harwich, a real estate research specialist with Security Pacific National Bank, confirms this. "Home prices have continued to rise throughout the current downturn, and I don't expect any break in that pattern," she told a reporter in May 1982. "Things aren't selling as fast as they used to, of course, but values are still appreciating."

Sales-price figures collected by the National Association of Realtors from forty states show that the California and Washington patterns are common across the country. What does all this mean to you as a seller?

Yes, There Are Cash-Rich Buyers

For one thing, it means that inflation has cooled at least temporarily. The September 1983 inflation rate was only half the level of a year earlier. Property prices can't skyrocket when other factors in the economy, such as wages, salaries, energy prices and transportation costs, are in the doldrums. However, any new surge of inflation is sure to hoist property values again.

There's also another meaning in the data you've just read.

With two million used homes selling in a year, and average prices rising at 6 to 8 percent, it means buyers are still around—buyers with enough cash not to need today's dangerous mortgages. "The buyer for cash is the only one totally unaffected by interest rates," notes Richard Fletcher, one of my instructors, who says he sees more cash transactions lately.

Who are the cash buyers? Where do you find them? Try these ideas:

1. If you own a rental home, ask your tenant if he would like to buy. He is your most logical buyer. Maybe he's been saving up for a house of his own. (Even if his savings are comparatively small, maybe you can offer terms that would be good for both of you. See Chapter 17 about financing arrangements, as well as the section headed "Renter Becomes an Owner" in Chapter 18.)

2. Look for older homeowners who have so much equity in a high-priced present home that they can easily convert it into enough cash for a smaller, cheaper "empty nest" home— or for investment in rental property.

3. Look for someone who has been transferred by his employer. Many companies provide relocation subsidies, enabling employees to pay more than other buyers, and to act more quickly.

4. Look for unrelated adults who want to share a home for family reasons and/or economic reasons. For example, two or more divorced women and their children might be prospects. Each might have part of the cash you need. Rentals that allow children are hard to find, so there are many single mothers searching desperately for homes these days. Maybe you can remodel a property to give privacy to several groups and accommodate a variety of lifestyles.

5. Consider listing your property with the biggest, best-connected realty brokerage firm in your area. It may use national relocation and advertising networks that pull in moneyed buyers from far away. Today there are surprising numbers of newcomers from Taiwan, Hong Kong, the Middle East and Latin America. Some are political exiles with lifetime savings, looking for places to settle down. Others are fat cats seeking safer investments than they can find in their homelands.

Here Comes the No-Interest Mortgage

If you do get a nibble from a prosperous prospect, but he hasn't quite as much money as you need, you might sound him out about a zero percent mortgage (ZPM), a financing idea that is cropping up across the country. The buyer ends up owning his house free and clear much sooner than with other kinds of mortgages. This could be good for both sides if he's elderly, or if you are.

Let's say you want one-third or one-half of the purchase price down, and the prospect will go along provided he isn't saddled with a heavy debt. You offer a no-interest (principal payments only) mortgage for five or seven years on the remainder. (Naturally you set a higher price to make up for the interest you won't get. In my real estate investors seminar I teach, for example, that a $105,000 home conventionally financed should be boosted to $119,000 when financed with a ZPM.)

The buyer still comes out ahead, not only in monthly payments but in total cost. He buys your $119,000 house with $40,000 down, which is roughly one-third. Paying off the rest of the principal in seven years will take $940.48 per month.

On the other hand, monthly payments would be $1198 if the buyer had qualified for an $84,000 mortgage payable over thirty years at 17 percent—and if you had therefore cut your price to $105,000 with a down payment of 20 or 25 percent. In thirty years the buyer would pay a total of $431,280.

As for you, the seller, you get more cash right now with a ZPM —and if you need still more cash, you can sell the no-interest note, although it naturally would be discounted heavily.

There's still the tax angle to be considered by the buyer if he's subject to U.S. income tax. A ZPM gives him no deduction for mortgage interest. But wait. A section of the tax code declares that simple interest may be imputed at 10 percent when less than 9 percent is charged. So maybe ZPM buyers can deduct 10 percent a year for interest. The IRS says, Ahem, it hasn't made a ruling yet. Another possibility for a buyer willing to fight it out with the IRS is claiming an interest deduction for the higher house price, since it was raised to compensate you for giving up interest.

Some Brokers Get Mortgages for Buyers

Wouldn't it be delightful if a real estate broker, after showing your property to a prospect and getting him enthused, could reach into a pocket and simply lend the mortgage money he needed, at the going rate?

Well, it's beginning to happen—mainly in the New York metropolitan area, but occasionally elsewhere. The magic is worked through Citibank's program called Mortgage Power, which is being watched prayerfully by real estate people nationwide.

The program started in the summer of 1981. More than twenty major real estate firms have signed up. For a fee (usually 1 percent) Citibank promises to make available a specified chunk of mortgage money. For example, a broker pays $20,000 for the right to get $2 million in mortgage loans for his clients. Of course the clients must qualify for the mortgage as they otherwise would, but they know exactly what the mortgage terms will be. Sometimes they can prequalify—that is, get cash earmarked for their loan before they find a property they want to buy.

To Mortgage Power clients, Citibank lends up to 80 percent of the first $150,000 cost of a house, plus 60 percent of the rest. Even the bank's own preferred customers don't get this much, normally.

If you, as a would-be seller, are working with a broker who can draw on Mortgage Power, he'll probably urge you to "buy down" the Citibank mortgage rate to make it easier on the buyer. For example, let's say you want to sell a $150,000 home, and the going rate for mortgages is 16 percent. The broker may tell you, "I can get my client a $100,000 mortgage from Citibank, but the interest rate bothers him, especially since the mortgage must be renewed after thirty months at whatever the rate is then. You can reduce my client's interest rate by 2 percent for those thirty months if you pay Citibank 2.2 percent of the face value of the mortgage. That's $4,400. Better still, if you pay $8,800, the mortgage will carry only a 12 percent rate until renewal time. . . . Look, this is better for you than simply reducing the price of the house. Your expense in buying down the mortgage is a tax-deductible sales expense. But if you just cut the price, you're out that money, with no tax deduction for it."

The new breed of real estate brokers who represent only buyers, not sellers, have been quick to sign up for Mortgage Power. They charge a modest flat fee to their clients, plus a commission ranging from 2½ to 4 percent of the original asking price—not the selling price—of whatever home they buy. Consequently such brokers have no interest in trying to sell for top dollar. By having Mortgage Power available, they can often help a seller work out financing that benefits both buyer and seller.

How does Citibank benefit from its liberality? One way is by getting more borrowers at less expense for screening and paperwork. The brokers screen out ineligibles and do the talking with clients that banks must normally do. The client saves time and effort too. So he feels friendly toward Citibank and may move all his accounts there—which is another of the bank's motives for starting this program. As a sweetener, one point is knocked off the mortgage of any borrower who agrees to bank exclusively with Citibank.

If you want a list of real estate brokers who offer Mortgage Power, get in touch with Judith Mann, real estate sales manager at Citibank. Her phone number is 212-750-5577. The address is 200 Park Avenue, New York, N.Y. 10166.

Three Ways to Unload Without Selling

When you think about disposing of property, don't limit your thoughts to selling. If you can't find a buyer, there are other ways to liquidate. You won't get cash in hand, but you should be money ahead soon afterward.

One way to liquidate property is simply to abandon it. The seldom-noticed IRS regulation 1.165 (d) and Revenue Ruling 54-581 permit a loss deduction when property is abandoned. The owner can claim ordinary losses without any set limit.

Two steps are required under the law. First you take fully documented measures to get rid of the property, such as quit-claiming it to the county tax collector or deeding it to the lender before foreclosure—meanwhile moving out all your belongings and writing off the property on your books.

The second step is to establish the worthlessness of the property. A lack of available buyers (after it is advertised and/or listed by brokers) is generally considered valid cause for abandonment. You must abandon it in the year it becomes worthless and must take the deduction for that same year.

Since there's no exchange or sale, there's no capital loss. It's an ordinary loss, and clearly allowable, although the IRS may try to whittle down the amount you claim. Before you abandon the property and claim the deduction, get help from professional advisers. You can find a more detailed explanation in Paul Anderson's excellent book *Tax Factors in Real Estate Operations,* available through Prentice-Hall.

A second possibility is to give property away, if it represents a large taxable gain. By donating it to charity, you transform your gain into a tax *deduction* that may be much bigger than the gain.

This opportunity arises most commonly for people who've owned a house a long time. Maybe you or a parent bought your home decades ago for $18,000. Now it's worth more than $300,000. Under certain conditions, $125,000 of the profit may be tax-free if you sell, and you'll get favorable capital gains treatment on the rest—but even so, the federal and state taxes will bite painfully. To avoid these taxes legally, and simultaneously lock in a lifetime income for yourself, you can give the house to any charity registered with the IRS as a nonprofit organization under Section 170 (c) of the code.

Let's imagine you offer it to a hospital. The hospital establishes that the property has a fair market value of $340,000 and that several real estate developers want to buy. So it accepts your gift through what is called a "charitable remainder trust," then sells it and invests the proceeds. Since you gave and did not sell, you have no tax liability. In fact, your taxable income will be reduced by 30 percent each year for some years to come, putting spendable money in your pocket. Furthermore, you will receive income on the full market price of the house, $340,000. Nothing will be taken out for taxes, commissions or anything else. (Only after you and your spouse have died will the hospital get unrestricted use of the $340,000.)

Here's how it works. The $340,000 is invested in a group of securities supervised by investment professionals. Taking into consideration your age and your spouse's, the professionals will determine how much income should be allotted to you—proba-

bly at least 10 percent. If so, you'll get at least $34,000 a year for
the rest of your lives. The amount will never change.

This arrangement is called an annuity trust. If you prefer, you
can choose a "unitrust" arrangement instead. This means that
the monthly amount *will* vary, because it will be 10 percent of
whatever the market value of the securities happens to be. So if
inflation continues during your lifetime, and the securities grow
in value as they should, your income should keep pace with the
cost of living. With either an annuity trust or unitrust, donating
property that has risen markedly in price may leave you better
off than selling it and paying the tax. (See my book *How You Can
Become Financially Independent by Investing in Real Estate* [Re-
vised], Simon & Schuster.)

The third way to unload property is to exchange it for something else—which, if done right, can mean that you indefinitely
postpone some or all tax on your capital gain.

An exchange is most likely to help if you own a property that's
nearly free and clear and is worth much more than you paid for
it. If you want to trade up into as large a property as possible, a
Section 1031 tax-deferred exchange could be the best answer. Or
this might be a way to dispose of property that has an uncertain
value and a very limited market.

The field of tax-deferred exchanges is a big one (the above-
mentioned book gives it a whole chapter), and I won't try to
cover it here, since I'm focusing now on ways to cash out, not
enlarge your holdings. I'll just say that you ought to seek the help
of exchange specialists. Realty agents who handle residential
sales are seldom qualified to set up tax-deferred swaps—but they
can often recommend people who are. Be sure to get someone
who understands the new kinds of delayed transactions called
Starker and Biggs exchanges. If you don't find anybody through
a realty office, check with a university or community college
offering courses in real estate law and taxation. The instructor is
probably a real estate or tax attorney who knows all about tax-
deferred exchanges.

Getting Ready to Sell Your Property

For the rest of this chapter let's assume that you definitely want to sell your property rather than exchange it, abandon it, or give it away. In that case your first step should be to make it attractive.

If property is dirty or shabby, only hard-boiled bargain-hunters will bid on it. They aren't numerous, and they don't buy except at low, low prices. You'll sell faster and get a higher price by first making whatever minor improvements are obviously needed and then "staging the house," as salespeople say. This way you'll appeal to those seeking a nice place to live.

Don't start major renovating. Just take care of defects that catch the eye. Often $100 spent for improvements can return $1,000 in your sale price. Fix any torn screens, broken tiles, drippy faucets, cracked plaster. If it's the rainy season, new gutters can suggest that the whole building is structurally sound, while leaky gutters may be seen as a signal that the place is falling apart. If it's summer and the house is like an oven, maybe you should invest in a secondhand room air conditioner.

Home buyers seldom visualize how a house will look after it is spruced up. So do the sprucing up before they come. Start with the outside to give it "curb appeal." Hose it down, rake the yard, mow the lawn, trim the hedges. Maybe put a few potted plants around. Polish up the brass on the front door. Consider a paint trim in a neutral color.

Then go to work inside. Wash the windows. Clean the walls, floors and carpets. Straighten the closets. Get rid of the smelly rags in the basement, and don't let junk pile up anywhere. Scrub out the kitchen and bathrooms, and make them as attractive as you can; to many buyers, they're the most important parts of a home.

Make a Fact Sheet

Now you're almost ready to put the property up for sale. But first you need a fact sheet. This is a paper to be handed out to prospects, telling them nearly everything they'll want to know. Start with your name, address, phone number, and a capsule description that highlights the home's most desirable features, such as extra storage areas, favorable location, two-car garage, large screened porch, a home office or study or game room, trees in the yard, or whatever else might make it attractive. Don't misrepresent anything; this might kill a sale or leave you liable for repairs.

List the number of rooms, bedrooms, baths. Below that should come the following items, in column style:

Architectural style	Type of heating
Age	Air conditioning
Construction type (frame, brick, etc.)	Method of sewage disposal
Size of lot	Brand and age of kitchen and laundry appliances
Size of each room	Special closets
Square feet of living space	Schools nearby
Rugs and drapes	Shopping centers nearby
Attic features	Public transportation.
Basement features	Property taxes
Garage Size	Mortgage

Your sheet should include a photo of the house so a prospect can remember it. It should also state the house's asking price—but leave this blank for now, because you don't know the price yet, and you'll need help in setting it.

Pricing Your Property

Too high a price means no prospects. Too low means a fast sale but a loss of some profit. A realistic asking price is important in getting negotiations started—but remember that terms, not price, will be the key to closing the sale. What you need now is an in-between price, perhaps 5 or 10 percent higher than fair market value, to give yourself negotiating room—although in some cases you can eventually raise the price if you ease the terms, as I'll show you.

Home buyers aren't dumb. They learn values by comparison shopping. Most of them have been looking for months, trying to find the best buy for their money. They may know more about the current worth of local homes than a realty agent who hasn't kept tabs on recent sales. So you'd better set your asking price in a range that will interest them.

One way to find the market value is to hire a professional appraiser, whose fee may be $150 to $350 but could be worth it. Look for appraisers in the Yellow Pages, or ask your bank or S&L for recommendations. Just be sure to get someone whose business is mainly in homes rather than commercial properties, and who is thoroughly familiar with your neighborhood.

If you don't want to pay for an appraisal, do some scouting. Find houses similar to yours that are up for sale, and see what their prices are. If someone recently moved into such a house, maybe he'll tell you what he paid. However, your scouting can give you only a rough idea of the right price range. To narrow it down, get help from a few local real estate brokers.

Show them the first draft of your fact sheet and explain frankly that you're undecided about using an agent. Ask if they'll look at your property and suggest a price, telling you how they arrived at it. Some won't bother, but most will, especially when business is slow. They'll prepare a free, written "comparative market analysis," showing what properties like yours have sold for recently, the sales terms, and the current asking prices of unsold properties that will compete with yours.

Agents hope to get your listing by doing this work. Those who won't try aren't worth considering. You should also steer clear of any whose price estimates are much above the price range you've identified; they're playing the game called highballing, trying to get an exclusive listing even though they know they can't deliver a buyer at the price they recommend.

At this point you're not committed to a broker. Should you use one? There are some arguments for doing your own selling, and I'll touch on them later. You can try it on your own as an experiment. But in a buyer's market, if your property is competing against similar ones, I think you'll soon decide you need an agent.

What Kind of Listing?

Every agent you talk with will want an exclusive right-to-sell listing contract, probably for at least ninety days. This is a good bet if you're in a hurry to sell. It means that you allow only one broker to list the property and try to sell it. This provides a real incentive to work on it. Even if you find a buyer yourself, you'll owe the broker his or her commission. However, if you already have a prospect when you call the broker, you can usually exclude that particular person from the right-to-sell agreement.

One of your alternatives is to give a broker an exclusive agency listing, which means you won't let any other broker show it, although you can still sell it yourself and save the commission. Your broker won't like this because he suspects you'll try to snatch away any prospect he finds, as well as anybody who rings the doorbell. Therefore he'll probably put in less advertising money and less effort.

Another alternative is the open listing, which is scarcely a listing at all. You send your fact sheet to as many brokers as you please. It will produce activity among the brokers—not so much to sell the property as to wangle an exclusive listing. As long as the listing stays open, it's a race between you and the brokers to find a buyer; if you win the race, the brokers earn nothing. They won't gamble their time on it unless they have nothing better to do.

Or you may choose the most common selling method—multiple listing. Many areas have listing services that distribute information on local properties to all subscribing brokers. You list the house with one broker who in turn shares it with the others. Listing and selling brokers split the commission.

Some brokers resist using a listing exchange. They want to keep the commissions to themselves. But of course they're limiting your property's market exposure; other members of the exchange may have buyers looking for just what you're offering. Weigh the factors and personalities, and decide on the type of listing after you choose a broker.

Games Brokers Play

As we saw in Chapter 13, unethical sellers often try to trick buyers into paying more than they should. (One trick I didn't mention is to stall off a buyer until a realty listing contract expires, then make the sale themselves. I don't advise you to try this; not only is it unfair, but it's illegal in some states. That is, if a prospect is first shown a property by a broker but doesn't buy it until months later, that broker is still legally entitled to his or her commission no matter who negotiates the ultimate sale.) Brokers have tricks too, which you should guard against.

For example, having given an exclusive listing to someone, you may find the property no longer offered for sale after you've turned down an offer at close to the listed price. Why? Because the broker is trying to clinch the commission by temporarily taking your property off the list, hoping you'll give up and accept the offer.

Similarly, a broker who supposedly is cooperating with a listing service may try to freeze out other brokers who phone to inquire about your property. He may say it has been sold. Or he may have "lost" the file on it. So you'd better check to make sure your property stays on the market until *you* take it off. You can get a friend to phone brokers and ask about it.

Sometimes, too, a broker makes a side deal with a friend to pick up property at bargain prices. To protect the friend, he discourages other prospects—maybe even conceals actual offers. This is illegal too. Every offer must be presented to the owner during the listing term, even if the broker considers it totally unreasonable. Not reporting an offer is grounds to revoke an agent's license. If you find any evidence that a broker is holding out on you, notify the state real estate commissioner.

Occasionally a broker plays the risky game of misrepresenting a property in order to sell it. If a buyer finds he was cheated, he may come back at you as the seller—but it's the agent who is usually liable. For example, if the agent says, "This house has a sound cement foundation," and the new owner finds patched-over cracks in the cement, necessitating a costly rebuilding job, the agent is liable for damages. To keep yourself in the clear, disclose all pertinent facts in the sheet you yourself prepare, and make sure the agent and buyer read it.

Choosing a Broker

Most brokers conscientiously try to serve the interests of buyer as well as seller. A first-rate broker provides experience and know-how. Even in the years when property was easy to sell, licensed brokers and salesmen handled three fourths of all homes that changed hands. Today, home-mortgage lenders throughout the country report an average of eleven sales arranged by realty agents for every mortgage on a "for sale by owner" (FSBO) home sale. There must be reasons why eleven out of twelve sellers use agents.

A good broker has an accurate idea of how much a house will bring in the current market. He'll advertise it. He'll show it to a stream of prospects. He'll separate "lookers" from qualified buyers. If he finds a buyer, he can help with the financing that may make the sale possible. For all this he charges 5 to 7 percent of the selling price—although he may be willing to trim his commission, if you ask, rather than kill a sale.

In a buyer's market, you should give serious thought to listing only with the biggest, best-connected realty firms in your area. Tough economic times are when the big firms can do the most for you. Sometimes they can get financing for your buyers via Wall Street and mortgage banking sources unavailable to small firms.

To find the broker that's right for you, you might begin by phoning several offices or dropping in briefly, just to see how you're received and what your first impression is. Start with those whose "sold" signs or newspaper advertising caught your eye—but don't be dazzled by the fancy ads of some nationwide franchise organizations. Remember that their offices are locally owned and independent.

A realty office should be attractive, easily accessible, and open seven days a week for residential business. In making your first calls avoid any serious discussion. Spend just enough time to get a feeling—"I like them," or "I'm not particularly impressed." If you're uncomfortable with one, or sense a lack of interest, move on. With those you like, try to arrange an appointment with the head of the firm; otherwise you'll get (and be stuck with) whoever happens to be on duty.

Ask brokers how long they've been in the business, and what marketing and financing help they can give if you list with them. Watch out for superstars with a reputation for big-money sales. They tend to concentrate on easy properties and ignore hard ones; they may pressure owners to accept a poor offer for the sake of a quick sale. Contrariwise, don't be afraid of new agents. Often they're ambitious and work harder than the established winners who are coasting toward retirement.

When you've narrowed down the field, ask the surviving candidates for reference names of past sellers. Then phone the last three sellers and ask, "Would you list your property again with this agent?" and "Were you unhappy with the service in any way?" Check out the firms at the local Better Business Bureau and the realty board.

When you've found a broker you like and can trust, follow his advice on price. Fill it in on the first draft of your fact sheet. You'll need plenty of copies of this sheet for potential buyers. Ask the agent if he'll get it printed, with the photo at the top. If he seems reluctant, you can take it to a printer yourself—or type it perfectly, attach the picture at the top, and take it to a place that will make photocopies.

For serious prospects, compile some extra data on a separate sheet—your average monthly bills for utilities, garbage removal, and any other operating costs. Give the figures for your insurance and mortgage payments. You'll need only a few copies of this sheet.

Showing the Property

Whether you live in the house or a tenant does, it should be shown only by appointment (except, perhaps, for an "open house" on weekends) so that you can always have it at its best when prospects come.

Whenever the house is to be shown, keep pets and children out of the way. If there are tenants, give them lunch money the day of the open house, and maybe send them to a movie. Be sure the beds are made and the pillows plumped up. Do what you can to warm the atmosphere—with a crackling fire, for example, if there's a fireplace and it's cold outside. Turn the TV off and the lights on. Put on soft music. Fill the house with pleasant aromas. (Better forget the old-time stratagem of baking bread when the house is to be shown; you could accumulate a heap of bread before you make a sale. Instead try cinnamon on foil heated for half an hour in the oven—or vanilla extract.)

Don't follow the broker around as he shows the house. Get lost if you can, or else just sit down and shut up. Some buyers won't ask negative questions if you're there, for fear of offending you, but if you're out of earshot they may bring up difficulties that the broker can resolve. Then too, your attempts at salesmanship can damage the sale. For example, if the broker doesn't explain the wonders of your automated kitchen, you may feel bound to—but the broker may know that the client hates cooking and wants to move along to other parts of the house. Owners always tend to talk too much. Assume that the broker knows the customer better than you do.

Could You Sell It Alone?

This brings us back to the question I mentioned earlier: Would it be better to sell without a broker?

There's no certainty that realty agents can sell your property any faster, or for a higher price, than you can. In fact, buyers like to buy direct from owners, since they know they're saving a broker's commission. However, they'll expect your price to be lower because of this.

If you sell alone, you'll need to do your own advertising, put a sign in front of the property with your phone number on it, answer telephone inquiries at all hours, and be in constant readiness to show the house. You'll need to screen out potential troublemakers and even thieves.

Maybe you're willing and able to do all this. And maybe you're so familiar with real estate investing that you can handle the negotiations, help a prospective buyer arrange financing if necessary, and avoid legal pitfalls. (You'll be tempted to make promises on the spot in order to get the property sold, but you could regret them later. Before starting to sell on your own, talk with a lawyer and learn the danger spots.)

If you feel competent, there's no reason you shouldn't make the experiment. You can always switch to a broker if you get discouraged. Meanwhile there are good guides available at bookstores. Look up *For Sale by Owner*, by Louis Gilmore, or *How to Sell (and Buy) Your Home Without a Broker*, by Kenneth S. Gaines. Or send for a short helpful booklet called *For Sale by*

266

Owner published by Maine's Bureau of Consumer Protection, available for $1.00. Write to the bureau at the State House Office Building, Augusta, ME 04333.

Whether you do the selling or leave it all to agents, as soon as potential buyers appear the question of financing is bound to come up. Except for the rare all-cash buyers, the big question is whether they can afford the monthly payments.

So you'll need to be flexible about financing. There's a baffling array of new mortgage options. To help you (and perhaps your broker) forage through the financial thickets, you may want a brochure called *Home Financing Blueprints for the '80s,* which offers help in comparing basic differences among mortgages. It's for sale at $10 a copy, plus $2 in mailing and handling costs, from the National Association of Home Builders, 15th and M Streets N.W., Washington, D.C. 20005. I understand you can order it by phone, calling toll-free to 800-368-5242.

Working out the terms of a sale, as I said earlier, is more important than setting the price. There are so many ways to help a buyer that they're worth a chapter in themselves. So that's what the next chapter is about.

KEY POINTS TO REMEMBER

· Cash-rich buyers are plentiful. Learn where to look for them.
· By taking a no-interest or low-interest mortgage you may get a bigger down payment and higher price.
· Watch for brokers who can get prearranged mortgage loans from a bank.
· If you can't find a buyer, consider abandoning the property, donating it to charity, or exchanging it. There are tax advantages in doing these.
· In preparing to sell property, take pains to make it attractive. Prepare a sheet listing all pertinent facts about it.
· Find out a property's market value, and set your asking price within 10 percent of it.
· When you give a broker a listing, make sure your property stays on the market until *you* take it off.

__17__

Don't Cut Your Price; Change Your Terms!

Okay, so the market is against you. Property you're trying to sell hasn't sold. There are too many other would-be sellers, too few potential buyers. What to do?

Figure out a way to help a buyer solve his financial problem.

Financing is the key to moving property when buyers are scarce, money is tight, and business is slow. If you've set your price fairly, you needn't knock it down. Instead, change the terms. With affordable terms you may actually find you can raise your total price.

Come-Hither in Headlines

Here's an example. Suppose you own a one-family home you want to sell for $100,000. You owe $60,000 on an old VA-guaranteed loan, which is still assumable—that is, transferable to a new buyer—despite the famous June 1982 Supreme Court decision allowing federal S&Ls to enforce due-on-sale clauses. You're waiting for a buyer who will assume this loan and put $40,000 down, thus turning your equity into cash. But buyers back off despite the low interest they'd be paying. Nobody is willing and able to write you a check for $40,000.

Then you see the solution. You instruct your broker to run an ad headlined "$10,000 down—no qualifying—seller will carry at 12 percent." The broker does this—whereupon his phone starts ringing.

When he brings the eager prospects to you, you explain your proposal: You will sell on a wrap-around mortgage for $100,000 at 12 percent. The payments on the principal will be as small as if it were being amortized over thirty years, although the outstanding balance will fall due in twelve years. (Long before then, buyers figure, interest rates will drop and they'll be able to refinance at better terms.)

With part of the money the buyer pays you each month, you'll continue to pay your lender. As for the buyer, he avoids the long, slow rigmarole of qualifying for a new loan from a bank or S&L. His closing costs are delightfully low. He's willing to owe $100,000 at 12 percent. Where else could he borrow at such a low rate just now? He doesn't even mind the total price of $110,000.

"But I still haven't got my cash out!" I hear you mentally protesting. Relax. Here's how to get it.

So far you've received $10,000 cash and a mortgage committing the buyer of your property to pay you $1,000 per month (the 12 percent annual interest on the $100,000 he owes you). Out of this you'll pass along $350 per month to the original lender, as payments on the underlying $60,000 loan at 7 percent. Thus you're ahead by $650 per month or $7,800 a year. (Of course the exact numbers will change a little each month as the loan balances are reduced.)

Now, to get your cash, you can run another ad headlined "Earn 19 percent legally, secured by mortgage paper on real estate."

An investor answers the ad and buys your wrap mortgage for $40,000 cash. So he gets the $7,800 per year you've been netting. This is a 19½ percent yield on the $40,000 he paid. If the loan is paid off early he gets what is owed to him ($100,000) minus what he owes ($60,000).

But what if interest rates are so high at the moment that a 19½ percent return isn't tempting enough? In that case you can discount the paper you hold—in other words, sell it for less than face value, sacrificing some long-term profit for immediate cash. If you sell the mortgage for $30,000, the $7,800 interest the buyer collects will be about a 26 percent return.

The point of the whole example is simply this: If you have high equity in a property and are paying low interest on an existing loan, consider arranging a wrap-around mortgage and then selling the mortgage. It's a way to help a buyer get around those hurdles of high down payment and high interest rates, while you get more cash than he could pay.

Selling by Lending

Few people now remember a world without long-term, fixed-rate mortgages. Before the New Deal, a home buyer had to save up a third or even half the price of a house for the down payment. The rest was due in five years, with no assurance that the mortgage would be renewed. But the New Deal set up agencies like the Home Owners Loan Corporation and the Federal Housing Administration that enabled home buyers, for the first time in history, to make monthly payments that were as cheap as rent. The mechanism was the long-term, fixed-rate mortgage—to be paid off during twenty-five or thirty years rather than five.

But in the 1970s those old mortgages became a bonanza for property owners while nearly crippling the lending institutions that had issued them. The owner with the 6 or 8 percent mortgage got property-rich as real estate values soared, and he often borrowed against his equity. Meanwhile the savings institutions were losing their depositors to money market funds and to other instruments that could pay higher interest rates.

So the institutions that concentrated on housing loans are now in a painful squeeze; most of their capital is locked up for long terms at low interest. They're too busy trying to replenish their funds to make many new loans.

Hardly anyone is willing nowadays to put money out at any fixed rate for twenty-five or thirty years. A home buyer's payment schedule may be set up as if he'd gotten a thirty-year loan, but in the third or fifth year he is obligated to pay the loan off with the fearsome "balloon payment." If he signs such a contract he's gambling that in five years he can refinance the hefty balance; otherwise the property goes back to the lender. Prudent borrowers balk at signing, or prudent lenders refuse to let them do so.

It wasn't that way between 1975 and 1979. Remember those

good old days? It seemed money flowed everywhere then. If you were a seller, you got just about everything your own way. You could refuse to carry back a second mortgage, and buyers still would buy because money was readily available—at low interest —from hard-money lenders and mortgage brokers. Who would moan about paying 10 percent interest when the properties bought with those loans were appreciating at 15 or 20 percent a year?

But today lenders want higher interest, because they lent too cheaply in the past and they fear rates may go up again. Even though inflation has slackened, interest rates have stayed much higher than they were in the 1970s. The result is that sellers reluctantly become lenders themselves, charging below-market interest because they think that's the only way they can sell.

Six out of ten existing homes now carry back second mortgages, according to a survey by the National Association of Realtors. As recently as 1980 it was only four of ten. The same survey also showed that when a seller carried back a second mortgage he usually accepted an interest rate of 12 to 14 percent, which was comparatively low at that time. Only one in each fifty of the sellers surveyed was able to get full market interest.

Nevertheless there are ways you can sell today without having to take your money in dribs and drabs. I showed you one way at the start of this chapter. The rest of the chapter will show you other ways.

"Due on Sale" May Not Be

Most people trying to sell property today are under the impression that an old low-interest mortgage can't be taken over by a new buyer. In many cases they're mistaken.

The 1982 U.S. Supreme Court decision, which I mentioned early in this chapter, applied only to federally chartered institutions. It didn't affect the approximately 30 percent of home loans issued by state-chartered S&Ls and banks across the country. In at least fourteen states, legislatures and courts have made it difficult, if not impossible, for lenders to enforce their due-on-sale clauses. This is the situation in Arizona, California, Colorado, Florida, Georgia, Illinois, Iowa, Mississippi, Michigan, New Mexico, Ohio, South Carolina, Utah, and Washington.

The states' own policies were reaffirmed—for three years, anyhow—by Congress in September of 1982. Congress passed a law providing for certain mortgages to continue to be assumable during a waiting period of three years after its bill became law. In general, this law means that current state rules will apply until fall of 1985 unless a state legislature changes the rules in the meantime.

I don't think many legislatures will vote to let lenders raise mortgage rates when property changes hands. The California legislature has refused in the past to overturn the famous 1978 "Wellenkamp" decision of the State Supreme Court, which declared due-on-sale clauses unconstitutional. This influenced legislatures and courts in other states to act similarly.

As a matter of fact, many older mortgages—mostly those issued before 1976—don't contain any "due-on-sale" clause. Get out your mortgage or trust deed and read the fine print. Usually the due-on-sale clause, if any, is lurking in Paragraph 17.

If there is no due-on-sale clause, you can offer an attractive proposition to prospective buyers of your property. They can take over your mortgage, continuing whatever payments it specifies. Often the payments are 60 percent or more smaller than a 1980 mortgage would require for the same property.

If there is a due-on-sale clause, it probably can't be enforced until 1985 if your lender is state-chartered rather than federally chartered. Local real estate brokers will know for sure.

However, let's say your old mortgage is held by a federally chartered S&L, and does contain a clause about assumptions. You still may be okay. Read the clause closely. If it says the loan comes due "in the event of assumption," that's easy to beat. Just have your buyer take title "subject to" your old loan.

Beating "Due on Sale"

This means you retain all personal liability for the loan, so there has been no "assumption" in the eyes of the law.

Therefore the buyer gets a deed and makes payments directly to the lender, just as if there had been a regular sale. The only difference is the wording used in the purchase agreement and in the deed drawn up by the closing company. Your banker or S&L loan officer may frown, but he has no right to call in the old loan, or to jack up the interest rate, or to charge an "assumption fee" or to reject the buyer as unworthy of credit, because—to repeat—there hasn't been any "assumption" of the loan.

272

Who Owns Your Mortgage Now?

Maybe Paragraph 17 (or some other paragraph) in your loan document does say the lender can demand immediate payment of the entire debt if the house is sold. The wording will be to the effect that "if there is a sale or transfer of either equitable or legal title, or any interest therein, the loan becomes due and payable." Even so, your apparently nonassumable low-interest mortgage may have invisibly been transformed into one of those beautiful old assumable mortgages through a quick shuffle by the "secondary mortgage market." (The phrase refers to a secondary market, not to second mortgages particularly.)

To find out whether your loan can still be assumed, you must know who holds it now, and whether FHA, VA, or FNMA are involved.

The millions of loans insured by the Federal Housing Administration or guaranteed by the Veterans Administration are nearly all assumable with no rate change; the Supreme Court ruling doesn't apply to them, even if your VA or FHA loan was made by a federally chartered S&L.

Also, a nonassumable mortgage may become assumable when the Federal National Mortgage Association, known as Fannie Mae, buys it. FNMA allows assumptions of government-backed loans it holds and, under certain conditions, of older conventional loans. It also is beginning to help sellers in other ways, as we'll see in a moment.

Fannie Mae is a $66 billion mortgage investment company— America's fifth largest company in terms of assets. Its granite headquarters in Washington, D.C., swarms with twelve hundred employees. Congress set it up to provide a big "secondary market" for mortgage loans—that is, to buy mortgages from the original lenders. Later it was converted to a stockholder-owned company, although it still holds its federal charter, and its bonds are considered virtually as good as government bonds. It is the nation's largest home-mortgage lender. In fact, it owns one of every twenty home loans outstanding in this country. In some subdivisions and condominium projects, it owns the loan on *every* home.

Three Ways Fannie Mae Can Help

This colossus in far-off Washington may have bought your paper in a block of mortgages years ago, without your knowledge. The bank or mortgage broker who originally lent to you can still collect your monthly payments, still send you regular statements of the mortgage balance, tax escrows and so on. Usually lending institutions don't inform a property owner when they sell his or her mortgage in a secondary market, and they aren't required by law to give out this information.

However, most of them will tell you if you ask. Or you can ask your real estate broker to find out for you. If you get no help from either of these, write to FNMA, 3900 Wisconsin Avenue NW, Washington, D.C. 20016.

Let's say your loan does turn out to be owned by Fannie Mae. If it is assumable by a new buyer, fine. Even if it isn't, there are two other possibilities.

In 1981 Fannie developed a "Refinance/Resale" plan to benefit owners and investors alike. And in 1982 it came up with a "Seller Finance" program designed to enable you to provide below-market financial assistance to a purchaser of your property, yet get nearly all of your money out of it.

Here are the details of the first plan, which refinances nonassumable loans at bargain interest rates.

Let's suppose you own a small, conventionally financed townhouse which is now worth $65,000. You'd paid its original 8 percent mortgage down to $30,000. The mortgage does contain a standard anti-assumption clause, barring you from passing along the 8 percent rate if you sell the house.

Without Fannie, this would mean you'd either have to "take back" a large mortgage at a cut rate—letting the buyer owe you most of the purchase price plus interest, and collecting from him in monthly payments over a term of years—or else you'd have to put the house on the market with no special financing attached whatever. Then the only possible buyers would be people who qualified on their own for a conventional loan at current high rates. To attract such buyers, you might have to slash your asking price by one-fifth or more.

But if you're one of the lucky owners with a Fannie Mae mortgage, you can offer buyers a "resale" loan. They'll be able to obtain a new $58,500 loan—nearly twice the size of your existing mortgage—at a discounted rate that won't change in thirty years. The old 8 percent loan disappears, and you stroll away with all cash and a full price. You don't have to hold any mortgage from the buyer. Fannie does that.

What will be Fannie's rate to the new buyer? Somewhere between 12 and 14 percent. You can estimate it by these steps of arithmetic:

(1) Take the amount you now owe on your current loan, and express it as a percentage of the new loan requested.
(2) Take the difference between the existing balance and the new loan, and express that too as a percentage of the new loan.
(3) Take the rate you've been paying on your current loan, and multiply it by the percentage determined in step 1 above.
(4) Multiply .175 by the percentage determined in step 2.
(5) Add together the results of steps 3 and 4. That's your rate, unless the answer is below 12 percent, in which case the rate will be 12 percent anyhow because that's Fannie's current minimum. Still, it's not a bad incentive to a buyer who needs help in acquiring your property.

Now about the other program, "Seller Finance."

Fannie started buying first mortgages from home sellers in 1980, then expanded the program in 1982 to include second mortgages as well. Hence you can probably offer a would-be buyer a purchase-money mortgage, then turn around and sell it to Fannie Mae, ending up with cash instead of an IOU—although Fannie won't pay the full face amount. The price it will offer for the mortgage depends on the interest rate you are getting and Fannie's rate at the time. In any case its discount will be smaller than most other mortgage buyers demand. The higher the interest rate on the mortgage, the greater its value—and therefore the smaller the discount.

At any rate, this program relieves you of the chores of collecting monthly payments, as well as the possibility of having to foreclose. And it enables you and the purchaser to work out your own mortgage terms, within limits. You might offer him an 11 percent, fifteen-year second mortgage, say, for $50,000 or even $100,000, depending on the appraised value of the property. (Fannie will insist on a written appraisal.)

Fannie will lend up to $108,300 on a single-family home, $136,800 on a two-family home. If you live in the home, you can borrow as much as 80 percent of the property's value in the total of both the first and second mortgages. If you are the landlord or the seller, you can borrow up to 70 percent of the total. The term of a second loan can be from three to fifteen years.

Fannie won't automatically buy every loan made by an individual. The main requirement is that you get your mortgage from a FNMA-approved lender. For a fee, this lender will "service" the loan, including property appraisal and credit qualification.

To take advantage of this opportunity, you should approach a local lender who deals with Fannie Mae, such as a finance company, bank, S&L, or mortgage banker. Explain that you plan to offer seller financing to prospective buyers in the form of a purchase-money mortgage, and that you'll want to cash in this mortgage as soon as the sale is completed.

The lender will write up your loan application on standard Fannie Mae forms. Then you'll have to wait awhile. Fannie insists on plenty of paperwork and careful checking. Your purchaser will have to meet nationally standard tests of creditworthiness. (However, these usually aren't as stiff as the local institution's own standards.)

You can charge your buyer whatever interest rate you choose. But if Fannie Mae wants new second loans in its portfolio to yield more than you charge, it will discount your loan accordingly. For example, if you offer the purchaser a 13 percent mortgage of $30,000 for ten years, and Fannie's current standard is 16 percent, it will probably pay you only about $28,500 to make up for the low rate.

To offset this discount, you can probably ask and get a higher selling price for your property, just as you would have done in the case of the wrap-around mortgage transaction I suggested at the beginning of this chapter. And remember, a borrower can pay off a Fannie Mae loan at any time, without the prepayment penalty imposed by most banks and S&Ls. Interest is charged only for the time he uses the money.

Your real estate broker should know all about these new programs. If he or she doesn't, a phone call to Fannie Mae will bring full details.

Other Ways Government May Help

Remember the equity-sharing arrangements I suggested in Chapter 16? Recently, since I wrote that chapter, the FHA has notably enlarged its own equity-sharing program, in which it helps sellers pair an outside investor with a purchaser. It will insure shared-equity mortgages. This means, according to national housing officials, that the number of such transactions will double within a year. Contact my office to tell you more about equity sharing via FHA and other plans (*The Lowry Group,* 3390 Duesenberg Drive, Westlake Village, CA 91362 1-800-255-6979).

loosen federal restrictions on mortgage bond financing by state and local governments. Under these programs cities, counties, and state agencies use some of their money to provide cut-rate mortgages (sometimes at 10 to 12 percent) for home buyers whose incomes are in or below the middle tax brackets. Where does this government money come from? From the sale of tax-exempt municipal bonds. Call your local housing agency to see if some of the bond money might be lent to a prospective buyer of your property.

All this competition from government lenders is pushing down mortgage interest rates charged by private lenders. Also, money has been leaving the money market funds since their interest rates dropped, and some of it is again finding its way into mortgages. So you may be able to sell your mortgage without government aid and not have it discounted as deeply as in the past. According to a *Wall Street Journal* article in September 1982, "Home sellers are seeing their contracts being discounted 15 to 20 percent instead of the 25 to 30 percent of just a few weeks ago. [A mortgage broker] says he expects the discount rate to drop even further."

Lenders Are More Liberal Lately

When you have a loan that definitely can't be assumed without the lender's okay, try talking with the lender to see if the new purchaser can be allowed to take over the loan at only a moderately higher rate. Many banks and S&Ls around the country now permit their old-fashioned, low-paying mortgages to be assumed at compromise rates set three or four percentage points below existing quotes for new mortgages.

Some even offer to give a buyer a break by "blending" the older mortgage into a new one. The borrower gets the amount left on your mortgage at a below-market rate, and the remainder at the regular rate. In this way the borrower shaves a few points off his loan and the lender retires your low-yielding mortgage.

Why are financial institutions showing this unaccustomed kindliness? Partly for the reason mentioned above: competition is pushing rates down. Then too, some institutions are eager to find borrowers for their current funds at current market rates—which is hard to do, since the rates are almost prohibitively high. Money men must keep lending to stay in business. They can't liquidate all those low-interest loans in their portfolios, on which they're losing money, unless they somehow make it possible for old owners to sell their houses to new buyers who need loans.

Save Money by Giving Two Mortgages

Here's another strategy for getting more cash than the buyer can pay, without selling his note at too deep a discount. Just divide the note into two parts—a second and a third mortgage.

For example, if the buyer wants you to carry back a $14,000 note, and you need an extra $5,000 in cash over and above his down payment, you can have the buyer give you a $6,000 second mortgage and an $8,000 third one.

You can probably sell the second for $5,000, which is about a 17 percent discount. Then you keep the other note and continue to collect interest on it. Obviously that's much better than giving up a 17 percent discount on all $14,000.

Why do you sell the note in second position rather than the third? Because it is in a more secure position and therefore easier to discount. You may also be able to insist that the buyer agree to pay a little higher interest rate on the second, or shorten the due date on it to three years, so it won't be discounted more than $1,000 when you sell it.

Incidentally, there's nothing very unusual about having three or more mortgages on a piece of property. There can be as many as the lenders agree on, although you should make sure there's enough equity in the property to serve as collateral for all the mortgages. Have you ever thought of offering your real estate broker a mortgage for the amount of his commission? Quite often a broker will agree, if you ask him. He'd rather wait for his money than lose a sale.

Maybe you're willing to help a buyer in order to make the sale, but you hate the thought of taking back any kind of mortgage. Instead, you might consider subsidizing the buyer's payments early in the mortgage. You can do this by putting a lump sum in a special account at closing. Part of the money and the interest it earns will go toward the buyer's payment each month until the sum is used up.

If you're willing to buy down a buyer's payments by helping out on those early ones, you may attract a qualified purchaser without cutting the price of your property much. Lenders are likely to qualify an applicant who can meet the first year's monthly payments on the theory that his income will rise later. "A buyer who can get $200 a month assistance for one year can probably buy $14,000 more house," says Bernard Hale Zick, a prominent real estate broker and consultant in Overland Park, Kansas.

A Smorgasbord of Mortgage Plans

Don't automatically assume that you'll have to take back paper in order to sell your property. It's always best to let the financiers do the financing, although a buyer might prefer it the other way. With you, he doesn't even have to fill out those tiresome loan papers. So he may not search out other resources if he's got you. It's up to you to do the buyer's searching if necessary. Your goal is to sell your property with as little personal risk as possible.

Make calls to your own sources for loans to the buyer. Shop around for terms he can afford. You and your broker can steer him past a smorgasbord of home-mortgage plans and help him choose the terms he can best afford.

The new mortgage plans are known by the initials of their complicated names. For example, GPAML means Graduated

Payment Adjustable Mortgage Loan. GPRM is short for Graduated Payment Renegotiable Mortgage. These and other types of VRM—Variable Rate Mortgage—shift all risk of interest-rate escalation onto the borrower. Borrowers with brains are bound to resist such risk.

They'll be slightly more receptive to GPM (Graduated Payment Mortgage) and TIP (Tailored Installment Program). Both offer bank loans—if a borrower qualifies—at 3 percent below market in the first year. Then the payments are stepped up each year for five years, on the theory that the borrower will be making more money thanks to promotions, inflation, Providence or something. If his income *doesn't* increase, too bad for him. Unless he can refinance or find some other way of scratching up the money, he'll lose the property. (But the average S&L will probably try to help him refinance. It won't want to foreclose, because foreclosed property is considered a black mark on an S&L's balance sheet.)

If you'd like to study the wide array of plans, there's a whole new book devoted to them, and I recommend it. It is Robert Irwin's *The New Mortgage Game,* published by McGraw-Hill. Bob has been a successful California real estate broker for twenty years.

One plan which he doesn't mention, because it has come along so recently, is the Growing Equity Mortgage (GEM). Like most mortgage alternatives, it has various advantages and disadvantages. GEM may be most suitable for a buyer who can only make a down payment of 10 percent or less but can afford to make increasingly high monthly payments, and would rather have a fixed rate instead of gambling on a rate that goes up or down according to money market fluctuations.

The interest rate of a GEM is about 2 percent less than on a conventional thirty-year mortgage. The home buyer agrees to increase his monthly payment by a specified percentage each year. Because his interest rate stays the same, the bigger payments are used to pay down the loan principal. Consequently his whole debt will be paid in ten or fifteen years, depending on the repayment schedule he chooses, rather than thirty years. He may be the first in his block to burn his mortgage.

For example, he buys your house for $130,000, using a $20,000 down payment and a $110,000 GEM at 14¾ percent. His monthly payments start at $1,388 per month, and will rise each year by 3 percent, so he'll be paying $1,562 monthly in the fifth year and $1,811 in the tenth. At the end of the fourteenth year the mortgage is paid off. By contrast, a conventional mortgage at 16 percent would keep him paying $1,479 per month for thirty years.

With GEM he knows from the start exactly what his monthly payments will be each year. They are not based on external indexes such as the six-month T-bill rate or the Consumer Price Index, which are used as scales for payment on variable-rate mortgages. And he has the nice feeling of seeing his equity increase—as the loan principal decreases—by a sizable slice each month. Under many other plans his equity might actually decrease with the passing of time, if inflation heats up again.

One drawback to GEM is that the borrower loses the normal tax deductions for interest payments during his high-earning years, because he pays down the principal so fast. Those big principal payments are entirely out of pocket. On the other hand, since his total cost is much smaller, he owns the home free and clear in about half the time, and will have more cash available for other uses.

How to Stay Safe if You Lend

If worse comes to worst, and you find that your buyer of choice can't qualify for (or afford) as big a loan as he needs from a financial institution, you may decide to defer part of the sales price, carrying that yourself as the junior lender. Look out!

If you don't sell the paper, it will be nice to have him paying you interest on your money for five or seven years or whatever term you and he agree on; if you had the money you might just put it out at interest somewhere else anyway. On the other hand, it's not quite so comforting to contemplate the risks involved. Real estate and consumer protection attorneys across the country say that seller-assisted financing is bringing more and more foreclosures, litigation, and serious financial losses.

You'll be taking the same risk as any lender—that the borrower may slow down his payments, and even default. Getting your property back through foreclosure can be laborious, as we've seen in earlier chapters. And there's no telling what condition the building will be in when you take possession. Here's how to guard against these risks:

(1) Don't sign any sales agreement that commits you to finance a buyer until your own attorney okays the wording. A real estate agent helping you may be using "standard" forms, and nevertheless get you into deeper legal shoals than necessary.

(2) Use one of the "servicing" programs for sellers that are offered by banks. For a relatively modest fee the bank will check the creditworthiness of your would-be buyer, and will warn you in advance if it feels your loan is too risky. It will also handle the monthly payment collections and accounting.

(3) Make sure the terms you give your borrower are within the standards of the secondary market for mortgages. This will enable you to turn your loan into cash, through sale to Fannie Mae or a mortgage bank or perhaps a private investor, if you need the money before the payment term is up. You or your lawyer can get information on these standards by writing to Fannie Mae.

(4) Take out "private mortgage insurance" on your loan. This is the most important precaution of all.

Private mortgage insurance companies refused at first to cover seller mortgages, but now that volume has grown, a number of them stand ready to protect you against default. While you're negotiating your sale, talk with your realty broker or attorney about arranging for insurance. You may be able to get the buyer to pay the premiums as a condition for your loan.

The biggest private mortgage insurer in the country, known as "Magic"—Mortgage Guaranty Insurance Corporation, MGIC Plaza, Milwaukee, WI 53202—will insure first or second mortgages, deeds of trust and wrap-arounds. American Mortgage Insurance Company of Raleigh, N.C., and Investors Insurance of New York City also offer protection.

Their insurance is available everywhere in the country through about 20,000 lending institutions—mortgage bankers, S&Ls, banks. The insurance compensates you if the buyer defaults during the term of the mortgage and you have to start foreclosure proceedings. You are reimbursed for foreclosure expenses, outstanding and delinquent principal, back interest and taxes, and the cost of maintaining the property. The insurance company will either pay you a percentage of your total claim—usually 20 to 25 percent for first mortgages—and let you keep title to the property, or pay the full claim and take the property.

Of course the mortgage insurance company doesn't insure mortgages for free. It charges a first-time fee (¼ or ½ of 1 percent of the amount of the mortgage is common) and a renewal premium each year. It also protects itself by requiring that the professional lending institution fill out standard mortgage documents and run a tough credit check on the home buyer/borrower.

The borrower is usually willing to pay for the insurance because the institutional lender may lower the down payment if the loan is insured. Sometimes a small down payment like 5 percent becomes acceptable. That's a tempting sweetener for your buyer, isn't it?

How Options Can Solve Sales Problems

An option is a written agreement in which an owner of real estate (called the optionor) sells to another (the optionee) the exclusive right to buy that property at a certain price and at specified terms within a specified time.

It isn't a sales contract because the optionee has no obligation whatsoever to buy. But he can compel the owner/optionor to sell in accordance with the agreement simply by making the specified payment and saying "I exercise my option." Once the option is exercised, a binding sales contract is created.

To you as owner, one advantage of selling an option instead of selling the property is that you receive cash undiminished by any transaction costs such as brokerage commissions, loan fees, appraisal costs, title insurance, escrow fees, or the like.

Sometimes selling an option to buy will get around an enforceable due-on-sale clause in a mortgage. Get a good real estate lawyer to draw up an option contract through which your buyer, instead of making a down payment on the property, pays the same amount as "consideration for the purchase option" to be exercised in five or seven years or whatever time you agree on. Under this contract he must make monthly payments to you to hold open the option. You use part of this money to keep up the payments on the old mortgage. The rest goes to pay off what the buyer owes you—that is, what the purchase price would be if the transaction were a conventional one. It's like a wrap-around mortgage. Since there has been no title transfer, the lender can't enforce the due-on-sale clause. Moreover, the optionee can sell his option to someone else without interference from the lender.

Some lawyers say the IRS considers such a transaction to be a sale for tax purposes. Others say the optionor (seller) pays no income taxes on the option price until the option is either exercised or expired. Ask your own favorite tax expert, if it's important.

Another point about options you should think over carefully: How does the buyer know he'll get a valid title to your property? He can buy title insurance on options, but this doesn't necessarily mean that the title will still be good a few years from now when he exercises his option and gets the deed from you. Maybe your attorney can work out a way for you to guarantee the title.

An option can help you cope with a prospective buyer who wants to leave himself a loophole to back out. All too often, deposit receipts provide for contingencies—"back-door" provisions that let a supposed buyer cancel the deal without liability. For example, he may stipulate that his purchase is contingent upon selling his own house, or upon getting specific financing. So you don't know whether you've made a sale or not.

If a buyer tries to give you a deposit while leaving himself loopholes in the receipt you're supposed to sign, you can counter by proposing an option contract instead. The buyer will pay a certain sum for the right to complete the purchase—but only for a stated time. That sum would be the equivalent of (or bigger than) the deposit he offered you, but wouldn't be refundable. "The option money is payment for the risk I take in keeping the property off the market," you can explain to him.

I think an option agreement is an honest and fair way of dealing with whatever uncertainties may bother a prospective purchaser. It gives him flexibility, but gives you some protection too.

An option can likewise be handy when you need to dispose of

284

a rental house or an apartment property. Instead of buying the property, your prospect can take it over on a lease option, take care of management and upkeep for five years (or whatever period you mutually decide on), and then exercise the option. He'll probably need to take out a new conventional loan at that time, when interest rates probably will be lower. But in the meantime he can simply sell his option, at a nice profit if the property has appreciated in value. It's far easier than taking out a new loan and then selling. If the person who takes the option can't keep up his monthly payments to you, the option lapses and you still have title, without the trouble of foreclosing. The best and most complete information on the use of options is available from Dave Glubetich, President of Impact Publishing Company, 2110 Omega Road, San Ramon, CA 94583. Ask for his Impact Report on the subject.

So you see, there are plenty of ways to move property today —perhaps more than ever before. Don't be panicked by a real estate market that's hit bottom and is likely to bounce back. Don't "give away the whole store" just to liquidate your property. Make the property more marketable by tailoring your terms to attract buyers.

KEY POINTS TO REMEMBER

· If you have high equity in a property, and are paying low interest on an existing loan, consider arranging a wrap-around mortgage and selling the mortgage.
· To sell, you may have to help a buyer with financing.
· Check your mortgage to see whether it contains a due-on-sale clause. If not, a buyer can assume it at the same interest rate.
· A nonassumable mortgage may become assumable when the FHA, VA, or FNMA is involved, or they may grant favorable financing.
· Competition is forcing institutional lenders to be more flexible about mortgage terms. Shop around.
· To get more cash than a buyer can pay, divide his debt to you into several notes, and sell one or more of these.
· If you buy down a buyer's early mortgage payments, he may pay you a higher price.

· A Growing Equity Mortgage may suit a buyer who can't afford
  a big down payment but can make high monthly payments.
· If you finance a buyer, take out private mortgage insurance.
· Selling an option is often a good alternative to selling the property.

18

Get Ahead by Sharing Ownership

In the last few chapters I showed you numerous ways to find and acquire residential properties for prices far below their potential worth. In Chapter 15 I showed how your properties can prosper under rent control.

But what about selling? Most of the real estate you may have bought—and probably wish to continue buying—must eventually be resold if you're to continue building your wealth. Selling brings us to some special problems that arose with the downturn in the economic cycle, and may continue for years after the downswing reverses itself.

Sellers and investors, as well as buyers, have faced new difficulties in a time of widespread unemployment, tight money, factory closings, flat housing prices, and high interest rates.

To cope with these difficulties, a remarkable type of financing arrangement—the shared-equity deal—is emerging. It isn't really new. Commercial and industrial real estate people have often used it to solve many of their problems, by setting up joint ventures with lenders. But it's virtually new in residential real estate, and in my opinion it's here to stay. A real estate revolution, "the most far-reaching in half a century," according to *Fortune,* is in the making. You can be part of it and profit handsomely from it with a little patience.

Where Will Mortgage Money Come From?

We hear on many sides that the real estate market is sluggish or spotty at best, "frozen" at worst. Home resales, as tracked by the National Association of Realtors, dropped 50 percent between 1978 and 1982.

The main housing lenders—the savings and loan associations —are no longer attracting savings and no longer making loans, at least to typical borrowers. The S&Ls are stuck with all those low-interest loans made between 1950 and about 1978.

But depositors are not stuck with the S&Ls. Passbook savers have been flocking to withdraw their deposits and switch into high-yielding money market funds. The "thrift" industry, as it is called, began as a benevolent financial aid to ordinary working folks but now has little money to lend. Likewise, the insurance companies have seen much of their cash waltz out the door as low-interest policy loans. Consequently mortgage rates took off for the sky, and the old long-term fixed-rate mortgage seems to have gone, for awhile, the way of the wrap-around porch.

During the forty years when mortgage interest rates lagged behind inflation, many aggressive borrowers became millionaires. But now the conventional lenders have awakened and changed. They're shortening maturities on their loans, demanding high interest, insisting on cushions against inflation through floating-rate mortgages, or pressing for a piece of the action in the form of "equity kickers," as financial people call them. Why not? How else could they survive?

Five Problems with One Solution

Let's see how the current situation looks through the eyes of five imaginary families, typical of five huge groups.

Mr. and Mrs. Otto Vonderlust, as we'll call them, bought their house for $40,000 in 1970, have paid down their 6 percent mortgage to $20,000, and own a house currently valued at $120,000, which means that their share of it (their equity) is worth $100,000.

Now they'd like to turn that paper profit of $60,000 into real money by selling the house so they can move elsewhere. Maybe they have to move because of a job switch. Maybe they hanker for a different climate, or just want to keep up with the Joneses by moving into a better neighborhood.

But to sell their home they may have to knock the price way down. Or they may have to help a prospective buyer by accepting a huge purchase-money second mortgage—the difference between what a buyer can put down in cash and what he can get from a conventional lender.

By helping with the financing, the Vonderlusts will reduce their return on the sale. Worse yet, if the buyer defaults, they may have to sue to recover their money—or repossess their house, which by then may be badly neglected.

However, there's a better solution available to the Vonderlusts, as you'll see in a minute.

Mr. and Mrs. Struggles have been renters all their lives. They want to become owners, because they realize that paying $400 a month rent means an outgo of $48,000 in ten years with no tax deductions, no equity, no protection against rent increases, no place they can call their own.

Joe Struggles has held a good job for five years, with a raise each year, and he sees a key promotion on the horizon. But when the Struggles find the home they'd like to buy and think they can afford, they're shocked.

Suppose it's a home like the Vonderlusts' with a price tag of $120,000. Their friendly S&L tells them, "You'll need at least $30,000 for the down payment. Also we'll have to charge you closing costs, one-time fees and 'points' of about $10,000. For the $90,000 mortgage loan, the interest will start at 12 percent but we may have to keep raising it every few years, or adding to the loan balance you're paying off. Now then, what's your monthly income? . . . Sorry, folks. Under our formula you don't come close to qualifying for a loan. You'd need an income of $5,000 a month."

So the Struggles must find another way to finance their dream of home ownership. There is a way. We'll get to it.

Mr. and Mrs. Nelson D. Richman are well off financially because they've been buying properties, improving and reselling them, for some years. Their problem is how to keep investing their gains. They've been driven out of the stock market. They've gotten burned on gold and diamonds and collectibles, which all dropped in price. They don't want the work and worries of being a landlord.

They're looking for a reasonably safe investment, trouble-free, that will shelter some of their income from taxes. But just a tax saving isn't enough. They want an investment that is likely to be worth considerably more in five or ten years. Yes, there is such an investment available to the Richmans. Read on.

Builders in the Same Boat

Walt Carpenter and his family are wealthy because he started small, building and selling a house at a time, and gradually expanded. Now he's a builder-developer sitting on a multimillion-dollar project, with most of his wealth tied up in it.

Until about 1979 financing was no problem for people like Carpenter. It came in two stages. First a money-center commercial bank doled out funds to cover costs during the two years or so a project might be under construction. The bank was assured of a commitment from an insurance company or thrift institution for a permanent mortgage, or "take-out," when construction was finished. At that point Walt paid off the bank with proceeds from his permanent loan.

The bank was happy, having collected interest at a hefty markup over the prime rate. And Walt was happy because he usually lined up thirty-year financing that not only "took out" the bank but also gave him an extra 10 percent or more—a builder's profit in his pocket before the first house was sold or the first dollar of rent rolled in. The mortgage, of course, was based on the value of Walt's completed project, worth more as a whole than the cost of its parts financed by the bank while he built it.

Whatever the financing source, lenders routinely required an "equity kicker" from Walt in the form of a convertible mortgage, participation in the project's revenues, or a share in the profits when he sold or refinanced. This was a good deal for both sides, because the dramatic appreciation of apartment complexes and realty tracts in the 1970s made equity financing an attractive hedge against uncertain interest rates and inflation.

But Walt's sources of long-term funds shriveled as the thrifts and life insurers found themselves paying higher, and variable, rates to get lendable cash. So they refused to finance his current project unless he could get it 40 percent leased or sold before he broke ground. He couldn't meet such a tough requirement.

Nevertheless he thought he'd be okay, because he paid part of the construction costs with his money, and his bank dispensed the rest even though no lender had promised to make the take-out loan. (Developers call this "going naked.") Walt and the bank felt sure his solid reputation would bring him a mortgage loan at the end.

Walt's project is completed now, but sales are slow because would-be buyers can't qualify for residential-mortgage loans. Nor can Walt qualify for the usual long-term mortgage on his project. Meanwhile the bank is pressing for payment of its short-term loan. Bankers adore certainties, deplore uncertainties. So do their cousins the S&L people.

Walt is selling some homes, but mainly by offering big "buy-downs." That is, he gives the buyer a sum of money to reduce mortgage payments for a set period, often three years, which helps the buyer qualify for a bigger loan than he could get other-wise. Walt pays buy-downs to provide interest rates as low as 11.75 percent in the first year of the mortgage.

Normally the cost of the buy-down would be passed along to buyers in the form of higher purchase prices. But Walt is afraid to do this for fear his homes will stop selling.

Other builders feel the same. This has produced what they call a "profitless boom" among builder-developers. They're willing to accept paper-thin profits to stay in business and be ready for the time when a robust housing market returns.

The fifth family in our cast of characters is that of Marge and Tom Deale. They are real estate salespeople. They've done well in the past, but now they're suffering through the worst year for residential sales in their area since 1945. Legions of would-be sellers aren't selling. And legions of would-be buyers aren't buy-ing, even though the Deales keep telling them, "This is really the best time in recent years to buy," which is true.

Except in terms of size, all our characters are in the same boat: the big builder, the small broker, the well-heeled investor, the frustrated seller, and the poor renter looking for his first home. They have a common problem. And equity sharing can be the solution for each of them.

What Is Equity Sharing?

Equity sharing, equity partnerships, equity participation purchase (EPP), shared appreciation mortgage (SAM), shared equity mortgage (SEM)—there are many names for the basic idea, and many variations.

They all stem from one simple thought: to team a potential buyer with an investor, sharing ownership of a property, so that both benefit when it is resold or exchanged or refinanced at a profit.

The investor can be an individual, a corporation, a mortgage lender, a builder-developer, or even the former owner of the property. This investor may assist a buyer by putting up all or part of the down payment and/or monthly payment. In exchange for this help, the investor gets an equity.

Here's an example. The lender—let's say he's a homeowner wishing to sell—underwrites the buyer's purchase when the buyer can't otherwise swing it. After a number of years, usually five or seven, the home buyer thus assisted will either sell his home or refinance. At that time he and the investor (or home seller) will split the gain in the home's value—normally in proportion to their contribution: 50–50, 60–40 or whatever.

This buyer–seller pooling of interests is so highly regarded that in 1979 the Federal Home Loan Bank approved it for use by the nation's savings and loan associations. So far only a few S&Ls have used it, because most thrifts are so painfully illiquid that they don't want to wait even five years to collect their share of a home's appreciation.

The first S&L to dip a toe in the unfamiliar waters was Florida-based Coast Federal. "We sold $2.5 million in three days," reported Emily Etter of Coast. "We reduced the going interest rate, which was then around 12 percent, down to 8½. It was good for young people who could never qualify otherwise, and for older couples who didn't mind giving up part of their future appreciation." In return for reducing the interest rate, Coast will take one-third of the profit on the houses when sold.

Advance Mortgage Company, the nation's fourth-largest mortgage banker, pioneered its version of the SAM in 1980. It set up a $10 million pool of thirty-year loans at fixed rates well below market. "That $10 million commitment was gone in record-breaking time," said Ed Lindlow of Advance Mortgage. "We took stacks of backups."

The Trouble with SAMs

Under the most common SAM arrangement, lenders provide funds at a rate one-third lower than the prevailing mortgage rate, then cut themselves in for a one-third slice of the profits when the house is sold. But they protect themselves with a stipulation that even if the house hasn't been sold after ten years, the borrower must pay the lender his share of any appreciation. This bothers borrowers. Suppose they're short of money when that time comes?

Often the lender's answer is "We'll guarantee to provide you with new long-term financing after ten years, with any type of mortgage (and interest rate) we're offering at that time." But if real estate prices keep climbing at annual rates of 10 to 20 percent or more, as they did in the late 1970s, the new mortgage in the 1990s could be so large, and the monthly payments so heavy, that some SAM borrowers might be forced to move.

Even if inflation subsides and mortgage rates come down, a home buyer who can get a fixed-rate mortgage now at 12 percent and who keeps his home more than ten years should be slightly better off than a SAM borrower. On the other hand, if the SAM borrower can hold onto the $200 per month or so that he saves on mortgage payments and stash this away in securities yielding 12 percent, at the end of ten years his savings (with dividends reinvested) would total about $46,000 pretax. Added to the equity he would then have in his house, his total holding would be better than the fixed-rate borrower's.

The first few institutional lenders, like Coast Federal and Advance Mortgage, haven't continued to offer SAMs. "We didn't stop because the buying public cooled off, but because the secondary market for SAMs shut down," Mr. Lindlow explained. "Investors simply didn't think it was good business to be tied up for thirty years. The secondary-market people might become more comfortable with a shorter commitment and some other changes."

The "secondary market" is where mortgage loans are either

sold outright to long-term investors or packaged into mortgage securities and sold, via Wall Street, to institutional investors or pension funds. This resale market has become a sorrow to the thrifts. During the forty years when rates were relatively stable, outstanding mortgages kept their value. If an S&L had any need for cash, it could sell old mortgages for almost 100 cents on the dollar. But when interest rates went through the roof, these low-yielding mortgages became worth only about 60 cents on the dollar in the secondary market.

You might think SAMs wouldn't be discounted so heavily in the secondary-mortgage market. Usually they're not. But the trouble is that the biggest buyers in this market are such federal entities as Government National Mortgage Association (Ginnie Mae) and Federal Home Loan Mortgage Corporation (Freddie Mac). These outfits won't buy a mortgage if the borrower's monthly payment exceeds 30 percent of his pretax income.

This rule made most new mortgages, of whatever kind, unsalable to Ginnie Mae and Freddie Mac in 1981. By that time annual payments on new mortgages nationwide were running at more than one-third of the average household income. In several big cities payments on conventional mortgages represented 40 or 42 percent of the household income, according to the *Wall Street Journal*.

Investors to the Rescue

In short, the market's judgment has gone against the S&Ls, and they may never again be much help in real estate investment. (In California, where S&Ls have always been bigger and stronger than in any other state, fewer than one in five home sales were financed by an S&L loan in 1982.) More than a thousand thrift institutions could merge or fail by the end of 1983, according to a Brookings Institution study.

But to other kinds of investors, various equity-sharing arrangements—particularly the shared equity mortgage (SEM) and equity participation purchase (EPP)—are increasingly attractive. Electronic Realty Associates, in Kansas City, started a SEM program in March 1982. It matches buyers with investors who are willing to make down payments or subsidize monthly mortgage payments. In return, the investor, who becomes co-owner, is entitled to 75 percent of the home's appreciation. Electronic Realty's president, Michael Jackson, says the program has been doing fine even though housing prices mostly stopped rising in 1982. "The American consumer believes residential real estate will ultimately appreciate," he says.

California's most vocal salesman for shared-equity buying is Richard Palowski, president of Help-U-Buy System, Inc. "It's just a matter of making the seller a partner," he says. "What could make more sense for a seller than to sell half of his home at 80 percent of its value?" Through seminars and direct sales campaigns he is promoting HUB as a computerized data base to bring home buyers and investors together.

The agreement form available to HUB's 250 members (primarily real estate brokers) is usable "in 90 percent of the cases, and it doesn't cost you anything to walk into a broker-member's office and use it," Mr. Palowski says. "Of course you can have your own agreement drawn up, but the chances are it won't be approved by the IRS." He says he paid $60,000 to attorneys for designing his agreement form.

Home Partners of America, a corporation based in Washington, D.C., is promoting a plan called Shared Equity Participation. The corporation will pay three-quarters of the down payment (which is a tremendous help to home buyers in an era when the down payment may be more than the whole house cost in 1965) and will pay half of the closing costs as well as half of the monthly mortgage payment including taxes and insurance. The corporation becomes half-owner in the house, but its generous concessions take most of the sting out of giving up equity. The buyer signs a lease agreement for a monthly rental over and above the remaining half of the mortgage payment. This lease covers the corporation's share of the mortgage payment plus a reasonable return on its investment.

Dave Del Dotto's real estate agency in California has become widely known as a leader in putting together equity participation purchases (EPPs), even though his brokers find it a "hard sell," to prospective home buyers. One broker told a reporter, "It's difficult for people to swallow the idea of owning half a house. But after they've been out there in the marketplace a while, they come back and want to hear more about it. Lately it's coming more and more our way." He added that an investor in Arizona who owns thirteen houses had just asked the agency to sell them all on EPP.

Mr. Del Dotto's book on equity participation, *101 Purchase Offers Sellers Can't Resist,* is available for $49.00 from Impact Publishing Company, 2110 Omega Road, San Ramon, CA 94583. It gives details of dozens of innovative equity-sharing offers in actual use.

His examples are structured for properties in the most popular and affordable price range of about $80,000 or under. The formulas are workable even in the huge Southern California market, where the median home price is $104,000, according to a 1981 survey by the National Association of Realtors. The same survey, and others, have pegged the median home price at $64,000 in Chicago, $70,000 in Atlanta, $77,500 in Denver and $88,500 in Houston. (In 1968, existing homes sold for a median price throughout the country of $20,000. This gives you an idea of the nationwide appreciation in homes over the long haul.)

Big New Sources of Mortgage Money

In equity participation the seller, the buyer, and the investor can all be winners. But usually they must wait a few years for their winnings, since these winnings depend on the property's going up in price. When the inflation rate was in the high double digits, prices of homes and apartment buildings rose every month. But as I write, with inflation eased off, at least temporarily, nobody is likely to make quick killings in shared-equity deals—or in any other sound investment, for that matter. If you're the type who wants to multiply your money in a hurry, take it to a racetrack or a roulette table, or try some speculations in penny stocks.

Americans have pretty much lost the habit of individual saving. They've been penalized by inflation and the tax system, so that the old passbook savings account looks foolish. Still, two forms of saving remain widespread: the equity built up in houses, and the pension funds of corporations, unions, and state and local governments. Aha! The pension funds! Could they be a source of mortgage money for shared-equity buying and selling? Yes indeed.

Pension funds needn't set such stiff standards as Freddie Mac and Ginnie Mae, which must answer ultimately to Congress and immediately to the Federal Home Bank Board or the U.S. Department of Housing and Urban Development, respectively. Therefore the pension funds will probably become a receptive secondary market for SAMs, SEMs, EPPS and other new types of mortgage instruments.

In addition these funds seem almost ready to pour millions directly into shared-equity investments. Because of their tax exemptions and their long-term mission, pension funds prefer to defer their income (unlike S&Ls, whose needs now are for current income). The fund managers are looking for low-risk investments payable five or ten years from now, and preferably even farther in the future, if these investments keep growing in value.

From observer after observer we hear mentions of pension funds as potential co-investors in real estate. For instance, Help-U-Buy's Palowski says he has lined up one pension administrator with $10 million at his dispoal. And the *Los Angeles Times* for June 13, 1982, reported:

"A spot check of representative pension plan administrators would suggest that interest is high in shared equities as an investment outlet. Max Sullivan, director of the Arizona State Employee Retirement Fund, concedes that his people have 'talked about it and certainly have an interest in it.' . . . In San Francisco, C. Bruce Sutherland, administrator of all the fringe benefit funds in Northern California for the Carpenters Union Pension Fund, says his organization 'has the idea under very serious consideration' and is definitely considering SAMs under an arrangement where his pension fund would offer mortgage interest rates at one-third under the prevailing market rate in exchange for one-third the future appreciation of the home."

Other mountains of money are also moving toward this type of investment. *Barron's,* the national financial weekly, reported on June 14, 1982, that "More and more real-estate investment trusts (REITs) have become equity-oriented, owning properties rather than dispensing construction loans and mortgages, and the equity REITs have performed creditably." As you may know, REITs are private corporations that give small investors the chance to share in leveraged investments and tax shelters of the sort that have made the rich richer. A REIT pays no taxes as long as it passes on to its shareholders virtually all its earnings.

A few insurance companies, which likewise get helpful tax exemptions, are rescuing some small homeowners who couldn't meet balloon payments on second trust deeds. The insurers land enough to pay off those debts, in return for a portion of the homeowner's equity.

More spectacularly, some major insurance companies are bailing out builders unable to get either construction loans or take-out commitments. Recently Prudential Life Insurance teamed up with a small midwestern building company. The Pru has agreed to provide $20 million to complete a $30 million office building. When the building is rented, two-thirds of the profits will go to the Pru, plus a guaranteed 10 percent annual return on its $20 million. (This of course is a considerably lower interest rate than the building company could have gotten elsewhere.) In addition, if the building is sold or refinanced, the Pru will get not only two-thirds of any appreciation in the price but also a kicker in the form of an extra one-tenth of the appreciation.

This imaginative deal was worked out by a Los Angeles accounting firm, Kenneth Leventhal & Co., a specialist in real estate with eleven offices across the nation and a remarkable record of financial innovation. Unlike other accountants, Ken Leventhal and his partner Stan Ross spend much of their time helping clients find ingenious ways to solve financing problems. Ross recently told *Fortune* that the next great wave of change in real estate will be renewed interest in the field by non-real estate companies.

Two Leventhal clients, Ford and Sears Roebuck, have both been making realty investments for some time. In 1979 Sears created a new subsidiary to put Sears money into mortgage loans with equity kickers. Ford owns most of Detroit's big office and shopping complex, Renaissance Center, and has developed a lot of land in Dearborn.

How Individuals Can Benefit

On a much smaller scale, any cash-heavy bargain hunter can use equity sharing just as Sears, Ford, the Prudential, the REITs, and the pension funds do. He or she can share the risks—and the potential profits—with individual buyers and sellers of real estate. To these buyers and sellers, giving up a share of equity to an investor will often enable them to make transactions that would be impossible otherwise.

Let's see how equity sharing can help all those imaginary unhappy families I sketched earlier in this chapter.

Consider the Vonderlusts—and the multitudes of actual homeowners in similar predicaments. They've dreamed of cashing out all their bloated equity in a sale to some eager home buyer. But now it's a buyer's market. FOR SALE signs have stood in front of many houses for months.

Families forced to move because of a job transfer are finding out the hard way the difficulty of trying to sell one house and buy another. Some owners who've moved are giving up trying to sell and are renting their previous homes, or have sold at sacrifice prices and become renters themselves. Other families are in worse shape because of unemployment: maybe they're still facing a $900-a-month payment on their first trust deed and $450 a month on a second. So they can't trim their asking price by much.

But let's say the Vonderlusts are visited by a rescuer—someone like Marge Deale, who shows them several ways to get out from under.

Seller Becomes a Partner

"You've probably heard that about 85 percent of all real estate sales this year have been made by the seller becoming a lender," she tells the Vonderlusts. "In other words, the seller provides most of the financing by taking a second trust deed for three, five or seven years, at a lower interest rate than a lending institution would demand. But if you do this, at the end of those years you say, 'Mr. Buyer, you've got to go out and find your own loan to pay me off, or I'll take back the house,' which will be a nuisance all round. So it's a risky sale.

"Instead of that, I can bring you together with an investor named Mr. Richman. He doesn't want to live in your house. He wants to buy a piece of it as an investment. In return for part ownership, he'll write you a check for $25,000 or whatever you need immediately. He'll assume the mortgage, but you'll make payments to him at below-market rates. Maybe he'll rent the house to someone, if he and I can't sell it soon at a profit.

"You'll still be a part owner too—what the lawyers call a 'tenant in common.' Assuming your present equity in the house is worth $100,000, you'll be a 75 percent owner—so when the house is eventually sold you'll get 75 percent of the profits."

"What if it's sold for less than $100,000?" Otto asks.

Marge says, "I think I can get Mr. Richman to guarantee, in your equity-sharing agreement, that you'll get $75,000 back before he starts taking his share. So you're safer than he is. I know you'd rather sell the whole house, but where can you find a buyer who'll put $25,000 down? This way you're getting part of your payoff now, and you're retaining a chance for a juicy profit a few years from now."

Renter Becomes an Owner

Marge also suggests another equity-sharing possibility to the Vonderlusts:

"I know a family, the Struggles, who do want to buy. They're renters now. First-time home buyers usually need bushels of money nowadays, because of the high interest rates on mortgages. The Struggles don't have a bushel. However, they can afford to pay you $15,000 now plus $600 a month. So instead of just renting to them or someone else, why not let the Struggles move in as owners of 15 percent? They'll make payments for as long as five years, at which time—or before—they can buy you out, or vice versa. If the property goes up an average of 10 percent a year, and it's worth $120,000 now, it will be worth $180,000 in five years. Your share of the $60,000 profit would be $51,000, theirs would be $9,000."

The Vonderlusts, who never fancied themselves in anything but full-owner roles, carrying a thirty-year mortgage, gradually adjust to the idea of part ownership and the attending uncertainties of dividing a profit with a co-owner not too many years from now.

They like the idea of letting the Struggles move in as co-investors rather than renters. In effect the Struggles will be paying "payments" to the Vonderlusts, of course, but they'll feel pride of ownership, and will do their own property management instead of phoning the Vonderlusts whenever anything goes wrong, as tenants do with a landlord.

Thus the Vonderlusts can escape the headaches of absentee ownership, without having to lose out on all the future value of the property. Moreover, they convert their home to an income property, and thus can begin depreciating it and sheltering some income.

The Struggles too would rather buy the house outright, with help from a bank or an S&L, so they could get the full profit when they resell. But purchase isn't possible for them in today's market. Becoming part owners is better than renting. They'll probably get deductions on their joint-ownership interest, will avoid the closing costs and points they'd have to pay in getting a mortgage, and will be making smaller monthly payments than an S&L would require. Because of these various savings, they'll probably end up with as much spendable cash each month as they did when they paid only $400 a month rent.

The co-tenancy agreement protects them from all the hazards of a renter's life, such as intermittent rent increases, possible eviction at the whim of a landlord, and dependence on the property manager for whatever upkeep will be needed.

An Investor Can Help Buyer and Seller

If the Vonderlusts need more cash than the Struggles can scrape up, the Deales may bring in the Richmans to share ownership with both. Or it could be anyone else with spare T-bills, an inheritance, a chunk of cash from the sale of a business or other property. It could be an oil-rich Arab, a prosperous attorney or accountant, or a well-to-do relative of the Struggles or Vonderlusts.

Whoever it is, he or she can make the down payment for the Struggles and/or monthly payments, in exchange for part ownership of the house and a share of the profit when it is sold. By combining forces, the *two* new owners will qualify for a new mortgage, and the Struggles can move in.

For many investors, this sort of silent partnership is much more attractive than owning an apartment building or a string of rental homes. There's a prospective high total return on investment. Meanwhile there's no worry about negative cash flow, no difficulties with tenants or any of the other management problems that sometimes confront owners. They can own a stake in more properties for less investment. They'll probably get tax write-offs for their share of depreciation, interest, and property taxes. (Be sure to consult a tax expert in figuring the tax consequences of any particular equity deal.)

Sometimes investors like Richman, with help from brokers or advisers—or on their own if they're aggressive and experienced —can put together their own equity-sharing packages, and cash out quickly by selling half to an investor/occupant and half to a new co-investor. Here's one way it might be done.

Richman contracts to buy a home. Then he runs an advertisement:

$1,500 DOWN

buys half ownership of 3 bedroom, 2 bath home in good area. Payments like rent at $476 per month. No qualifying. Call owner at 555-1234.

This attracts someone like the Struggles who agree, for a 50 percent equity, to pay Richman $1,500 cash, to pay the monthly payments, and to live in the house and maintain it.

Thereupon Richman runs another ad:

GOOD YIELD

Only $4,500 cash buys half ownership of rental home. No management, no maintenance costs or work, no negative cash flow. Call owner at 555-1234.

Another investor sees the ad and pays Richman $4,500 for his remaining 50 percent share and position.

This is one good way to dispose of properties you've picked up at foreclosure sales, at some other types of auctions, or from owners facing foreclosure. Another good way is to make a deal with a distressed owner, letting him become the investor/occupant.

There are countless other possible combinations. Equity-sharing agreements can be as flexible as you and your prospective partners require. From time to time my associates and I give one-day seminars in equity sharing in various parts of the country. Here are some of the combinations we describe:

Nine Ways to Set Up an EPP

(1) Buyer puts no money down. He assumes existing mortgage, which is half the sales price. He executes a twenty-year second note and deed of trust to seller (at no interest) for the other half of the sales price. Seller lives rent free for up to twenty years, after which time house is to be sold and note paid.

(2) Buyer-occupant assumes existing loan and pays one-third down payment. The other two-thirds is paid by another investor. Each owns half. Seller carries second mortgage for two years at 10 percent with no payment until maturity.

(3) Buyer assumes high existing FHA loan. He makes no down payment. Seller carries $10,000 equity for two years at no interest. Then buyer receives one-half proceeds from escrow and $10,000 original equity.

(4) Buyer assumes existing first mortgage, and obtains second mortgage with proceeds paid to seller and to lender, thus covering points and closing costs. Buyer executes third note to seller for two years at no interest. Seller owns one-half; receives half of tax deductions. Seller receives half of the proceeds from sale in two years plus third note payoff.

(5) Buyer obtains maximum FHA 245 loan. Co-investor makes down payment and partial monthly mortgage payment, for agreed-upon ratio of ownership and term of partnership.

(6) Co-buyers obtain FHA 234 Plan 111 loan. Owner A will occupy. Owner B makes down payment. Each owns half.

(7) Seller refinances for maximum assumable loan, at lowest interest possible. Buyer assumes seller's loan. Buyer executes second note and trust deed to seller (interest free) for five years, in exchange for seller's equity. Seller still owns half, and receives half of net proceeds from sale plus cash payment to third note.

(8) Seller obtains maximum assumable refinance. Buyer assumes loan and executes second note secured by trust deed to seller in the amount of seller's equity. Interest rate and term are

agreed upon. Payment on second note to be made at time of sale. Seller to be one-fourth owner.

(9) Buyer assumes existing loan, subject to obtaining co-buyer to make down payment. Buyer owns two-thirds equity above present purchase price. Co-buyer owns one-third plus second note secured by trust deed in the amount of down payment. Co-buyers work out terms of partnership.

An Escape Hatch for Builders

This book isn't primarily addressed to builders of homes or developers of realty tracts. But you may be able to help them (and yourself, of course) by teaming up with them. That's why I mentioned Walt Carpenter earlier in this chapter. He is one of the five typical participants in this kind of financing vehicle.

You remember Walt, our imaginary builder-developer. Developers have been badly battered in the early 1980s. By mid-1982 there were more than a million unemployed construction workers, and more than 1,900 building firms had failed during the recession that began in 1979 (the seventh cyclical recession for the construction industry in this century). In California alone, three-fourths of the state's 5,000 home builders were idle because so few people could afford new homes.

If you look around, you can probably find someone like Walt, saddled with a bunch of unsold houses. Explain equity participation to him and see if he won't let you pick up a few of his houses on good terms.

As an investor or co-investor, Walt could refinance his unsold homes up to 80 percent of their value. This would release his money tied up in construction loans and get him a lower interest rate. Then those houses could be sold as no-down deals, with the co-investor/occupant taking over the payments on the 80 percent loan. The builder could carry back the remaining 20 percent for his half interest in the property.

This is good for the builder, the buyer, and the banks. Consider:

The builder can free up his construction loans, pay his workers, sell out of this project, and go on to another one—so more houses may get built. He'll have money coming in down the road, too, when his original co-investors sell their homes and he collects his half of their future appreciation. Or if he needs the money sooner, he can sell his interest to other investors.

Buyers would get no-money-down homes. And with more houses being built, more people could buy.

The banks could liquidate their construction loans instead of foreclosing on a whole development of houses that they'd then have to try to sell. Moreover, with the builder paying off those high-interest construction loans faster, he wouldn't have to price the houses too high in order to cover his costs.

I think equity sharing is far better for builders and everyone else than those builders' buy-downs, which are often deceptive. Newspaper and magazine ads for condominiums, cooperatives, and new single-family homes often trumpet rates of 9¾ percent, 10½ percent and the like. In reality the buy-down periods for these loans are sometimes as short as six months, after which buyers are faced with the full rates. This fact escapes some buyers' notice because it may be disclosed only in small print, and is seldom stressed by sales agents eager to close a sale. And as I mentioned earlier, when builders can get away with it they tack their buy-down costs onto the price of the home.

What If Property Values Stop Rising?

For equity sharing to be profitable, obviously there must be upward price movement. The same is true of virtually all investments in real estate and other commodities.

If America should go through a deflation like that of the 1930s, some owners of real estate would face a loss in selling. So would owners of almost everything else. (However, their fewer dollars would buy more during a deflation, so they might not be as badly hurt as they fear.)

As I write, the housing market is sluggish in most parts of the country. Net prices are down when the effect of financing by sellers is figured in. Yet history would indicate that this is only temporary. For the past sixty years housing prices have gone up an average of 13 percent yearly. (Of course they shot up much more than that in some years.)

Occupancy rates are near saturation in most parts of the country. With housing scarce, it's hard to visualize prices staying flat for more than a year or two. The demand for homes and apartments is growing as the supply is slipping. Our number of households is increasing at twice the rate of our population. This pent-up demand for housing seems sure to push prices up.

Kenneth T. Rosen, chairman of the real estate and urban economics program at the University of California, sees the price decline as temporary. "This is normal and to be expected due to high interest rates. A price drop has happened during every housing recession, although this one is more severe than usual. Nothing is fundamentally wrong. As soon as the economy grows, housing will roughly keep pace with inflation."

In California alone the population has grown by 755,200 since the 1980 census, according to the state Department of Finance. Nationwide, about 600,000 existing homes need to be replaced each year. Fewer than a million new units were built in 1981—the lowest number since the early 1940s. No building boom is in sight.

On June 23, 1982, the *Wall Street Journal* headlined: "Rental Apartments Becoming a Healthy Investment Again." Why? Because the rental housing market is tight and getting tighter. So there's a deepening shortage of all kinds of residential units.

To me, this means that the long rise in housing prices must soon resume, even if other prices slump. We don't need a runaway inflation for housing appreciation: the law of supply and demand is enough.

The best way to cash in on future housing appreciation, if you're a small investor, is by sharing ownership. The highly respected Marvin B. Starr, editor and publisher of the *Real Estate Tax Digest,* sees this as I do. "The shared-equity concept can stand on its own investment merits," he writes. "If it is allowed to do so, it will probably make a significant contribution to the home-buying market."

KEY POINTS TO REMEMBER

· Buyers, sellers, and lenders may all profit through equity sharing, which divides the profit when a property is eventually resold or refinanced.

- Pension funds may become co-investors in real estate. So may REITs and insurance companies.
- A renter may be glad to pay extra for part ownership.
- Look for investors willing to share ownership with a buyer and seller.
- There are countless possible combinations for sharing equity. Study them.
- If you buy or sell or invest with an equity kicker, don't expect it to bring a quick profit. You may have to wait until property values start climbing again, which is almost sure to happen in a few years.
- Be sure to seek the help of an attorney who is skilled in structuring equity-sharing contracts. A well-written contract will protect each participant from various contingencies that may occur.

_19_

Syndications: Power Through Pooling

Ever daydreamed about having millions of dollars to invest? Sure you have. We all fantasize about how we'd use megabucks.

In your daydreams, where did you decide to invest your millions? Probably in real estate—buying big apartment complexes, office buildings, shopping centers, right? That's where countless millionaires really do put their heavy cash, for excellent reasons, which we'll see. We'll also see how a small investor really can become part owner of such big properties.

How to Invest Where Millionaires Do

One of the big changes in American life during recent decades has been the gradual discovery by small investors that they can join together in groups to rake in the safe, steady, solid profits previously reserved for huge investors.

In the 1950s thousands of people found out about mutual funds, through which they could invest in diversified packages of stocks and bonds chosen by professional investment managers.

For the average investor this was far better than bucking the market on his own, risking his cash on just a few securities, any of which might turn sour enough to destroy all his profits. He could spread his risk by owning a fraction of each stock in the fund's large and varied portfolio. He would share proportionately in a multimillion-dollar pool managed by well-paid experts who studied the market intensively and could buy cheaply, since they bought in wholesale lots. And he would have little paperwork— in fact, none at all if he chose; he could just sit back and cash the regular dividend checks from the mutual fund.

This type of investing revolutionized the stock market by bringing millions of people into it. Of course they all lost during periods of broad market decline, but by the late 1970s there were more than six hundred different funds serving small investors.

Proving again that there's no limit to man's inventiveness in the pursuit of profit, a brand-new type of fund was born in 1974. This was the "liquid asset" fund, concentrating its investments in the short-term money market, where money is literally bought and sold via bank, corporate, and government IOU's. These are extremely safe and liquid investments, but they aren't available to ordinary people. Treasury bills are sold at a $10,000 minimum. Most banks won't go below $25,000 in short-term negotiable certificates of deposit, and won't offer a worthwhile rate of interest on less than $100,000. So people with only a few thousand to invest were shut out of the money market's yields—which ranged from 8 to 16 percent, and sometimes higher, according to the prevailing rates each day—and had to park their savings in a bank or S&L for a humdrum 5¼ percent. But now the "money" funds make it easy for the little fellow to prosper with the bigs. The response has been colossal. By mid-1982 almost $200 billion was invested in these funds.

Armchair Buyers of Real Estate

The pooling idea gradually spread into several kinds of real estate investment. The earliest of these were the real estate investment trusts, known as REITS (pronounced "reets" by money men). They were created to attract money from small investors and make it available to realty promoters and builders.

REITs are somewhat like mutual funds and money funds, except that they invest in real estate (mostly mortgages, in the beginning) rather than securities or short-term commercial paper. They raise money in two ways. First they sell shares to the public, as do all investment funds. Then they go out and borrow.

Some borrow from banks, others sell bonds to the public. Either way, the debt gives the shares leverage. Thus, without ever leaving his armchair, an investor can put money into leveraged investments and tax shelters of the kind that attract the rich.

Like the mutual funds, a REIT pays no taxes as long as it passes on to its shareholders virtually all its earnings. These earnings arise mainly from the spread between what it pays for its money and what it gets when it lends—just like a bank. (If it has tax losses, these can't be passed through to stockholders.)

In the early 1970s you could find many varieties of REITS. Some bought and held property for income. Some specialized in construction lending. Others did nothing but write mortgages. All were borrowing for short terms (supposedly at lower interest rates) to lend at longer terms (supposedly at higher rates).

In theory they could borrow from banks more cheaply than builders and developers could, because the cushion of the stockholder's equity made the loan safer. In 1973 HUD estimated that REITs were financing one-fourth of all new apartment-house construction in the country. At their peak in 1974 REITs controlled about $16 billion worth of real estate.

But that was the year of a painful recession. Suddenly the real estate market looked overbuilt. Lending institutions' rates rocketed upward. In two years many REITs went back to their cocoons or down the tubes, as they and their stockholders discovered that it hadn't been safe to invest in real estate and construction projects far from the eye of a guiding expert. ("You buy property in an area you don't know," one executive said, "and it's with you a long, long time.")

By 1976 most REITs were choking on defaulted condominium loans and busted apartment deals. It will be years before Florida bulldozes away the unfinished, shoddy condos and unwanted shopping centers built with money lent through REITs. However, REITs that had been organized by insurance companies had been more prudent. They were less eager to establish tax losses to make profits tax-free, more interested in long-term profits. In the late 1970s more and more of them abandoned their one-time roles as lenders and became equity-oriented—owning properties rather than dispensing construction loans and mortgages.

Those that survived into the 1980s are, in general, much more soundly financed than they were a decade earlier. Their total assets are back up to $13 billion, and some of them pay dividends of 13 percent or more. If you like real estate investments and leverage, you might learn about REITs and the varieties thereof. They offer a chance for better-than-average future income and capital gains. But before buying shares, check on their individual managements. How skilled are they? Is theirs a professional and highly motivated team?

One of the real estate trusts now praised (mildly) by the respected Value Line Investment Survey, which compiles quarterly analyses of most New York Stock Exchange firms, is BankAmerica Realty. In 1974 about 48 percent of its total capital was short-term debt—hardly gilt-edged. But at this writing (1983) debt due within one year is less than 20 percent of its total capital. Equitable Life Mortgage, also rated a medium-good investment by Value Line, likewise has only 20 percent of total capital in short-term debt, down from more than 60 percent at its peak.

Perhaps the best-looking of the REITs covered by Value Line is First Union Real Estate Equity and mortgage Investments. Since mid-1978 it has boosted its dividend nine times, while earnings per share have grown about 25 percent yearly. The stock price has nearly doubled to $15 a share in that time. But take a close look before you buy. I'm not personally recommending the stock, because I don't know much about it, and even Value Line rates it just "average" for safety and for price performance during the next twelve months.

The New Trend: Limited Partnerships

In its issue of June 14, 1982, the authoritative financial weekly *Barron's* called attention to "the explosive growth of publicly offered real-estate limited partnerships, tapping investment dollars that in an earlier day might have gone to the REITs." Explosive? Indeed, amazing. Balcor Company, just one of the so-called Big Six real-estate syndicators, currently manages about $1.5 billion in real estate assets for about 35,000 investors, according to *Barron's*.

Other statistics highlight the new trend. The National Association of Securities Dealers says there were almost twice as many public syndications (limited partnerships, that is) buying real estate in 1981 as in 1980. They raised more than a billion dollars in 1981. This is a continuation of a growth that has kept speeding up since 1978.

Yet public syndications are less than half the story. Private syndications (I'll explain the difference in a moment) don't have to be approved by federal authorities, and they invest three to four times as much capital as the public syndications do, by the calculations of the Real Estate Securities and Syndication Institute (RESSI). This means that private syndications in 1981 probably totalled about $8.8 billion. RESSI has projected that the total would be around $12.5 billion in 1982, according to Alan Parisse.

Twelve and a half billion bucks. What kind of properties could you buy if you used a tiny fraction of that bankroll, say, half a million, in your own real estate investments?

You can, you know.

Every month in every city, limited partnerships are forming to invest in real estate. With just a few thousand dollars you can buy into one or more. It's not unusual for one to command capital in the high six figures.

For People with Extra Money but No Time

Like the other types of pool I mentioned earlier in this chapter, a real estate syndication is designed for people who want to put their spare money to profitable use but haven't time or expertise to buy and sell on their own account.

It's a way to be a silent partner in a big-money enterprise guided (usually) by an expert. For passive investment, I think it's better in some ways than the other types of pooling.

One way it's better is that the profit potential is bigger, because of the leverage and because major real estate holdings tend to rise automatically in value. (Sometimes they multiply tenfold in ten years, with very little risk during the holding period.) You can't reasonably hope to multiply your money by putting cash in a money fund, which seldom yields more than 10 percent interest per year—or buying stock in a REIT, which sometimes pays fairly high interest and sometimes rises in price but seldom doubles—or by investing in mutual funds, which likewise tend to show good gains over a period of years, but may suffer a few down years. You can buy all these, or any individual stock, through a stockbroker—who will probably warn you that the only stocks with a chance of doubling or tripling in a few years are speculative. Historically, real estate has outperformed stocks and bonds year after year.

Another way realty syndications are better than most other investments is that they provide tax benefits available only to real estate investors. You probably know about the depreciation write-off, the deductible expenses, the lighter tax on installment sales. These and other benefits are passed on to partners in the syndicate for use in their own tax returns, just as if they were individual owners. In Chapter 20 I'll explain the tax advantages of syndications in more detail.

However, there are two disadvantages I'd better make clear right now.

The Liquidity Factor

First, your investment isn't very liquid. If you want easy access to your money, put it in a REIT or a mutual fund, or a money-market fund. In the first two of these, you can redeem your shares for whatever their market value may be that day—maybe more than what you paid for them, maybe less. In a typical money-market fund your shares are always at par ($1 each, normally) so you'll get back whatever you've put in plus accumulated interest, just as in a bank.

Of course you can't do that when you buy real estate, either as part of a pool or as an individual. Sometimes unsophisticated people say to me, "We have a number of investments in real estate limited partnerships. Can you tell us how to go about liquidating them? We need the cash for other purposes." Sadly, I have to explain that real estate partnerships are nonliquid by their nature, just as houses and apartment buildings are. Nobody should invest in a real estate syndicate if he thinks he may need his capital before the investment's sponsor expects to sell the property.

This doesn't mean it's impossible to liquidate. Sometimes

there's a small secondary market for units in public syndications; if investors want out they should get in touch with the broker, if any, who may have sold them the units. Even in a private syndication, the general partner or a broker will sometimes buy out a limited partner who wants to sell his share. Either way, this share won't sell for its full current value, because anyone buying it will want some discount for taking over the nonliquidity.

Another possibility is to call Liquidity Fund (415-652-1462), a company based in San Francisco. It buys units of most limited partnerships, public and private. It will evaluate an investor's units and make an offer based on the current value. Quite often investors can sell to Liquidity Fund for considerably more than their original investment. It all depends on how long the partnership has owned property, how much the property has appreciated, how high the cash flow is, and how soon the property is likely to be sold.

Still another possibility is for the cash-hungry investor to talk to his acquaintances and try to get someone to buy his interest in the partnership. Naturally he'd better be prepared to explain all the facts about the investment and its current value as well as potential future value. Any buyer with his or her head screwed on right will offer less than the investment is worth—but the value of becoming liquid can be worth the discount, especially if the seller can still make a profit on his original investment.

Waiting Can Be Worthwhile

I hope everyone who buys property understands that it's a long-term investment, especially in times when the market is depressed. There may be a wait of one to three years, or longer, to roll over your capital. (The bigger the property the longer the wait, as a rule.) However, this fact discourages more prospective investors than it should. Human nature being what it is, there's a primitive urge to keep a very high proportion of our assets in liquid investments. (That's why so many uneducated types have always kept their wealth in cash, under the mattress or buried in the backyard.) And yet, how many people ever need all their net worth in ready cash?

One reason real estate averages bigger payoffs than more liquid investments is that the marketplace generally rewards buyers for accepting the "liquidity risk"—the risk of needing their capital on short notice, not the risk of losing their capital.

You can see this principle at work when you buy a bank's certificate of deposit instead of putting your money in a passbook account at the same bank. The safety of principal (the "business risk") is identical. But because you're willing to wait for the return of your capital (the liquidity risk) by putting it into a CD, you reap a substantially bigger return. So too with real estate.

The fact that many investors shy away from real estate because reselling takes time is the very reason why those who do invest in it can normally expect higher returns. I advise investors to ask themselves what fraction of their capital they can afford to put into less liquid investments in order to collect bigger profits down the road. If their assets are modest, maybe 5 or 10 percent is all they should tie up in real estate—and of course the easiest way to do this is through a pool. If they're comfortably fixed, with ample spare capital, their percentage of realty investment might go to 30 or 50 percent.

A Cautionary Tale

The other factor you should fully understand before buying into a private syndicate is that you're staking your investment on the honesty and ability of the general partner. You should be very sure about him. And you should watch his operations carefully.

To help you realize some of the things that can go wrong, let me tell you a sad, true story, pieced together from partners who got burned.

Two food-company executives, Ed Shrood and Phil Covette, each invested $5,000 as limited partners in a home-building venture organized by Don Cope, a successful young builder who was himself investing $10,000 as a limited partner but would also be the general partner. (The names are fictitious.)

Their agreement was that the limited partners, including Cope, would share all profits pro rata until their yield reached 30 percent on a yearly basis, or 2½ percent for each month their money had been tied up. After that, all profits would be Cope's as general partner.

Cope's record was good. He had built and sold seventy-five houses in five years. He paid all bills promptly. His total assets were above $300,000. He'd never been involved in litigation.

The deal worked out nicely. In eight months Shrood and Covette each collected $6,000, representing their original investment plus $1,000.

So they jumped into another partnership with Cope, and then another. All houses were sold from the drawing boards within three months. Shortly after construction was completed, the two investors got their money back plus the agreed profit.

Next time, three acquaintances who'd heard about the marvelous results decided to invest along with them. Cope also lined up three more friends of his own. As time went by, word of the tasty profits began to spread. Astute businessmen pleaded for chances to invest with Cope. Their faith was fortified by his promptness in buying out any investor who requested it, paying back the investment plus 2½ percent for each month the investor's money was tied up, even if he himself was a year or more from cashing out that particular partnership.

But Ed Shrood was so cautious that he wouldn't even believe a calendar without double-checking. After several years he asked his banker to run another credit check on Cope. The report was mostly favorable—but the credit agency noted that Cope declined to answer some of its questions for what he called "competitive reasons."

Shrood noticed other small changes. Cope was no longer putting in much of his own money. And the newer partnership agreements permitted the partnership to do business with other firms in which the general partner had an interest.

So Shrood gave up those handsome yields and stopped investing with Cope. But Covette paid no attention to Shrood's doubts, nor did the other partners. "When you're riding a winning horse you don't get off to ask questions," one big investor said.

After ten years Cope announced a slight cut in the maximum yield he would pay to his investors. It could be only 26 percent thereafter, he said. In four years he cut the yield again, to 22 percent. By then he had more than 450 partners in his various projects, with shares ranging from $2,500 to $200,000.

Suddenly some of Cope's most valuable properties were in

default to lenders. The partners who hadn't put money into these particular ventures figured they were safe enough. Soon they found that it didn't matter which projects they were backing; all were in the red. People began asking him to buy them out—but he wasn't doing that anymore.

Finally Don Cope was adjudged a total bankrupt. He had overstated the value of his properties and other assets. His partnerships had bought land at inflated prices, sometimes from dummy corporations he controlled. None of his partnerships could pay their debts.

The partners took a close look to see what they might salvage. Certain projects could be saved if more capital was put in. But the capital wasn't forthcoming. The wealthiest investors, who could have written a check for as much as was needed, chose instead to write off their losses as tax deductions. They couldn't spare the time and effort needed to save the projects, they explained. Other investors, who had bought their way in with borrowed money, were destitute.

What Went Wrong?

How could such a successful operator go broke? I think Don Cope, basically honest, worked himself into a quicksand.

Somewhere early in the game, one of his ventures brought a smaller profit than he expected. He dipped into his own pocket, secretly, to pay off at the stipulated rate. Otherwise his reputation might have been hurt.

He got into the habit of using his funds to pad the profits whenever necessary. It was partly pride, partly a need to keep investors happy so they'd reinvest. Then the areas in which he was working got overbuilt. His investors' capital got tied up in overpriced land. Cope's only hope was to attract steady streams of fresh money from new investors. This meant always paying off in full when he liquidated ventures, and always thinking up attractive-sounding new projects so he could sign new partners and pay old ones. Finally his debts ate up the new money faster than he could bring it in.

What precautions should the limited partners have taken? First, they should have taken time to learn about the business.

There are plenty of books on land development. Any banker could have told them about the possible snares.

And they should have limited their investments to what they could afford to lose. Once in, the investors as a group should have insisted that Cope send them periodic, audited financial statements. They foolishly felt that it didn't matter how much (or little) Cope made, as long as their returns were the maximum he'd offered. The few who did ask for statements got polite evasions. This was a danger signal that almost everyone overlooked.

Investors should have exercised their individual rights to inspect the books from time to time. Nobody took the trouble. Few bothered to visit the sites of projects they were backing. And none worried when their partnerships abandoned projects, because they still got paid in full.

They should have taken into account what can happen to big builders and developers when money gets tight and renters lose jobs.

They put too much faith in one man because of his impressive "track record." Maybe they didn't realize that the best executives can make blunders or can get lax about ethics if nobody is watching them.

Worst of all, these investors were like sheep. They followed the crowd. A venture couldn't be bad when so many people were pushing to get in, they thought. The big yields lulled them into dreaming that the yields would never stop.

It's an old, old story—repeated in many kinds of "investment" from the Ponzi schemes and Florida land bubbles of the 1920s down to the Home Stake and Equitable Funding frauds of the 1970s. Let them be a lesson to you.

Public Syndicates Are Safer

You're protected against most of these hazards when you invest in a "public" rather than a "private" syndication or partnership. A key difference between the two categories of partnership comes from the way shares in the partnerships are offered for sale.

Real estate limited-partnership interests are legally classed as securities, like stock in a corporation. This means that shares can't be offered to anyone until the partnership is either registered with the federal Securities Exchange Commission (better known as the SEC) or is exempted from registration.

"Private" partnerships are exempt. Why? Mainly because the organizers don't solicit members of the public—strangers, as it were.

Before a general partner can even discuss his private syndication with a prospective investor, he must be sure the individual meets certain standards of financial strength and is knowledgeable enough to evaluate the risks. Because of this, reputable general partners usually keep a low profile and select their investors carefully.

Also, public syndications are usually much larger than private ones, and therefore need to sell shares widely. If an organizer budgets several million dollars to buy or develop a property and control it in escrow for a year or so, he'll definitely have to set up a public partnership.

Public partnerships must meet some of the toughest governmental regulations that exist today. Uncle Sam has plenty to say about what can and cannot be done in peddling securities. So do state securities laws (often called "blue-sky" laws) in whatever states the securities will be offered.

The state and SEC codes are voluminous. They stress the theme of disclosure. They require a seller of securities to disclose to the potential investor all facts that are relevant—especially the unfavorable facts. If a seller omits information that might make his proposition look more risky, he is breaking the law and can be jailed. The same goes double, of course, if he makes a misleading statement.

Prospectuses for public limited partnerships look and sound dull. They're printed in black and white with no pictures, no fancy language. But when you read one you can get a good insight into any and all weaknesses that a salesman might prefer not to mention. Most important, they are required to provide a detailed financial history of all investment programs ever operated by the organizers. This requirement alone would have been fatal to Don Cope if, in the final years before he went broke, he had tried to set up public limited partnerships. He would have had to reveal the concealed losses of some previous projects.

Writing a prospectus is a horrendous job, costing upward of $25,000 in fees to accountants and attorneys. Six months or a year may pass before the first shares can be sold. Still, these high initial costs are often outweighed by the marketing advantages of offering shares to thousands of people.

A typical public limited partnership may sell for $500 per unit, with a minimum of three to five units. This puts it within the reach of small investors. Each must review the prospectus before investing. Even though the SEC and the states refuse to endorse any investment—and say so right on the front page—the fact that they've approved the offering says it all. The investor knows that their job is to study every word, for the protection of unskilled investors.

How to Get Into a Public Partnership

With the growing popularity of real estate syndicates, public partnerships are often marketed through Wall Street firms that sell stocks and other securities nationally. You can easily find and buy public partnership shares just by talking to one or two brokerage firms in your town.

However, you shouldn't assume that all brokers are equally well informed about real estate. They've spent years learning about stocks and bonds and puts and calls and straddles and margins. Some of the best stockbrokers haven't studied tax shelters and real estate. So don't just walk in and sit down with the first available representative. Phone the manager first and ask for a specialist in this field.

No brokerage firm offers all the public partnerships that may be on the market. But local brokers do try to keep available a range of offerings with different objectives, different types of properties, and suitability for different income levels. Syndicate organizers realize that many new investors want to get into real estate, so they're working hard to provide facts and guidance. They often hire regional managers to tour the country giving talks to groups of prospective investors. Local brokers often sit in on these talks. Consequently some are quite expert in assisting investors.

When you buy through a major stockbroker, you can be sure

320

that the firm has thoroughly screened the general partner and the syndicate, so you needn't worry about fraud or ineptitude. Just keep in mind that even a corporate general partner can suffer reverses—like any corporation. There's a chance that you may have to wait longer for capital gains than you expect. And there's even an outside chance that the biggest syndicator can get over-extended and go broke—as did Bill Zeckendorf, after putting together the world's largest real estate empire. So don't hock the family jewels to buy real estate through anybody.

Blind Pools for Lower Brackets

Another key difference between public and private limited partnerships is that public offerings seldom pinpoint a particular piece of real estate to be purchased. They'd rather not buy or tie up a property during the long time needed for registration. So they usually set up the partnership as a "blind pool" instead. Their prospectus merely specifies the general type of property to be bought or developed after the investment funds are raised.

This has important implications for investors. It means that public syndicates tend to focus on producing just enough tax shelter to protect their properties' cash flow. They seldom are set up (as private partnerships often are) to provide big deductions that will shelter investors' other taxable income. This makes public partnerships better for people in lower tax brackets, who needn't worry much about heavy taxes on unearned income. These people want a good, stable rental income while holding property, plus a nice capital gain at resale some day. Contrariwise, people who need big tax write-offs are more likely to find them in private syndications, as I'll show in the next chapter.

If you decide to start small and work into bigger investments gradually, public partnerships are a good place to start. Later, when you know more and are stronger financially, you'll probably venture into private pools—because they do have important advantages, despite the hazards I've outlined.

Tax Shelter Digest says that nine-tenths of all tax-advantaged investments are made through private limited partnerships. There are weighty reasons for this.

You'll find the reasons in Chapter 20, where you'll also see how to find private syndicates, size them up, and protect yourself when you're a limited partner.

Tony Hoffman has a super course available with workbook and tapes. For more information call toll free 1-800-843-8687.

KEY POINTS TO REMEMBER

· Limited partnerships that invest in real estate are growing fast. They may be good investment vehicles for you.

· Real estate partnerships, like individual ownership, are not very liquid. Don't put in money that you might need soon, or that you can't afford to lose.

· Before joining a partnership, make sure of the general partner's honesty and ability. Watch operations carefully if he heads a private syndicate.

· Public syndicates are safer, although they provide less tax shelter. You can easily find and buy shares.

_ 20 _

An Investor's Guide to Private Syndicates

When you buy partnership shares in a public syndication, the differences between a "general" partner and a "limited" partner needn't concern you much. You're rather like a small shareholder in any large enterprise. You just cash the checks sent by the partnership. Your tax consequences are computed for you by the partnership.

But it's sometimes different when you buy into a private syndication. There you may be one of a very few partners. Are you sure you understand your legal and financial position?

A "limited" partner (in either a public or private syndication) can't lose more capital than he or she contributes. A limited partner isn't liable beyond that for debts of the partnership, can't be sued for its misdeeds, if any, and is free from all its managerial chores. Still, if you're a limited partner, you must be careful to behave like one. Otherwise you could lose your limited liability protection and become a general partner in the eyes of the law. Behaving like a limited partner means not meddling in day-to-day operation of the partnership or its properties.

The "general" partner, together with his paid staff, does the work. He usually puts together the partnership. He manages its affairs. He'd better be a very good manager, because he is personally liable (without limit) for the partnership's debts. All his personal assets may be seized to satisfy a court judgment against the partnership.

Since he takes bigger risks, and does far more work, he can expect a proportionately bigger payoff than the limited partners. How much bigger—and when? It should be spelled out in the partnership agreement.

The Beauty of Being a Non-Person

Partnerships are usually preferable to corporations for the purposes of real estate investors. Here's why.

Under the law a partnership isn't a "legal entity"—isn't a person, legally speaking. By contrast, the law insists that a corporation actually *is* a person—at least it is considered to behave like an individual and must be treated as one. It can enter into contracts. It can buy and sell, sue and be sued. It files its own tax returns and pays its own taxes.

Its owners, the shareholders, enjoy the same limited liability as do the limited partners in a partnership. The corporation's debts aren't theirs. That's soothing for shareholders. What isn't so nice is that they're taxed on the dividends the corporation pays them. Thus the profits made by their enterprise are in effect taxed twice. First the corporation as a "person" is taxed, leaving less income to distribute. Then the shareholders are taxed again on what is distributed to them.

That's not all the bad news. If corporate property (such as real estate) is sold, the profit is taxable at ordinary corporate rates, not at the lower rates available to genuine people when they have a capital gain. And if the corporation loses money, shareholders normally can't claim a tax deduction on the loss.

Therefore, buying stock in corporations is seldom a royal road to El Dorado. (Of course if you happened to get in on the ground floor of IBM or Xerox, that's another story.)

However, lots of people do get rich in limited partnerships. Since a partnership is a non-person, it isn't taxed. This means that the tax consequences to partners can be delightful.

A partnership's profits and benefits are divided among partners in the same proportion as their shares of the partnership. Likewise their percentage of any real or paper losses, of depreciation

324

allowances and other tax breaks, is passed through to them for use in their own tax returns.

Beware These Tax Traps

However, before you leap rejoicing into a private limited partnership, ask your lawyer. Ask him questions like "Is this syndication paperwork properly drafted?" and "Is my legal liability definitely limited to the amount of my investment?"

What's meant to be a partnership can be transformed, if the paperwork is bungled, into an "Association taxable as a Corporation," in the uncharitable view of the Internal Revenue Service auditors. If this happens, the IRS will strip you of the tax benefits of your investment. Suddenly you're not a limited partner, you're just a poor little corporate shareholder to be taxed twice.

It means that your previous tax returns, claiming partnership, were incorrect. You're disallowed various deductions you took. The finding by the IRS may be announced two or three years after your original investment, and it is retroactive, so the effect on your personal finances can be dire. The IRS refigures your taxes for each of those years. You not only have to pay more taxes, but also penalties and interest.

I'm not urging you to shun private limited partnerships because of this hazard. That would be like saying everyone should stay out of forests because of forest fires. What you should do is try to verify that the partnership is set up correctly so that it will indeed be a partnership, not an Association taxable as a Corporation. Here are steps you can take during the formative period:

1. Ask about the possibility of getting an advance ruling from the IRS on the partnership's tax status. This may or may not be possible, or even desirable. It depends on the circumstances.
2. Ask about getting a detailed tax opinion from a reputable firm of tax attorneys. A tax opinion is good for the peace of mind of the syndicator as well as the limited partners. It is a kind of insurance policy. If the IRS later takes an opposing position, the firm of attorneys who issued the opinion are bound to defend it in court. A general partner who goes to

the trouble of getting a tax opinion is showing that he's prudent and painstaking. Conversely, if he doesn't bother about this, he may be too bold for his own good.

3. Make sure that the attorney who drafts the partnership agreement is thoroughly familiar with tax angles of partnerships. This is a must!

You May Be Liable for More Than You Think

Another kind of disaster, a worse one, occasionally befalls unwise limited partners. Their liability expands. Worse, sometimes they even turn into general partners, fully liable for all partnership debts, without knowing it.

Let's take these two hazards in order.

As we've seen, a limited partner is liable only to the limit of whatever capital he puts in. This capital is shown on the limited-partnership certificate that is filed with the state government (and published in two local newspapers) as a public record—theoretically putting the public on notice that the limited partners' liabilities extend so far and no further.

But whenever cash distributions (from rent or other income) are made to limited partners, this certificate can and should be amended to reduce the invested capital it shows.

As capital is returned through cash flow, and as the certificate is changed from time to time to reflect the smaller capital pool, each limited partner's liability for claims is reduced accordingly.

Maybe you think of cash flow as dividends, not as a refund. Nevertheless, under partnership law, it really is a partial return of capital. This leaves less money that any creditors of the partnership can snatch away from you. The lawmakers confected this sweet little surprise as another way of encouraging people to go into partnerships.

For a general partner who knows his business, it's standard practice to keep amending the partnership certificate to show the dwindling capital accounts. If he doesn't do this, limited partners remain liable for the full capital contributions shown on its face. Then if something awful happens and the partnership gets sued successfully, a court may force the limited partners to disgorge their cash distributions to satisfy a judgment. They can lose everything they've put in plus everything they've received.

I'll admit the danger is remote. But why take a chance? When you receive a cash distribution, ask your general partner, "Have you amended the partnership certificate?"

Now for the worst case. How might you become a general partner all unawares?

One way is for the general partner not to file the required limited-partnership certificate. Another is for him to file tax returns as a general partnership. Such sins might be a matter of ignorance or negligence—or of cunning by a general partner who sees a flood of red ink ahead and doesn't want to face it alone. A good attorney, checking periodically for the limited partners, can seal off these booby traps.

A third way people get trapped is by investing with a general partner who makes such a mess of managing the partnership that the investors are forced to become active to protect their interests. When they do this, they should realize they're gambling. Are the partnership's debts (current and prospective) bigger than they want to become liable for? If so, they might better walk away and take a tax deduction for their lost capital.

When Limited Partners Can Butt In

Limited partners aren't completely helpless. At certain times they can interfere without jeopardizing their protected status under the law. The partnership agreement should spell out these occasions.

Even if it doesn't, there is a concept of "democratic rights" for limited partners, which has been written into the securities laws of many states. The general idea is that partnerships should let the limited partners vote on key decisions like selling property, refinancing, dissolving the partnership, maybe even removing and replacing the general partner.

Limited partners are entitled to be told what the partnership is doing, and to receive fairly detailed (but not audited, necessarily) financial reports, as well as the tax information they need for use in their own returns. Furthermore, they can expect the general partner to answer questions they raise by letter or telephone. An uninformative, unresponsive general partner should trigger action by limited partners.

If you feel that your general partner isn't doing his job properly, your first step should be to get in touch with your state's Securities Bureau. Ask if the "democratic rights" concept is part of the state securities laws. Find out if there have been other questions or complaints about your general partner. Get advice from the bureau about what you can and should do.

Your next step: Talk with a good attorney. Have him review the partnership agreement—of which you did keep a copy, didn't you? He can help protect your rights while also preserving the limitation on your liability. Probably he'll advise you how best to join forces with other limited partners and arrange for whatever group action is needed.

To stay clear of the difficulties I've just described, the most important steps come before you sign the partnership agreement: (1) Make sure the general partner is trustworthy. Later in this chapter I'll suggest how you can form a judgment on this. (2) Find out what will happen if the general partner should die or be disabled. Make sure there's a well-qualified backup team, with legal provisions for continuity. Otherwise the partnership might have to be dissolved, which would mean selling its assets immediately, perhaps at a giveaway price.

The Brighter Side

Now that you've seen the nightmare side of private syndication —and how to avoid it—let's look at some advantages.

First, you're in a good field of investment. Owing real estate for rental income, then selling it for a capital gain (taxed at the favorable maximum rate of 20 percent (long-term capital gain under the 1981 tax law) is a low-risk way to build wealth, with helpful tax breaks along the way. Probably you already know this or you wouldn't be reading a book on realty investment.

However, in my previous books and in the early chapters of this one, I've concentrated on do-it-yourself realty investment. I've shown how you personally can find and evaluate properties, negotiate for them, manage them, improve them, sell them. I've talked about "sweat equity"—increasing a property's value by doing your own painting, cleaning and fixing up.

There's no need for do-it-yourself, no sweat equity, when

you're a limited partner. If you no longer want to do the physical and mental work, or if you're new to real estate, you can invest through syndicates. This takes less capital than you might need on your own in times when it's hard to find good buys an individual can afford.

In short, you don't need experience, spare time, or a big bankroll to get the advantages of realty investing. The syndicate provides all three.

Also, what I mentioned at the start of Chapter 19 bears repeating: Through syndication you can buy big properties, the kind millionaires buy.

Why Bigger Properties Are Better

Because it has more borrowing power, a syndicate usually has more leverage than you could command as an individual. Leverage is a way of controlling a big asset with a small input. Just as a lever enables you to lift a big rock with little effort, the combination of good credit and financial muscle often enables a syndicate to buy a big property with a surprisingly small fraction of its price in cash. Hence the potential net profit on invested cash is bigger.

A couple of famous examples. When the Statler Hotel chain was up for sale at a total price of $110 million, Bill Zeckendorf put together a small syndicate which was on the point of buying it with only $1 million cash. But Conrad Hilton hustled up a somewhat larger syndicate and snatched away the chain with $7 million down. His syndicate took about twenty years to pay the rest of the debt, meanwhile profiting from the hotels' steady revenues as well as the tax deductions for interest, depreciation, and many other expenses.

Similarly, when Henry Crown (son of a necktie salesman) assembled a private partnership that bought the twenty-year-old Empire State Building for $51 million, Crown got a 24 percent interest in the building with a cash outlay of only about $3.4 million. The land was immediately resold to the Prudential Insurance Company for $17 million. The remaining $34 million included some $20 million in mortgages. Thirteen years later, when the mortgages were down to $8 million, Crown's group sold the building to a syndicate of New Yorkers for $65 million, netting a profit of $50 million before the capital gains tax.

There are few bidders for big properties such as syndicates buy. Consequently a syndicate can usually negotiate better prices and terms. Then, too, bankers would rather make real estate loans than most other kinds—because real estate is immovable, insurable, in demand, and will probably become worth more as time passes.

The true price of real estate to a purchaser includes not only the price of the land and the structure but also the price of the money used to buy it—which generally means the monthly mortgage payments. I'm sure you know about the high interest rates charged borrowers. Probably you also know that big borrowers —like syndicates—pay far lower rates than the average borrower. Thus you can buy slices of real estate more cheaply as a limited partner.

Leverage Boosts Write-offs

When you invest in real estate as an active personal owner, leverage could turn out to hurt you rather than help you. In case of a serious loss, you'd be responsible for the borrowed money as well as your cash investment, so you might lose much more than you put in. However, we've seen that as a limited investor you risk only as much as you invest. Borrowing on your behalf, the syndicate not only gives your cash extra leverage but also boosts your tax benefits.

The depreciation allowance is the biggest bulwark in your tax shelter. "Depreciation" is defined as a loss in value through age, obsolescence, or wearing out. The tax code makes allowance for this, on the theory that any building has a limited useful life, and will be worthless someday. By estimating when that day will come, you can gradually lower the stated value of your property over the estimated time.

Another valuable feature of the depreciation allowance is that you can claim it against the total cost of the property, not just the partnership's equity. If a property is bought with 75 percent financing, say, then depreciation is credited against triple the partners' cash payment. Dear old leverage at work again.

Depreciation is an accounting myth, but real estate fortunes are built on it. The loss of value through depreciation is a paper loss—a "tax loss"—which takes no cash out of your pocket but actually leaves more cash in, because you pay a smaller tax. Every dollar of depreciation wipes out a dollar of taxable income at no current cost to you; you needn't spend a nickel repairing or preserving a building to claim depreciation.

In fact, you can subtract the "depreciation loss" from profits you actually make, whether in the partnership or elsewhere. Conceivably you'll owe no tax while tons of cash are cascading in.

New investors are often confused to find that a piece of property simultaneously brings them cash distributions and tax deductions, but some investments can be set up to do so. And if a building brings in no money at all, its owners can apply the deduction to income earned elsewhere. In effect the government gives them their "profits" by excusing some of their other income from taxes.

Real estate often appreciates in value while depreciating on paper, thus putting you ahead both ways. However, the proportion of tax that is avoided (or deferred indefinitely) can vary widely from investment to investment.

Some investments are deliberately designed to produce a tiny operating income, thus shifting over virtually all the tax shelter to protect unrelated income. This is preferable for rich and heavily taxed people who are happy to wait for capital gains later on. But it may not be preferable for you and other small partners. You may prefer investments that bring you steady income with just enough shelter to keep it untaxed. Some private partnerships plan their investments this way (as do most public partnerships).

Private syndicators often pick out one or more properties, buy them or tie them up, then start selling shares to limited partners. They'll show you in advance what your income and tax benefits should be, so you can shop for syndications that suit your needs.

A Lazy Way to Wealth

It's nice to have tax benefits computed for you. Each year, well before April 15, any well-run partnership sends you a filled-in IRS Form 1065. This printed sheet is headed "Partner's Share of

Income, Credits, Deductions, etc." and the filled-in blanks show precisely what your share of profits or losses were for the year, together with the amounts of tax deductions you should enter on your personal tax return.

Incidentally, there are many interesting tax considerations that I won't take space to cover here, because the general partner and his tax experts figure them into each transaction and include them on your Form 1065 when applicable: provisions for your tax basis, for nonrecourse financing, recapture of depreciation at sale, accrual accounting, and so on. Look them up in tax manuals if you're curious.

"The prudent way is also the easy way," counseled Paul Samuelson, nationally known economist, in a column he wrote for *Newsweek*. "Someone else does the research, someone else does the worrying. . . . What you lose is the daydream of that one big killing. What you gain is sleep."

And of course much more is done for you all year round. Managing the properties, for example. The professionals do this better, for less money. If you personally owned an apartment building and managed it yourself, you'd work very hard to handle more than twenty units. Or if you wanted to hire a manager, rental income might not pay for more than a mom-and-pop team working in exchange for an apartment. But when a syndicate buys an apartment property, it usually buys one with three hundred or more rental units. An operation that big can easily support a full-time professional manager, plus clerical, accounting, and maintenance people. You're part owner but you never need go near the place.

Have you ever managed apartments? If so, you know that profits hinge on a thousand day-to-day details—mechanical maintenance and repair, care of shrubbery, clearing snow, collecting rents, painting, advertising, showing vacant units to prospective tenants, keeping records, and so on. These requirements are the same for huge properties as for small ones, but "economies of scale," as the efficiency experts say, keep down the turnover and operating cost per unit. To say nothing of the wear and tear on owners.

Then, too, small problems that can be crucial in a small property are minor in a big one. Suppose the boiler blows out. Replacing it can eat up a small building's profit for a year. A big building can absorb this with only a slight impact on the bottom line. It not only spreads the cost among hundreds of units, but it probably buys boilers at a better price. A big organization has far more buying power than an owner of a few apartments.

I could go on, but I'm sure you see the point. Being an absentee owner, fractionally, of big properties takes none of your time and proportionately less of your money than being sole owner of one or two small properties.

There's another point too. Maybe you know how much time an individual invests in searching for properties, studying them, negotiating to acquire them. Your syndicate's general partner and his staff do all this for you.

They may consider thirty property offerings for each one they buy. They may spend two weeks inspecting one possible investment from roof to foundation, and combing its records. Usually they send in specialists in various aspects of realty work. They verify the rent roll and vacancy rate. They check the bills and payrolls for at least two years back. They examine original blueprints. Often they open up walls to look at wiring, plumbing, and structural soundness. A good syndicate buys scientifically, with a solid resale profit built in. You could do as well on your own but only after study and attending seminars.

The Art of Selling

In selling, too, a syndicate does better than an individual. It can more easily find and cultivate prospective buyers. And it can time a turnover for maximum profit.

An individual owner of a building may develop a pride as big as the Ritz, and hate to sell—especially if all problems have been solved, if cash flow is at high tide, and there are no troubles on the horizon. But this may be the perfect time to sell, especially if the economic cycle is at a point where nobody else is selling. Syndicates know that the biggest killings in real estate are made by going against the cycle—buying in recessions, selling into booms. Being far less emotional than individuals, syndicates do this when individuals won't or can't.

Timing isn't the only art involved in selling well. A transaction can be tailored many ways, and money men are better than the rest of us at choosing the best options—selling for cash, taking notes, exchanging for other properties, stretching or shortening payback periods. Net gains are weighed against risks and tax consequences.

The Importance of Deep Pockets

The best-managed properties can run into unexpected red ink. People do move out unpredictably. Accidents happen. Many contingencies are covered by insurance, but insurers are sometimes slow to settle. If the cash flow dries up meanwhile, an owner faces a hard choice: shall he postpone replacements and maintenance, or dig into reserve funds to keep the property in top condition? The latter choice is almost always wiser. But individual owners sometimes can't afford it. Needing cash flow, they're forced to bleed their property. It may be worth less when they try to sell.

A well-heeled general partner, on the other hand, will keep spending while running in the red. He knows that the best way to maximize resale profit is to improve property, not let it go downhill. A syndicate—or an individual—who sinks 100 percent of capital into property, or even 80 percent, is gambling that the revenues will hold up. If the property hits a streak of bad luck, revenues may not cover the mortgage payments, and there could be a disastrous foreclosure. Before you invest in a partnership make sure that its reserves give it plenty of staying power. Never, never go into an undercapitalized partnership.

And how about your own financial position? Would you feel a serious pinch if a syndicate stops making cash distributions? Usually you shouldn't keep all your eggs in one or two baskets. Why not diversify your risks and minimize the consequences of one mistake by buying a smaller piece of several partnerships?

Seven Ways to Find Private Syndications

Private limited partnerships stay underground, so to speak. There may be several near you without your hearing about them. They don't advertise, don't solicit strangers, seldom even mention themselves to prospective investors they don't know well. It's almost as if they wanted to keep their business secret.

There are good reasons for this. If you'll glance back at the previous chapter, in the section describing public syndicates and how they differ from private ones, you'll see that a private group could lose its exemption from SEC registration if it did any aggressive promoting. So it's generally up to you to make your own approaches to private limited partnerships. Where do you look? Who do you ask?

(1) Start with a quick survey of the Yellow Pages of your phone book. Look under Investment Securities, under Real Estate, and under Property Management. If any of the organizations listed sound like limited-partnership organizations, phone and ask if they are.

(2) The next place to search is among securities brokers in your area—listed in the Yellow Pages under Stock and Bond Brokers. Some local and regional ones now sell a few private real estate partnerships as well as the usual run of Wall Street securities. Skip the big national firms because they sell only public partnerships, if they offer real estate investments at all. Just phone less familiar firms and ask if they deal in private real estate limited partnerships.

Incidentally, you won't have to pay a broker's commission if you buy into a partnership through him. The general partner pays the broker's commission if a broker is involved.

These phone calls will probably produce a fair-size list of private syndications. But try to get a longer list before you zero in on a few.

(3) Ask your social and business friends; probably some are into real estate partnerships.

(4) Ask around among business attorneys, accountants, and investment counselors, even if you don't know them. They may have clients constantly seeking tax-advantaged investments. If you ask for a list of good partnership sponsors, you'll probably get it without charge on the chance that you may become a client later.

(5) Check with your state's Securities Bureau. Helping people find private syndications isn't the bureau's job, but it probably will be willing to give you a list of active syndicators, and may

also offer helpful advice. It can at least warn you against the shady operators.

(6) Telephone RESSI, the Real Estate Securities and Syndication Institute in Chicago, at 312-670-6760. It will be glad to send you a list of members in your vicinity.

(7) Look for big residential or commercial buildings that seem unusually attractive and well managed. They're probably the kind in which you'd like to own a partnership interest. Walk into the building office and ask who owns the property and who manages it. Maybe a private limited partnership is in charge. If not, the management company may work with other properties owned by private partnerships, and can point you in their direction. Tracking down a few syndicators who obviously do quality work may get you off to a good start.

How to Screen Your List

Now you can start narrowing down your list. Some private syndicators are just promoters. Realty developers bring them deals, for which they raise money and then turn the property over to a property-management firm. You can screen these out through quick telephone inquiries. The same phone calls may eliminate others whose units are priced higher than you can afford, or who emphasize tax write-offs when you want income, or vice versa.

You can eliminate others by one unannounced visit to the syndicator's office. Simply getting a feel for the office atmosphere and the personalities is useful, even if unscientific. You wouldn't be comfortable investing with anyone you subconsciously distrust or dislike.

Whenever one makes a good first impression on you, talk further. Usually there'll be a prospectus available for a specific limited partnership in process of formation, because these pools are being put together constantly. If there's nothing forming at the moment, just ask to borrow a prospectus or two from partnerships previously offered. These will give you an idea of how the general partner structures his investments.

In these same preliminary visits you can ask for names of a few limited partners who live in your area, or who might otherwise be approachable by you through being in the same profession or whatever. Of course these names are private information, and won't be given without permission of the individuals. But a general partner often can get permission, and he usually likes to provide names as a matter of pride.

One more thing to do in preliminary visits to syndicators: Ask what properties they currently own and operate. You'll want to visit some of these. You needn't be an expert to form a sound opinion. You can see whether the property looks neat and well maintained. If there's flaking paint or threadbare carpets, that's enough to scrub the syndicator from your list. However, if external appearances are good, don't be satisfied without probing a bit deeper. Try to chat casually with at least one employee, either a maintenance worker or someone in the building office. It's surprising how readily you can sense good or bad spirit and efficiency. And this is crucial. Remember that a property's real value depends mostly on what happens at the site, not in the partnership office.

Naturally you'd like to know how profitable a syndicator's past projects were in terms of annual after-tax return on investment. But this information is hard to get. Guide 60 of SEC regulations says that private limited partnerships can't give information selectively about just a few of the ventures they've organized. They must supply data for every partnership the company has run since it started—or for none. And if they do start giving the information, they must keep on giving it to all prospects for all future partnerships—in a special fully detailed form that is bothersome to compile. Therefore most general partners are reluctant to give out their success stories, if any. You may have to settle for whatever you can glean from past limited partners. Still, in casual conversation syndicators sometimes say more than they would put in writing. You should certainly try, politely and pleasantly, to get them chatting about past performance. (But double-check whatever they say, because oral claims aren't always accurate.)

What to Ask a General Partner

Your basic relationship with any general partner boils down to this: "You [the limited partner] put up the money. I'll provide know-how."

So it's up to you to evaluate his know-how—and his integrity.

One way to do this, as I've mentioned, is to find out what his previous limited partners think of him. Another way is to ask bankers, real estate brokers, and other financial people.

If the reports are good, you'll still want to check further before you put up much money. Sit down with him and ease into a few key questions:

"Have any of your properties gone bankrupt? Have any been sold for less than their purchase price?"

If so, you may choose to back off, or you may decide to listen to as much of the story as he wants to tell. Sometimes there are extenuating circumstances. How did his investors come out when it was all over?

"Have you ever had bad times during the ownership of a property?"

If he says no, either he's a beginner or his memory is weak. Real estate work is made up of solving problems. The best general partners are glad to talk about what they've done during unexpected maintenance expenses or a downturn in occupancies, because they know how to cope with bad times. If a general partner tells you he's taken money from his own pocket to bail out troubled partnerships, or personally guaranteed loans to them, you can mentally mark a big plus for him. It means that he takes pride in his reputation and backs it up with his money; that he believes his limited partners' first investment should be their only one.

On the other hand, if you learn that a general partner has previously written long letters to limited partners starting, "Dear investor: We need more money," this tells you he hasn't the deep pockets I mentioned earlier.

"Do you collect any broker's commission when the partnership buys or sells property? . . . Does the partnership deal with any other firms in which you have a financial interest?"

If he answers yes to either of these questions, go slow. As a

338

general partner his duty is to negotiate the best possible prices for the partnership, but self-dealing tempts him to pocket a profit by skinning his limited partners. Later, if you take home an offering circular from the syndicate, watch for any sections entitled "Conflicts of Interest" or "Interest of General Partner in Certain Transactions." Normally there should be no such interests. If they exist, they should be minor and manageable.

Sometimes a minor technical conflict of interest really saves money for investors by providing expert services below market rates. A general partner may set up subsidiaries to provide services to the partnership because they'll be more economical and dependable. (Outside contractors sometimes squeeze customers when emergencies arise.) But you should take a close look. How much do the subsidiaries charge? How good is their service? What is a fair price? How much profit should the general partner make on these dealings? A good general partner pushes hard to contribute to the success of the investment and won't take much profit on whatever in-house affiliates he sets up.

"Do the cash investors get priority in cash distributions?"

They should. While a general partner can charge fees that are enough to keep the organization running smoothly, his big payoff should come at the end, and only after the limited partners have made money. If a syndicate's plan of operation doesn't specifically put the limited partners in front of the general partner for return of capital plus a specified percentage, stay out. It's a mug's game.

What Should the Syndicator Cost You?

"As general partner, exactly what compensation, commissions, fees and other payments will he receive?"

Fees are the ruination of too many tax-shelter deals. The general partners deduct excessive amounts for themselves. So you should make sure that the offering materials clearly set forth the general partner's remuneration from all sources. If they don't, there's probably a reason. Ask about it.

Many states have laws limiting the amount of capital that can go to the general partner at the outset; a syndicate sometimes arranges (openly or secretly) to get around these laws.

The syndicator is entitled to be paid well for his work and expertise. But you should know how much. You should know that it's lawful. Then you must decide for yourself whether it's fair.

You undoubtedly realize that you'll be paying for the luxuries of favorable tax treatment, limited liability, and freedom from the worries of management. A general partner is bound to cost you money. In all fairness he should be compensated handsomely if he brings you a good return on your money. So look at the return. Given the payment to the general partner, is your projected return still high? It will be if the transaction is properly set up, and you should be willing to pay what he specifies.

Obviously a general partner who undercharges for his services is struggling to stay afloat and can't be expected to help in stormy weather—he just won't have the financial strength. Before you invest, be sure you clearly understand the personal financial status of the general partner. His compensation usually consists of fees plus a share of ownership in the property. Specific fees vary. But generally there's a front-end or syndication fee, which covers the syndicator's work in putting the deal together. Then there may be a monthly management fee for guiding operations throughout the lifetime of the deal. At the end he'll receive a stated percentage of the profits realized from the sale. But until sale, all profits normally flow to limited partners only, in proportion to the capital they've put in. It's best if the general partner's profit comes mostly from his ownership share and not from his front-end fee.

As I mentioned earlier, some syndicators buy property themselves at the lowest possible price, then raise money from investors afterward. There's nothing wrong with this. It's how several of the best and biggest syndicators work. It's a bit risky and ties up their capital—but it's good strategy if the property might not be available later. Cash is king in real estate, especially in a depressed market, and a syndicator with plenty of cash can negotiate remarkably good prices and terms. This kind of syndicator will often buy apartments for $2,000 or $3,000 less per unit than a new or struggling syndicator.It might mean a saving of $600,000 in buying a 300-apartment complex—which could be more than the syndicator's entire compensation.

But what if the syndicator, after buying the property with his own money, sells it to the partnership at a generous markup? Some syndicators do this, and may or may not disclose it. Even if they do disclose it, their profit certainly is an extra fee. The best syndicators transfer the property to the partnership at exactly their own cost basis. Whatever property your syndicate owns or plans to acquire, be sure to find out whether it's being bought from the syndicator himself, and if so how much he's making on the transaction.

And then there are builder-syndicators. You should be especially inquisitive if new construction is involved in a limited partnership. Sometimes a building or a tract of homes is constructed by a syndicator or his affiliate, then sold to his partnership at a price arranged in a cozy private conversation. This may be okay if the price is fixed in advance and disclosed in the prospectus. A builder-syndicator is entitled to a profit, since he's taking a risk in providing the finished building or tract at a fixed price.

The question that concerns you: Is the partnership's purchase price reasonable? If it wasn't arrived at in the open market through arm's-length dickering, it might be much too high. Look at the prices of similar properties.

"Why do you give away part of the profit to investors instead of putting in all the money yourself?"

This may sound like a stupid question, but it sometimes opens up unexpected insights. If the syndicator can't afford to put in all the money himself—as is often the case—does he have enough reserve funds to see him through a financial crunch without asking his partners for more money? On the other hand, if he is amply funded, why should he bother with the hassle of limited partnerships?

A lot of entrepreneurs do stop syndicating as soon as they strike it rich. Others find that partnerships give them a way to own a piece of more properties, and they want diversification. One of the biggest and most successful private syndicators, Craig Hall, of Southfield, Michigan, writes: "Personally I find it better to have my money in a few deals at a time, even though I may reflect back on the sale of any one property and realize that it would have been more profitable to have owned the whole thing."

"How much of my money will actually go into the investment?"

Hall's standard answer to this question is "All of it. Obviously all the partnership's capital won't go into buying the property, but all of it will go toward achieving the objectives of the partnership." Presumably he means operating expenses. These expenses, to some syndicators, include management fees.

Investors are entitled to wonder whether some management fees simply enrich a syndicator. This is natural, since two common ways to report fees are as a percentage of total capital raised, and as a percentage of total expenditures. But percentage evaluation can be misleading.

For example, if a partnership buys a $10 million property, it may need $2 million down payment—or only $1.5 million if the general partner is an unusually skillful negotiator. Let's say that in either case the general partner charges a $450,000 fee. If he negotiates the lower down payment, his fee is 30 percent. But his fee is only 22.5 percent if he settles for the $2 million down. Of course he receives the same amount of money either way, but his investors are obviously better off with the higher-percentage fee, which gives them higher leverage. Yet the 30 percent fee might sound "too high." This shows what can happen when investors think only about percentages when evaluating fees.

The example also shows why fees for tax-shelter deals usually seem steeper than for other real estate investments. For maximum tax advantage, you want high leverage. So the general partner tries to keep capital investment low, borrowing a high proportion of the purchase price. This makes his fee look high as a percentage of capital invested.

Maybe a better way to evaluate fees is to compute them as a percentage of the total price of real estate purchased—or of net profit—rather than as a percentage of capital. However you analyze it, fees should more than pay for themselves in results.

Full-time professional syndicators range from the small solo operator, with a few friends who back his operations for fixed percentages of the profits, to corporate organizations sponsoring either private or public real estate funds. When you begin this type of investment, your best bet is probably with a small but stable operator in your own area. Because he is located nearby, you'll have easier access to information from and about him. Because his reputation is his lifeblood, he'll be very likely to give you a square deal. To grow, he needs repeat investors and referrals, so he's highly motivated to make money for his investors.

If you yourself are a thoroughly experienced and successful buyer, manager, and seller of real estate, you may want to start small syndications of your own. For detailed suggestions on how to do this, read Chapter 24, "How to Start Your Own Limited Partnership," in the 1982 revised edition of my book *How You Can Become Financially Independent by Investing in Real Estate* (Simon and Schuster).

KEY POINTS TO REMEMBER

- Private syndicates aren't advertised. You'll have to search for them.
- As a limited partner in a private syndicate, be careful not to meddle in operations lest you become liable as a general partner.
- Make sure a tax attorney certifies that the syndicate documents are properly worded. If they are not, your profits may be taxed much more heavily.
- Before investing in a partnership, make sure it has an adequate financial reserve. Check the general partner's previous record and watch for clues to self-dealing.
- When you receive a cash distribution, ask your general partner if he amended the partnership certificate. He should.
- If you feel that your general partner may not be doing his job properly, consult an attorney at once.

21

Damn the Torpedoes!

"Damn the torpedoes—full speed ahead!" shouted Admiral Farragut at the beginning of a critical battle. It turned out the way he thought it would. No torpedoes hit his ships. And his words went ringing down the ages as a reminder to us all that boldness wins battles.

We all need such a reminder occasionally—especially as we grow older. We've kept telling our children "Look out, be careful," and the warnings have gotten deeply grooved into our own subconscious minds. They work like posthypnotic suggestions, influencing us to pull back automatically at any hint of risk.

Often we are blindly and unnecessarily cautious. We pay a price for this. Habitual overcaution can block us from seizing great opportunities.

There are times when we need to say to ourselves "To hell with caution, let's try something new!" I think this is such a time for you, if you're hesitating to make your first venture into real estate.

Open Your Eyes and Look Into Something New

Recently I heard of a lady in her sixties who took a trip to Alaska. Sure, it was a conducted tour, perfectly safe—until, at its farthest point north, she left the tour and ventured off on her own. She determined she would go into the Arctic Circle just for the pure

343

happy hell of it, to see it and feel it for herself. There were no taxicabs, no hotels, no rooming houses. She slept on a cot in a radio shack. But she saw the glistening, icy Arctic Ocean, which not that many people have actually seen. She came back feeling renewed, not only because of the adventure itself but because of the sense of freedom her bold act had given her. She'd shaken off the dead weight of overcaution.

I've read, too, that in Korea people think of themselves as beginning a new and different life at sixty years. Their national custom is to start unfamiliar activities at that age. One Korean told a reporter, "I became a resurrected person at sixty, and have been living as a new man ever since."

Many Americans who have long since outgrown the reckless-ness of youth are embarking on daring adventures of various kinds. Not all of us can abandon our whole way of life and strike off into something totally new like hang-gliding or wind-surfing or joining the Peace Corps. But we can all find ways to break through the conditioned reflex that tells our subconscious "It's new, don't try it, stay where you are." Your first investment in real estate is a way to do this.

Naturally you shouldn't abandon all caution or common sense or good judgment. We always need to be realistic—to sift and weigh the available facts. But the kind of caution that blinds us to opportunities is a fog of carefulness that blots out reality and beclouds reason. Often it actually leads us away from common sense and real security.

Think about this habit of caution. It enables us to survive. But it also makes us fearful. If you're careful when you drive a car, you're acting in a way that's necessary to your survival. But if you drive very slowly on an empty road with no living things nearby, then you're just fearful, not careful. Your survival isn't threatened but your reflexes make you act as if it were. You're going too slowly because of your gloomy imagination.

Drop Gloomy Thoughts and Come Alive

Since this book has been about real estate investment, I'm sure you see what I'm getting at. Don't let overcaution scare you away from using what the book has taught you. Take a good look at the facts, and you'll be ready to go ahead.

You've heard the gloomy talk about tight money, about unsold properties, about inflation, deflation, and even depression, about an "end of the real estate boom. Then, too, perhaps you think you're green and unskilled, too much of a novice to try even a modest venture.

As for the hard times talk, remember that hard times are when most fortunes are made. Bold investors buy when the market is bad, when self-proclaimed experts advise you to stock up on canned goods and head for the hills because money will soon be worthless and revolution is coming. I've pointed out several times in this book that the best bargains turn up when people are scared.

Are we in for deflation or more inflation? Nobody knows. But here's a surprising fact: For real estate investors, it doesn't really matter.

John McMahan, a San Francisco real estate consultant quoted in the *Wall Street Journal,* has reported after voluminous research that real estate's performance doesn't vary greatly between periods of low and high inflation. Based on a sample of sales by insurance companies, the real return on real estate during highly inflationary times (1969–78) was 11.2 percent a year, compared with an annual return of 9.6 percent for a period of low inflation (1951–68).

Should you be scared about real estate now? Only if you're speculating in overpriced mansions in Beverly Hills or over-priced office towers in New York. Only if your horizons are strictly short term. A sustained, widespread decline in real estate prices is virtually impossible. I'll show you why.

In the stock market or the diamond market or the collectibles market, price declines trigger selling, because people will sell something they believe is going still lower. Prices drop when there's a glut, or a panic.

On impulse, a pension-fund manager can make a few phone calls, sell ten thousand shares of Exxon or Anaconda and switch the money into bonds or Treasury bills. The market is slower to shift in postage stamps, paintings, and Oriental rugs, but never-theless it can go down steeply. Owners don't need stamps or art or rugs. They do need a place to live.

Say your neighbors paid $85,000 for their house. In 1978 they were told it was worth $200,000. Why didn't they sell?

In 1981 they saw the price drop to $180,000, perhaps. Why didn't they unload before it went lower?

They didn't because they asked themselves a simple question: "Where would we move?"

The housing shortage won't go away. Apartment vacancies are filled overnight, at least in California and other states where I own property. California needs about 280,000 new units of housing a year, but we're only building 200,000. Demographically, young couples in their late twenties and early thirties are a group that will expand by ten million nationwide in the 1980s. That's the home-buying age group. How can there be a "crash" in realty prices? I look for a resumption of the boom before long.

Fit Your Goals to Your Resources

Now, what about that worrisome inexperience of yours? If you've never invested in real estate, aren't you likely to lose your shirt?

Every single one of the tens of thousands of investors who've made barrels of money in real estate was inexperienced when he or she started. You can become experienced the way they did: by experimenting. Don't risk your shirt. Start small—but think boldly about growth. And do your homework. Plan ahead, invest what you can afford, and wait out the bad times, if such there be.

Set goals for your investments—reasonable goals, like steady rental income that will keep you comfortably in the black, or a tax shelter that will protect actual income, or a house you can easily renovate for resale. Don't aim to get rich in one quick buy-and-sell turnover. That's how speculators get burned.

If you were a runner, would you set yourself a goal of running a mile in three minutes? Not if you checked the facts about running. The facts are that only the world's best milers can break four minutes, and nobody has ever gotten close to three minutes.

Still it's interesting, if you study sports history, to read about the "mental barriers" and "psychological blocks" that long prevented runners from breaking four minutes. For decades no one believed it would ever be done. Then suddenly someone did it. Almost immediately there were dozens of races under four minutes, because runners now believed it was possible, and dared to push themselves. It was the same in the pole vault, where four-teen feet was believed to be the human ceiling, and in the high jump, where seven feet was thought impossible. Ask any sports-writer how many athletes have soared above those heights in the past few years. Or ask him whether women were believed capable of running a mile, let alone a marathon, a decade ago—and how many woman marathoners there are now.

"It's impossible" is the age-old thought that chills enthusiasm and kills many a project that could otherwise succeed. That's why you must eliminate "impossible" from your speech and thoughts. If a three-minute mile really is impossible forevermore, don't think about it, but decide what *is* possible for *you*. And let your decision be bold.

Set goals that challenge you without being over-risky. The best part of life is striving to reach a worthwhile objective or to make something better of yourself and your situation. The *worst* part of life is irrational fear. In fact, a distinguished physician, Dr. Karl Menninger, said, "The commonest and subtlest of all human diseases is fear."

In real estate, the guidelines for goal setting are simple: don't tackle a project that would take more of your own time or energy than you can spare; don't take on a bigger debt load than you know you can handle. Keep thinking in terms of *possibles*. Skip that *impossible* concept from now on.

Choose the Best Path for You

This book in your hand is a set of detailed maps. I've mapped different routes to financial independence, and to hidden for-tunes, all tested and proven—but not all for you. Pick one or two best suited to your own capabilities and situation.

If you're cash poor but handy with tools, hunt for shabby-looking low-cost properties—maybe at foreclosure sales or other auctions—and upgrade them with "sweat equity." You needn't necessarily count on quick resale, if would-be buyers can't qual-ify for loans right now. When you buy a single-family house, rent it to a steady tenant and raise the rent moderately every year, while you enjoy the tax shelter. Your house will increase steadily in value. After a few years you can refinance it and take out enough cash to buy and fix up a second house. The third and fourth houses will come faster.

If you instinctively understand people and talk easily with them, seek out owners of distressed properties and talk over the various ways you can help them while helping yourself as well. That's another route I've mapped extensively for you.

If you and your spouse feel capable of managing your own property—for a complete guide to this, see my book *How to Manage Real Estate Successfully—In Your Spare Time* (Simon and Schuster)—look for a fourplex or maybe an eight-unit property, live in one unit yourselves and take care of the others. Apartment properties are about the safest investment there is, haven't been depressed at all during recessionary years, and produce steady income unless they're badly mismanaged.

If you're a shrewd and experienced business operator, go into rent-controlled areas where others fear to tread, and use the methods I've shown you to make "impossible" profits.

If you have very little spare time but some spare cash, find other people like yourself and work out shared-ownership arrangements in any of the many patterns I laid out in Chapter 18.

If you have $5,000 or more to invest, and no time or inclination to manage your own investments, start investigating limited partnerships, either public or private. Having read my chapters on them, you know how to choose carefully so that your money and knowledge will grow year by year, and the time will come when you'll help put together bigger partnerships for bigger profits.

Get Help from Others

I've talked about setting goals and planning how to achieve them. In developing your plan, an important factor to consider is your own personality—including your quirks, Maybe you're a loner, preferring to do everything yourself. If you carry this quirk too far in real estate, it can lead you astray. Likewise for the very human quirk of laziness.

Sure, you can be your own boss in most real estate situations. But this leaves you free to make the blunders of inexperience, or to do nothing when you should be taking important steps to protect your investment.

You can save yourself much grief if you just take the trouble to find and use expert advisers—primarily, a competent lawyer, a good tax man, and a real estate agent with high integrity. You may also need an appraiser or a construction expert when you're buying property, old or new, to be sure you have an accurate idea of the property's intrinsic worth.

These experts can make and/or save you more money than they will ever cost you. Professional services are tax-deductible when you buy investment property. Even though you may never have a partner or a co-investor, be sure you obtain sound advice.

Beware of Falling in Love

As I pointed out a few chapters ago, another human quirk is to become emotionally involved with property. Sometimes people see a house and are smitten by love at first sight. Successful brokers know all about "curb appeal." The first impression in driving up to a home, or entering through the front door, may kindle a desire that overrides all considerations of the property's profit potential. *This is a property I'll be proud to own and show off to my friends,* a would-be investor thinks to himself.

Smart investors in income property are interested in appearance *only* if it can contribute to cash flow or resale profit. The financial analysis determines the price you can afford to pay. Sometimes a property without curb appeal or other delights will bring you more profit per dollar invested than one with decorative bridges and running brooks. So here again you may need wise counsel to protect you from your own emotions.

The same holds true about selling. If you've fallen in love with your property, you won't want to sell it. Yet the biggest profits come when you sell. Maybe you need unemotional advice about the right time to put a house or apartment complex on the market, and how to get the most money for it. This is where the experienced, unsentimental general partner in a limited partnership of realty investors can be most valuable to his partners. His business is to know when and how to sell—so don't stand in his way.

And if you're not in a limited partnership, you can get advice from a good real estate broker. Cultivate one you can trust. Naturally he'll tend to encourage selling, since that's where he'll earn

350

his commission, but at least he'll disabuse you of exaggerated notions about the value of your property. And at best he'll tell you when the time is ripe to take your profit and move ahead to a bigger property.

Keep Abreast of Changes

Real estate is a fast-changing business. Court decisions can have tremendous impact overnight on mortgage rates, sales methods, and other facets of the business. The Internal Revenue Service may change a regulation, with broad tax consequences for investors. Property sales may be hotter in some areas than in others. Prices fluctuate.

By keeping up with real estate news you can spot new opportunities, avoid pitfalls. But how can you keep up? The daily newspapers give little inside information about real estate.

At this point, let me blow my own horn temporarily. In 1981 I saw the need for a newsletter that would cover all news of importance to real estate investors. So I organized a staff to comb through hundreds of periodicals, keep in touch with insiders, and publish a monthly compilation of advice and information. This newsletter has been enthusiastically received. Our subscription list keeps growing, even though the price—$145.00 per year—is substantial. I think it's well worth the cost. And the cost is tax-deductible, of course, if you use it for investment guidance.

You can subscribe by calling toll free 1-800-255-6979.

What Others Say

I've written this book, like the newsletters, because the methods I teach are worth knowing and using. Others can speak for me, and do. Here's what the press has had to say:

"His seminars instruct sellout audiences across the country how to buy a first house, and also how to make money by investing in real estate," wrote Nancy Faber of *People* magazine.

"Albert Lowry has attracted his wide following by preaching that even middle-income people with no more than $5,000 to $10,000 to invest can still do very well by investing in real property. And even if they don't get as rich as an Astor, they should still be able to pass the acid test of investing today—beating inflation," wrote Robert Runde in *Money* magazine, one of the prominent Time-Life publications.

Enthusiastic letters come to me from people, and are filed in my offices at The Lowry Group, 3390 Duesenberg Drive, Westlake Village, CA 91362. If you're ever out that way I hope you'll drop in. You'll be welcome to browse through the files of correspondence from those who've profited by the advice in my books, seminars, and newsletters. Here's just a quick sampling:

Jon R. Swoager, of Coraopolis, Pennsylvania, writes: "I use the tools given to me under 'financial analysis' to close any deal I want, without spending cash. . . . You got my head out of the sand and made me a candidate for your Multimillion-Dollar Club, because we now have $408,500 in properties, since March of 1977."

William H. Hallett, of Webster Grove, Missouri, writes: "Here it is four months later and I am $31,000 richer! . . . I used your ideas to cash in on the value of my home. . . . I sold it last month for a profit of $41,500. This left me with $27,500 to invest in some income property; a month ago I had nothing in cash reserve. You inspired me to put my home equity to work . . . you taught me how to use leverage and thus the least amount of cash for down payment."

Noble Roberts, of Louisville, Kentucky, writes: "At present we are into about one-half million dollars' worth of property. Our goal is to use the Lowry approach and to be in one million dollars' worth of property in two to three years. . . . Let me assure the doubting Thomases: It works. I will stand on the highest mountain and shout that the Lowry approach to real estate investment works."

William S. Hawkes writes: "In ten months I increased my net worth by $100,000, established an income of $14,000, control property worth $135,000, have sixteen units under option, and now I have a believing wife. It works!"

John Caruso writes "At the age of 45 I have created more wealth in the past 2½ years than I have working for a living in the past 22."

Visualize Yourself Succeeding

If they can do it, you can. You have the knowledge. All you need is a positive attitude.

About seventy years ago a Frenchman named Emile Coué, a psychotherapist, began urging people to think positively. He was a persuasive speaker, so a good many people followed his advice, even if rather skeptically, only to find, sometimes to their surprise, that it worked in spite of their skepticism.

In lectures all over America he exhorted audiences to tell themselves something like this, over and over so it wore a groove in their subconscious: "Day by day in every way I'm getting better and better."

It sounded like a silly gimmick. But there was a sound psychological truth behind it. Coué illustrated this by asking the audience to visualize a plank six inches wide, laid across the living-room floor. Anyone could walk such a plank easily and confidently. That was obvious. But then Coué told his listeners to imagine the same plank stretched between two buildings a hundred feet high. Suddenly walking it seemed almost impossible. Yet it was the same plank. How people thought about it made all the difference.

So think of yourself as succeeding. Plan, and act, with confidence.

This isn't a book about religion. But I think there's a place in it—right here—for a reminder that a trusting faith in our Creator will help you succeed.

As you follow the principles in this book, you'll be doing business in an ethical way, never cheating anyone, arranging transactions that are good for everyone involved. So you shouldn't hesitate to ask for divine help. Expect to receive it whenever you need it.

The Bible's great promises sound on, century after century: "Ask and ye shall receive. Seek and ye shall find. Knock and it shall be opened unto you. . . . All things work together for good, for them that love the Lord."

I know a simple prayer that has helped me and many other people. When you face problems or difficulties, say to yourself:

I will do all that I can do about any problem.
Beyond that I trust in God.
I believe I am always divinely guided.
I believe God will always make a way where there is no way.

So now I've told you all I can. The rest is up to you. Go ahead confidently, knowing that you will do well—and go with God, as the Spanish say.

KEY POINTS TO REMEMBER

· Don't let overcaution blind you to opportunities.
· Start small but plan for possible growth.
· Examine the alternative routes to financial independence, and choose whichever is best suited to you.
· Instead of going it alone, use expert advisers.
· Mental attitude can make a big difference. Visualize yourself succeeding.

INDEX

355

362